Portraits of
Whole Language
Classrooms

Portraits of Whole Language Classrooms

Learning for All Ages

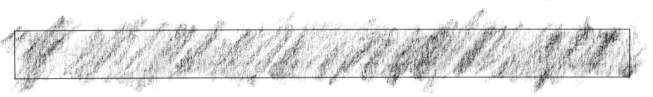

Edited by

Heidi Mills
University of South Carolina

Jean Anne Clyde
University of Louisville

Heinemann
Portsmouth, New Hampshire

Heinemann Educational Books, Inc.
361 Hanover Street   Portsmouth, NH 03801-3959
Offices and agents throughout the world

The authors and publisher wish to thank the following for permission to reprint material
appearing in this book:

Figure 7–1: *Children's Games* by Pieter Brueghel, by permission of the Kunsthistorisches
Museum, Vienna.

Page 140: "Hoopla" by Lorenca Rosal, from *The Dictopedia* by Pleasant T. Rowland. Menlo
Park, CA: Addison-Wesley Publishing Company, 1982. Reprinted by permission of the
publisher.

Page 141: "Jacks" by Kathleen Fraser. From *Stilts, Somersaults and Headstands* by Kathleen
Fraser. Copyright © 1968 by Kathleen Fraser. All rights reserved. Reprinted by permission
of Marian Reiner for the author.

Page 141: "Stilts" by Tonia Lapham, from *The Dictopedia* by Pleasant T. Rowland. Menlo
Park, CA: Addison-Wesley Publishing Company, 1982. Reprinted by permission of the
publisher.

Page 142: "Headstand" by Matthew Brock, from *The Dictopedia* by Pleasant T. Rowland.
Menlo Park, CA: Addison-Wesley Publishing Company, 1982. Reprinted by permission of
the publisher.

Figure 7–2: *Revolution of the Viaducts* by Paul Klee. Hamburger Kunsthalle, West
Germany.

Every effort has been made to contact the copyright holders and the children and their
parents for permission to reprint borrowed material. We regret any oversights that may
have occurred and would be happy to rectify them in future printings of this work.

All photos in each chapter were taken by the author of the chapter, except as follows:
Chapter 1 photos by David J. Whitin; Chapter 4 photos by David J. Whitin and Timothy
O'Keefe; Chapter 6 photos by Gloria Kauffman; Chapter 8 photos by Sharon Andrews;
Figure 12–1 by David J. Whitin; Figure 12–2A by Delbert Morgan; Chapter 14 photos by
Jym Wilson.

Library of Congress Cataloging-in-Publication Data

Portraits of whole language classrooms: learning for all ages/
    edited by Heidi Mills, Jean Anne Clyde.
       p. cm.
    Includes bibliographical references.
    ISBN 0–435–08510–7
    1. Language experience approach in education—United States.
I. Mills, Heidi. II. Clyde, Jean Anne.
LB1576.P67 1990
407—dc20   89–35937
                                                                 CIP

Designed by Maria Szmauz.
Printed in the United States of America.

10 9 8 7 6 5 4 3 2 1

Contents

Foreword

VIRGINIA A. WOODWARD

The following remarks about whole language come from undergraduates, graduate students, practicing teachers, public school administrators, and teacher educators:

"Are you doing it?"

"Whole language is what good teachers do naturally."

"I can't believe it! The whole world is turning whole language."

"I do whole language; I use Big Books."

"Whole language is a way of thinking about teaching and learning."

"We do whole language activities on Fridays."

"Whole language is not a bag of tricks. Whole language is a theory of literacy based on a set of beliefs about how people learn."

"It seems like whole language is just glorified language experience."

Sound confusing? It should. Why? Because the recent surge of interest in whole language and its enormous popularity bring to the classroom both exciting and educationally sound changes and unfortunate misconceptions. Many teachers have embraced this philosophy of instruction and have quite thoughtfully created ways to put the theory into practice in their own classrooms. Others, however, have attempted to develop a whole language orthodoxy and have misconstrued the approach. Hence we hear some of the remarks like those quoted above. This book was compiled to demonstrate what whole language theory looks like in classroom practice. It was also created to confront an age-old problem that has historically plagued education: "When bad things happen to good ideas" (Graves and Harste 1988).

Recently teachers have begun to examine their beliefs about teaching and learning, and many have adopted a whole language perspective. Bolstered by this new way of thinking, these teachers are moving away from fixed language and reading curricula. Instead, they are collaborating with their students to create and monitor their own theoretically based, process-oriented language arts programs.

The editors of this book have invited a select group of whole language teachers to share their individual experiences by highlighting a typical day in their classrooms. These teachers illustrate how whole language theory works for them and their students. They have made the theory their own in a variety of ways. Some teachers have organized their curricula thematically around the study of dinosaurs, family histories, literature study groups, and the learning of poetry through art. Others have used the authoring cycle as a framework. One teacher describes how she made the decision to change her assessment procedures by inviting students to take responsibility for evaluating their own learning. You will find that all of the teachers have created reading and writing events that are naturally integrated into the ongoing curriculum. Risk taking is also found in all of the chapters. Through stories of classroom events, the teachers share the importance of helping learners become risk takers to foster their growth. The teachers also continually reflect on their teaching and learning, the children's learning, and the effectiveness of various teaching strategies. Consequently, their curricula are in a continuous state of revision as they develop, through their teaching, new theoretical insights.

Portraits of Whole Language Classrooms is organized chronologically. We travel from a home day-care setting through preschool programs and elementary classrooms to junior high and high school. Along the way we visit special education sites and an English as a second language class. We conclude our journey in an educational laboratory staffed by graduate students in a reading methods course. This organization is not meant to suggest that a whole language theory of learning and the learning processes involved are different for each age group. Instead, the curricula discussed are united by a universal theory of learning that cuts across grade levels.

While this book is highly practical, it is certainly not a "how to" handbook. The ideas embedded in each chapter are not presented as a plan of action for all to follow. Instead, they provide a range of perspectives to be considered when implementing whole language. The stories these whole language teachers tell about their students and the learning environments they create are different — and they should be. Whole language teachers are learners too, and their chapters reflect their present understandings and working hypotheses. However, what ties them, and this book, together is a belief system about how people learn. It is not a fixed system that teachers hope to arrive at completely some day. It is instead constantly reshaped and refined as teachers continue to reflect and collaborate with one another.

John McInerney advises in the last chapter that teachers need to begin to implement their new theoretical beliefs even though they might not feel that all parts of their curriculum are in order. Through the process of reflecting on the experiences you have with your students—a critical aspect of the curriculum development process—your theory will continue to be revised. But you need not work in isolation. As a whole language teacher you may join a growing thought collective throughout the country and abroad. It is important that you seek out and share your successes, questions, and problems with other whole language teachers—just as these teachers do.

References

Graves, D., and J. Harste. 1988. "When Bad Things Happen to Good Ideas." Speech given at the annual convention of the National Council of Teachers of English, St. Louis, Missouri.

Acknowledgments

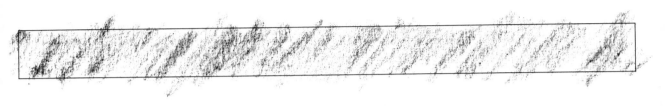

W e would like to express our gratitude to our colleagues, families, and friends who have supported our efforts throughout the production of this volume. Our families have been especially patient and understanding. We truly appreciate their encouragement.

Timothy O'Keefe, Mark Condon, and David Whitin were particularly supportive. Their insights have played an important role from creation through completion. David Whitin assisted tremendously in the development of the introduction by contributing ideas about the value of storytelling in learning.

Jerome Harste, Carolyn Burke, and Virginia Woodward supported our research at Indiana University and, in so doing, helped us understand the need for a book like this. Its framework originated with our dissertations; our committee members enthusiastically accepted our decision to share the theoretical underpinnings of our classrooms through story form. Hence, the idea of a day in whole language classrooms emerged. Our committee also celebrated the idea to edit a book written by classroom teachers, not only to demonstrate the theoretical commonalities and practical variations of whole language, but also to provide a forum for teachers' voices to be heard.

We owe a great deal to Kathryn Mitchell Pierce, one of the initial readers of our prospectus. We are grateful that she saw potential in this work and recommended that it be accepted for publication.

Philippa Stratton and Toby Gordon were unbelievably helpful. From the beginning they advised us in very thoughtful and cheerful ways. They acknowledged good work and helped us see when significant revision was needed. We soon came to realize that their suggestions were always on target.

Donna Bouvier and Kathy Traynor did a superb job of fine-tuning the text for publication. Their attention to detail was remarkable and greatly appreciated.

Pat Carver typed the original prospectus for this book. She was extremely conscientious and patient. We believe that the final form of the document supported the content, thanks to Pat.

Richard Kemper enhanced our efforts by providing practical support. His enthusiasm and appreciation for this project really made a difference.

Our special thanks to Janet Files, Laura Westberg, and Brenda Hawkins, whose dinner conversation gave birth to the title of this volume.

Finally, we would like to thank the teachers who contributed to this volume. Obviously, we would not have been able to complete this work without their efforts. But more importantly, the teachers writing about life in their classrooms expanded our vision of whole language.

About the Authors

DONELLE BLUBAUGH is a reading consultant and teacher of English for grades nine through twelve at Middlebury Union High School, Middlebury, Vermont. She was a contributing editor of *Whole Language Strategies for Secondary Students* (Richard C. Owen, 1988). She was educated at the University of Missouri—Columbia and is in her eighth year of public school teaching. She owes it all to Mrs. Bowman, her first-grade teacher, who thought she was teaching phonics but was really teaching the art of making meaning.

JEAN ANNE CLYDE is an assistant professor of Early and Middle Childhood Education at the University of Louisville. She has been involved each year in collaborative ventures cosponsored by the University of Louisville and the public schools. She values the opportunity to keep actively involved in early childhood and elementary classrooms. Formerly an elementary classroom teacher and teacher-researcher in a preschool, Jean Anne believes that she has learned the most about teaching from children. Her research at the Campus Children's Center is her most memorable to date, for it was the vehicle through which she discovered the benefits of collaborating, not just with colleagues, but with the children with whom she worked (and they were only three and four years old!).

PATRICIA TEFFT COUSIN, a former special education teacher, is currently an assistant professor in the graduate program of special education at California State University in San Bernardino, where she teaches graduate courses in reading and special education. In addition, she works with other special education teachers who are interested in holistic teaching. She uses insights gleaned from a collaborate research project at Sprunica Elementary School in Indiana as she works with other special education teachers.

MARGARET GRANT is a third-grade teacher in Missoula, Montana; her favorite way to learn is in her classroom. Margaret has shared her classroom through the video series *Teachers Teaching Writing* (ASCD-NCTE) and has conducted workshops and institutes for teachers throughout the country. A member of the Montana Writing Project, she offers courses in literature-based integrated learning for the University of Montana and for Missoula School District One. Margaret has been Teacher of the Year for the Montana Association of Teachers of English Language Arts and she has recently served on the Social Studies task force for the development of Accreditation Standards for the State of Montana.

JEROME C. HARSTE is professor of education at Indiana University in Bloomington. He has written children's stories as well as numerous articles and books on whole language, including his latest book, *Whole Language: Inquiring Voices*, written in collaboration with Dorothy Watson and Carolyn Burke. Jerry's research in early literacy with Carolyn Burke and Virginia Woodward is cited in *Language Stories & Literacy Lessons* (Heinemann, 1984), which received the David H. Russell Award for Distinguished Research in the Teaching of English by the National Council of Teachers of English in 1987. In response to teachers' requests to write about organizing process-centered reading and writing classrooms, Jerry wrote *Creating Classrooms for Authors* (Heinemann, 1988) with Kathy Short and Carolyn Burke.

REBECCA HUNTSMAN became a part of the Education Laboratory at the University of North Carolina at Wilmington as a graduate student in 1987. She has since completed her master's degree. She is currently an instructor of English and Written Communication at Miller Mott Business College in Wilmington, North Carolina.

GLORIA KAUFFMAN is a third-grade classroom teacher at Millersburg Elementary School in northern Indiana. Her first-grade classroom was the site of a collaborative research project with Kathy Short on literature circles and text sets. Some of this research is published in *Creating Classrooms for Authors* (Heinemann, 1988). Gloria continues to work toward developing a process-centered curriculum based on the authoring cycle. She also collaborates with Kathy Short on various research projects. Recently she was awarded the Barry Sherman Practicing Teacher Award for Whole Language Teachers. She is actively involved in local International Reading Association and Teachers Applying Whole Language groups.

ALANE LANCASTER is a special education resource teacher at Sprunica Elementary School in Ninevah, Indiana. Having gained many insights from her collaborative research effort with Patricia Tefft Cousin, she continues to further refine her curriculum and collaborate with the regular education teachers in her school, building supportive learning environments.

JOHN McINERNEY has been a primary instructor for eight years and currently teaches first grade at the newly opened Symmes Elementary school in Cincinnati, Ohio. His current goal is to maximize the number of days in which the children are so engrossed in pursuing their projects that they say, "But you didn't teach us anything." Recent projects he has been engrossed in include developing computer-generated, individualized spelling dictionaries drawn from a child's own writings and a grant tracking spelling development across different classrooms.

HEIDI MILLS is an assistant professor of Elementary Education at the University of South Carolina. A former classroom teacher, she attributes many of the important literacy lessons that she has learned to the children with whom she has worked. Although her students are now graduates and undergraduates, those lessons continue to play an instrumental role in her teaching.

Heidi is entering her third year of a collaborative research project with Timothy O'Keefe and David Whitin. Together, they are exploring ways to support the development of mathematical literacy in young children. They are the coauthors of *Living and Learning Mathematics* (Heinemann, 1990).

VERA E. MILZ, a former first-grade teacher at the Way Elementary School, currently teaches third grade at Conant School in Bloomfield Hills, Michigan. She received her doctorate from the University of Arizona in 1983 and continues to research and write about her experiences in the classroom in the areas of beginning reading and writing. In 1987, she was named Michigan Elementary Reading Teacher of the Year. She has consulted at various schools across the country and has presented at the National Council of Teachers of English and International Reading Association conferences.

TIMOTHY O'KEEFE has been a classroom teacher for ten years. He has taught Head Start through sixth grade. He has been a whole language teacher from the beginning of his career, having had Jerome Harste as an undergraduate. His work with Jerry not only influenced his thinking about teaching language arts but also caused him to think holistically about all areas of the curriculum. He is currently researching how young children learn mathematics. He shares his work in the transition first-grade classroom in a book entitled *Living and Learning*

Mathematics (Heinemann, 1990) and a video about working with "at risk" children in a forthcoming Heinemann video series. His chapter is dedicated to his father, Jack O'Keefe.

KATHLEEN O'NEILL took over as teaching assistant at the Education Laboratory at the University of North Carolina at Wilmington in 1987. She brought with her a love of art, and in time the lab began to reflect her interests. She now teaches reading at an elementary school in Hawaii.

LIA RIDLEY has been an elementary classroom teacher; an ESL teacher for elementary, secondary, and adult education; a drama instructor in a cultural arts program; and a reading/writing consultant for five elementary schools and one middle school. The United States is her third country and English is her fourth language. At present she teaches at Ponderosa Elementary School in Aurora, Colorado. She holds a master's degree in reading and writing and in English as a second language from the University of Colorado at Denver. She has coauthored curriculum materials for Cherry Creek School District in Aurora, Colorado, including *A Guide to Teaching Selected Children's Literature.*

KATHY G. SHORT teaches children's literature at the University of Arizona, where she is an assistant professor in the Division of Language, Reading, and Culture. She has worked extensively with teachers to develop curricula that actively involve students in using reading and writing to learn. Teachers know her especially for her interest in literature and her ideas for integrating children's literature into the curriculum.

While teaching at Goshen College in northern Indiana, Kathy worked with Gloria Kauffman and her students on numerous collaborative research projects. She is coauthor of *Creating Classrooms for Authors* (Heinemann, 1988) with Jerome Harste and Carolyn Burke.

BETTY SLESINGER taught English and reading to "remedial students" for about thirteen years in four states before she ever admitted that something was wrong with her teaching, the curriculum, the system, and the school environment. Through graduate courses in language arts and her participation in a Pennsylvania Writing Project she began to recognize the power of sharing and group work and the natural integration of oral language and reading with writing. She has begun to think beyond what she and her students are doing, to why and how they are reacting and are involved. She is now entering her twentieth year of teaching in a fifth state.

DIANE STEPHENS is currently a visiting assistant professor at the Center for the Study of Reading, College of Education, University of Illinois. She teaches classes for the College of Education and conducts classroom-based research. She has had several years' teaching experience with learners of all ages. After completing her doctorate at Indiana University in 1986, she spent two years at the University of North Carolina in Wilmington, first designing and then directing the Ed Lab.

ERIC STONE has been teaching with the Spencer—Owen Community School Corporation in Southern Indiana for nine years. He received a master of science degree in elementary education from Indiana University in 1984. He also has taken coursework in gifted and talented education and was the elementary gifted-talented curriculum coordinator and instructor at Spencer Elementary School for three years.

Eric was introduced to whole language primarily through two collaborative research studies: one with David Heine of St. Cloud University, and the other with Sharon Andrews of Indiana State University. He has spoken on his experiences with collaborative research at several national conferences and conducts workshops in local school corporations on holistic curriculum planning with students.

JENNIFER STORY is currently an educational consultant at the Bishop Museum in Honolulu, Hawaii. She is a writer with ten years' experience teaching reading, writing, and science in the elementary school. She earned a master's degree in Elementary Education from the University of North Carolina in Wilmington and was the graduate assistant in the Ed Lab during that year. She volunteered in the Lab part time, after school, during 1987–88.

JANINE TOOMES became a part of the Education Laboratory at the University of North Carolina at Wilmington as a graduate student in 1987. She has since completed her master's degree and is currently teaching eighth-grade language arts and reading at M.C.S. Noble Middle School in Wilmington, North Carolina.

VIRGINIA WATSON became a part of the Education Laboratory at the University of North Carolina at Wilmington as a graduate student in 1987. She now lives in Louisville, Kentucky. She is director of the kindergarten day-care program at Anchorage Elementary School in Anchorage, Kentucky.

THOM WENDT is a fourth- and fifth-grade teacher at Highland Park Elementary School in the South-Western City School District, Grove City, Ohio. Highland Park is one of fifteen elementary schools in South-Western City Schools and uses a unit approach to the curriculum with an emphasis on literature and writing.

Thom has taught in grades one, two, four, five, and six. He also serves as an in-service consultant to Ohio school districts interested in whole language and literature-based reading programs and was featured in a videotape series on reading and writing produced by Indiana University.

Thom has a B.S. (1980) in early and middle childhood education and an M.A. (1988) in educational administration from The Ohio State University. He is currently working on a children's book about the Ohio canal era.

DAVID J. WHITIN is currently an assistant professor of elementary education at the University of South Carolina. He taught elementary school for nine years in the Follow Through Program of Lebanon, New Hampshire. He was also an elementary principal of a small rural school in Wales, Massachusetts. Along with two colleagues, he recently completed a book entitled *Living and Learning Mathematics* (Heinemann, 1990). He enjoys reciting poetry, telling stories, and investigating mathematical patterns and games.

PHYLLIS E. WHITIN has taught preschool, elementary, and middle school in several states. While her three children were small, she ran a home day care. During this time she became fascinated with language development and spent almost two years documenting the language growth of her children. She has contributed articles to *LiveWire* and *The Whole Language Catalog* (McGraw-Hill, 1990) and has conducted workshops on the importance of preserving family history. She currently teaches seventh-grade language arts in Columbia, South Carolina.

Introduction

The Stories Whole Language Teachers Tell

W hole language teachers love to tell stories about the children whom they teach and about adventures in their classrooms. These stories are revealing, for they reflect the beliefs that whole language teachers hold and the reasons for the learning environments they create.

Stories are "one of the most effective ways of making one's own interpretation of events and ideas available to others" (Wells 1986, 194). They are an empowering force, a "means of crossing the threshold of awareness" (Erikson 1986). Essentially, they enable "storytellers" to adopt a reflective stance, to hold their beliefs up for inspection. They provide a vehicle through which we can confirm old beliefs or entertain new ones, a means for fine-tuning our own teaching. So while stories may be exciting to tell and engaging to listen to, they ultimately have the potential to propel teachers forward with new insights for exploration and new hypotheses for testing.

Not surprisingly, stories do not just benefit the teachers doing the telling. Hearing rich descriptions of authentic classroom events offers listeners the opportunity to construct their own meanings, to generate and articulate their own hypotheses, to fine-tune *their* own beliefs as well. Our appreciation of and respect for the generative nature of stories has led to the creation of this volume and the form that it has taken.

Although whole language stories are told by a variety of teachers working in different places under diverse conditions, they are alike in one important way: they are bound together by a common belief system — a research base — that reflects how children learn best.

Stories: A Reflection of Beliefs

These beliefs come to life when we view them within a context in which they are most easily understood: the whole language classroom. Here is a story told by a teacher in Grand Rapids, Michigan.

> The children in our classroom were delighted with the introduction of a message board in our room. In observing their reactions, we could soon see that it served a significant social function for them, providing children the opportunity to present — via writing and reading — personal information to class members in a meaningful way. Each day they jotted down "newsworthy" events to share during gathering (large group time), items that, for four- and five-year-olds, were likely to include announcements of the acquisition of new pets, upcoming trips to the dentist, or explanations of their latest cuts and bruises. However, the most popular theme for the message board revolved around loving family members and liking or loving friends. These most often took the form of "I like" and "I love" lists.
>
> Writing and sharing messages was one of five-year-old Christal's very favorite activities. And as can be seen [Figure I–1] the "I love" theme was clearly an important one for her as well.

While her message, particularly her decision to include art, may be unlike those we adults might produce, there is certainly no question of Christal's intention. Her text provides clear evidence that she recognizes that the function of language is the making and sharing of meaning. This understanding is central to a whole language philosophy of teaching and learning (Goodman 1986; Goodman and Goodman 1979; Graves 1983; Halliday 1975; Milz 1980; and Watson 1980).

In examining her message more closely, we notice that she has made some very interesting decisions in expressing her meaning. After having captured what she could of her message with print (quite conventionally, at that), Christal turned to art, including a smile heart, well known as her personal symbol. She then drew a second heart, this time writing the names of her family members within it. How fascinating to see her so naturally move from one communication medium — writing — to another — art. Each of them has unique communicative qualities, and when taken together, they expand and extend what Christal can "say" with them independent of one another.

Observations of Christal and other children in natural settings have helped whole language teachers to realize that to represent meanings through language alone actually limits meaning potential. Encouraging children to use various

Figure 1–1   Christal's message

forms of communication—for instance, incorporating art and math, or language and movement—allows them the opportunity to expand their communication potential and to express their intended meanings more fully (Harste, Woodward, and Burke 1984; Rowe 1986; Siegel 1984).

There is another assumption embedded within this story, one that is evidenced in the teachers' decision to utilize the Message Board. Their invitation to children to read and write "the best way they know how" reveals their understanding that children learn to read and write in the same way they learn to talk: they interact with language—written language—in meaningful ways (Baghban 1984; Bissex 1980; Calkins 1986; Clyde 1986; DeFord 1980; Harste, Woodward, and Burke 1984; Heath 1983; King 1982; Lindfors 1987; Taylor 1983; Watson 1980). The more children read, the more they learn about reading and writing, and the more they write, the more they learn about writing and reading.

Whole language teachers also recognize that language is inherently social, and that it always occurs within a social context (Kucer 1983; Scibior 1986; Shanklin 1981; Smith 1978). "Children build knowledge of themselves and the adequacy of their thinking through interaction with others" (Rowe 1986, 38). When considering written language, we recognize that a reader of a text presupposes the existence of an author; a writer presupposes a reader. In this case, as Christal shares her intended meanings with her friends, there is always the possibility that they may glean from this social encounter new strategies for effective communication.

Observing Christal's engagement as a writer/reader helps us see that literacy learning involves being strategic. That is, it involves using what we know in new and inventive ways. Strategic language users have the capability to reflect upon, manipulate, organize, share, and extend their experiences. The strategic use of language, then, empowers learners by providing opportunities for them to share their feelings and knowledge with others. "Literacy...allows us to actively manipulate our relationship to the world" (Harste 1986).

Taken together, these basic assumptions—that language is a meaning-based system; that learning to read and write is as natural as learning to talk; that literacy is multimodal (involving alternate sign systems); that learning is a social event; and that literacy involves being strategic—form a genetic pool of sorts, from which curricular decisions will be born. What teachers understand about language, language learning, and children will determine the kinds of educational experiences they will consider and those that they will avoid. Essentially, teachers' beliefs become operationalized as curriculum.

Whole Language: From Theory to Practice

Because of the philosophical beliefs embraced by whole language teachers, there will necessarily be some basic similarities in the ways in which they are implemented in classroom practice. While there is a refreshing uniqueness evident in each of the classrooms described in this book, examining them in relation to one another enables us to appreciate what it is about them that makes them "whole language." You will see that:

1. A whole language curriculum highlights authentic speech and literacy events. Teachers want to guarantee that children will encounter literacy in ways that are reflective of language in everyday use.

2. A whole language curriculum encourages risk taking. Teachers demonstrate the value of risk taking by accepting all rough draft efforts. They realize that errors or miscues are a natural part of the learning

process and present important evidence regarding children's growth and development.

3. A whole language curriculum provides choice for learners. Teachers allow children to select learning experiences from a variety of open-ended instructional invitations — invitations that ensure success for each learner at a personally challenging level.

4. A whole language curriculum is developed with a sense of trust in the learners. Teachers trust children as capable decision makers and believe that they will learn from an experience what they are cognitively ready for (Dewey 1938).

5. A whole language curriculum is collaboratively established. Teachers plan with, not simply for, children. The teacher relies upon the children as curricular informants, viewing their "errors" and accomplishments as rich sources of information upon which to make informed curricular decisions.

6. A whole language curriculum casts teachers in a variety of supportive roles. Teachers are participants, guides, and learners in their classrooms.

7. A whole language curriculum capitalizes on the social nature of learning. Teachers provide opportunities for children to learn from one another.

8. A whole language curriculum is multimodal in nature. Teachers incorporate music, art, dance, drama, and math into the curriculum. Each form of communication is nonredundant (Eisner 1982) and so naturally expands the communication potential of the curriculum.

9. A whole language curriculum encourages reflection. Teachers and children alike are provided opportunities to reflect upon their own learning and to monitor their own growth.

10. A whole language curriculum empowers all participants as teachers and learners. Whole language classrooms are neither teacher centered nor student centered; they are learner centered (Stephens 1986). All participants collaborate to establish the curriculum. This explains the practical variation of whole language teaching across contexts.

Whole language concepts were generated by studying children's literacy in natural contexts. Such data have revolutionized the profession. Given that our greatest insights about literacy learning have come from research in natural settings, it is appropriate that we return to the supportive learning environments of whole language classrooms to further our understanding of the teaching/learning process. When we do, you will see that whole language environments are as diverse as the teachers and children who create them.

As you read *Portraits of Whole Language Classrooms*, we invite you to search for the unique ways that these teachers' shared assumptions are converted into the day-to-day workings of their classrooms. Watch as they conduct their research; consider the nature of their observations, and the meanings they make from them. Then have a go at telling your own stories.

An Important Note

Our discussion of theoretical underpinnings is not intended to emphasize theory over practice. Instead, their inclusion provides a framework to assist readers in exploring the commonalities that unite whole language teachers.

References

Baghban, M. J. 1984. *Our Daughter Learns to Read and Write: A Case Study from Birth to Three*. Newark, Del: International Reading Association.

Bissex, G. 1980. *GNYS AT WRK: A Child Learns to Write and Read*. Cambridge, Mass.: Harvard University Press.

Calkins, L. M. 1986. *The Art of Teaching Writing*. Portsmouth, N.H.: Heinemann.

Clyde, J. A. 1986. "Talking on Paper: Exploring the Potential of a Quality Language Experience." *Forum in Reading and Language Education* 2, no. 1.

DeFord, D. E. 1980. "Young Children and Their Writing." *Theory into Practice* 19: 157–62.

Dewey, J. 1938. *Experience and Education*. New York: Collier Books.

Eisner, E. W. 1982. *Cognition and Curriculum: A Basis for Deciding What to Teach*. New York: Longman.

Erikson, F. 1986. "Tasks in Times: Objects of Study in a Natural History of Teaching." In *Improving Teaching: ASCD Yearbook*, edited by K. K. Zumwalt. Alexandria, VA: Association for Supervision and Curriculum Development.

Goodman, K. 1986. *What's Whole in Whole Language?* Portsmouth, N.H.: Heinemann.

Goodman, K. S., and Y. M. Goodman. 1979. "Learning to Read Is Natural." In *Theory and Practice of Early Reading*, vol 2, edited by L. B. Resnick and P. A. Weaver. Hillsdale, N.J.: Erlbaum.

Graves, D. 1983. *Writing: Teachers & Children at Work*. Portsmouth, N.H.: Heinemann.

Halliday, M. A. K. 1975. *Learning How to Mean: Explorations in the Development of Language*. London: Edward Arnold.

Harste, J. C. 1986. Personal communication. Dissertation committee meeting, Indiana University, Bloomington.

Harste, J. C., V. A. Woodward, and C. L. Burke. 1984. *Language Stories & Literacy Lessons*. Portsmouth, N.H.: Heinemann.

Heath, S. B. 1983. *Ways with Words*. Cambridge: Cambridge University Press.

King, M. L. 1982. "Language Foundations for Writing: A Research Perspective." Speech given at the Language in Education Conference at The Ohio State University.

Kucer, S. 1983. Using Text Comprehension as a Metaphor for Understanding Text Production: Building Bridges between Reading and Writing. Ph.D. diss., Indiana University, Bloomington, Ind.

Lindfors, J. W. 1987. "Perspectives on Language Acquisition." In *Children's Language and Learning.* 2d ed. Englewood Cliffs, N.J.: Prentice-Hall.

Milz, V. 1980. The Comprehension Centered Classroom: Setting It Up and Making It Work. Videotape in D. J. Strickler (producer and director), *Reading Comprehension.* Videotape series. Portsmouth, N.H.: Heinemann.

Rowe, D. W. 1986. Literacy in the Child's World: Preschoolers' Exploration of Alternate Communication Systems. Ph.D. diss., Indiana University, Bloomington, Ind.

Scibior, O. 1986. "Learning to Spell." In *Whole Language: Theory in Use,* edited by J. M. Newman. Portsmouth, N.H.: Heinemann.

Shanklin, N. K. L. 1981. *Relating Teaching and Writing: Developing a Transactional Theory of the Writing Process.* Monographs in Language and Reading Studies. Bloomington, Ind.: School of Education Publications Office, Indiana University.

Siegel, M. G. 1984. Reading as Signification. Ph.D. diss., Indiana University, Bloomington, Ind.

Smith, F. 1978. *Understanding Reading.* New York: Holt, Rinehart & Winston.

Stephens, D. 1986. Research and Theory as Practice: A Collaborative Study. Ph.D. diss., Indiana University, Bloomington, Ind.

Taylor, D. 1983. *Family Literacy: Young Children Learning to Read and Write.* Portsmouth, N.H.: Heinemann.

Watson, D. J. 1980. "Whole Language for Whole Children." Paper presented at the Third Annual Reading Conference, Columbia, Mo.

Watson, K., and B. Young. 1986. "Discourse in Classroom Learning." *Language Arts* 63, no. 6.

Wells, G. 1986. *The Meaning Makers: Children Learning Language and Using Language to Learn.* Portsmouth, N.H.: Heinemann.

Literacy Learning in a Home Day-Care Setting

DAVID J. WHITIN   PHYLLIS E. WHITIN

In this home day care in a small community in the central part of New Hampshire, learning is at the heart of each day's routine. Phyllis, a former elementary school teacher, and her husband David, a former third-grade teacher, often talked about the literacy learning they were both striving to support, at work and at home. Phyllis finally decided to stay at home with their own young children; she also provided care for the children of two other teachers, who continued to work.

The six children in the group, three of whom belonged to the day-care provider, will be referred to in this chapter as Megan (one), Becca (two), Chris (three and a half), Leslie (four), Brett (four and a half), and David (six and a half). David attended first grade but was home in the afternoon to play with the other children. Parents left their children at the home by 7:30 A.M. and picked them up at approximately 4:30 P.M.

The Day Begins

The woodstove is already warming the house as the children begin to arrive. It is a clear but cool New England morning in mid-October, and frost covers the pathway that leads to the house. Chris is the first one to come through the door. Although he is bundled up in a warm coat, he proclaims loudly, "No more cold, please. There's enough down here!" Phyllis laughs because she knows the history behind that clever exclamation. One of the children's favorite stories was "Tom Thumb" (Martin 1972), which had been read aloud many times. At one point in the story Tom is swallowed by a cow and he calls out from inside the stomach, "No more hay, please. There's enough down here!" The children enjoyed Tom's outcry and would chime in every time it occurred in the story. Chris took this familiar phrase, transformed it, and used it in a new context. His exclamation demonstrates that reading is its own experience; it can alter and enrich further experiences we have with our world.

As Chris arrives Brett is already busy at the kitchen table drawing and writing. He has drawn a picture of himself wearing some ice skates (Figure 1−1). Chris comes over and asks him about his writing and Brett reads it to him: "This is ice. I have skates on." Here Brett has cleverly combined an "8" with the letter "c" to create the word "skates." Phyllis encourages all the children to write for themselves and knows that they will invent their own unique ways to communicate if they are given ownership of the process.

Figure 1−1   Brett: "This is ice. I have skates on."

Other children begin to arrive as Chris takes off his coat and begins to warm himself by the fire. He then walks over to his mother, takes a large book of fairy tales from her hands, and gives it to Phyllis, saying, "You have to read this one! We read it last night!" Phyllis senses the excitement in his voice and invites the other children to gather on the couch to hear the story. Usually the children enjoy working with some of the materials when they first arrive. However, today would be different. Plans and schedules change because the needs and interests of children change. Good teachers write their plans in pencil (Burke and Short 1987) and are ready to capitalize on a current interest or episode when it arises. Chris's excitement about this story demonstrates a love for reading that the others eagerly respond to as they sit together, ready to enjoy a tale that comes highly recommended from one of their peers. The story is entitled "The Glass Hill" (Asbjornsen and Moe 1970) and is replete with knights, princesses, and magic coats of mail. Chris sits entranced throughout the story. Afterwards he begs Becca to act out the story with him. Drama is an open-ended activity that provides a rich problem-solving experience for children. They must make choices about how to use a certain space, which props to utilize, what roles people ought to play, and what parts of the story ought to be portrayed. Chris sits on the rocking horse and begins to direct the action: "I am the knight; you are the princess." As the reenactment proceeds, Chris jumps down from his horse and dashes to the coat rack to retrieve his winter jacket. "This is my coat of mail," he proudly announces and continues to call it so for the rest of the day.

Chris used drama to experience the story in a new way. He turned to drama because it had been used as a vehicle for expression many times before. Children often acted out stories, or parts of stories, as they played. Drama was viewed as an acceptable way to express personal meaning and interpretation. This allowed Chris to take increasing responsibility for his own learning.

An Environment of Choices

As the story ends other children scoot down from the couch and begin to use some of the materials that are displayed on the shelves of melon-crates. The materials invite multiple interpretations by the children. There are empty spice cans that still retain the smell of their contents; there are measuring cups, spoons, and various other dishes bought at rummage sales; there is a box of dress-up clothes, a set of wooden blocks, containers of buttons and shells, and several pillows and cushions (old sheets that are kept upstairs are occasionally used by the children to create houses, caves, and tents). There are some simple dolls and trucks as well as a mirror, which hangs horizontally at the eye level of a sitting child. Art supplies are also available, including Play-Doh, crayons, and an easel

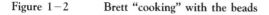

Figure 1—2   Brett "cooking" with the beads

for painting. Often scraps of material or seeds are laid out for children to use in collages. These materials are not structured for one particular use but are employed by children in a variety of ways.

Brett walks over to one of the shelves, selects a string of beads, puts them in a pan, and stirs them with a spoon (Figure 1—2). He walks over to Phyllis and says, "I'm making some stew. Do you want some?" These beads have proven to be one of the most popular items in the house. They were discovered outside in the grass the day after Halloween and have been used by the children in an endless number of ways. They have been chewed on and fingered by babies, dished up in stews both in and out of the water, pressed into Play-Doh to see the impressions, used as a necklace, made into "blueberries" or "spaghetti," counted, and curled carefully into a spider's web. The interpretations continue, and yet the beads did not cost a penny.

These materials encourage children to express their experiences in different ways. The environment promotes various solutions to a problem and not a syndrome of single right answers. It encourages children to be flexible thinkers, using the materials to fit their changing needs and experiences. In setting out these materials Phyllis was not envisioning any predetermined outcomes. She

Figure 1–3   Leslie bursts into song

trusted children to use them in their own ways for their own purposes.

Leslie sees that the easel is out today and decides to do some painting. She remembers to put on her smock before she begins. Leslie loves to sing and dance. As she finishes her first painting, she begins to sing a Mother Goose rhyme (Figure 1–3). Her singing increases her enthusiasm for the painting as she adds the last touches with a flurry of strokes.

Meanwhile, Chris and Becca are building a house; they have created a space with the small, plastic teeter-totter and several cushions from the couch. They gather together an assortment of quilts, which they drape over their structure for a roof. Carefully they crawl in and out, bringing with them small blocks, which serve as their food supply. Phyllis enjoys watching their imaginative play as she sits in a rocking chair nearby, giving Megan her mid-morning bottle.

Twenty minutes later Brett finishes making his stew and decides he wants to write a poem. He selects a piece of paper and a pencil and begins to record the poem "What Is Pink?" by Christina Rossetti (1924) (Figure 1–4). This poem he had heard read and recited for several years. He had learned to say it himself,

Figure 1—4   Brett writes

either alone or with a partner, in a typical call-response pattern. He had even recited it on several occasions for some guests who had come to dinner. Today he mumbles the poem as he starts to write it. There are eight stanzas and each begins with a question about a color: "What is pink?" "What is red?" and so on.

After Brett writes about half the poem, he starts to write the beginning of the next stanza, looks up and says, "There sure are a lot of 'whats' in here!" This shift in perspective from reader to writer causes Brett to experience this poem from a new stance and provides him with a broader appreciation. Brett knew the poem in his ear but he saw it in a new way when he wrote it down. He had heard the repetition of the "whats" before, and now he was seeing them as a writer. For the first time his eye was seeing and his hand was feeling the repetition of a sound that he had heard for so long.

Sharing Together at Lunch Time

Soon it is lunch time, and the children sit around the kitchen table to share a meal. Phyllis uses this time to relate some observations with the children. She takes from her apron pocket a piece of paper. "I wrote down this morning some kind acts that I saw happening as you all played, and I wanted to share them with you. Brett, I saw you share the dishes so nicely with Leslie. Chris, you were so kind to share your coat of mail with Becca. I wrote these wonderful things down so I wouldn't forget to tell you. Did anyone else notice something kind that happened?"

Phyllis sees herself as an active participant in this learning environment. She writes for different purposes and demonstrates that writing for children. As the children finish their discussion about this morning's activities, Becca looks around the table and asks, "Whobody's goin' have Jell-O?" Phyllis smiles at this creation of "Whobody." She is always intrigued by the children's linguistic inventions. She recalls the time David said after Christmas, "Let's undecorate the tree," and the time he remarked, "He's going fastly." Children do not learn language by merely mimicking what they hear; they take hold of language and use it for their own purposes, often running risks and making predictions about how it works. Phyllis views herself as a learner, allowing children the opportunity to share with her the insights they have gained about oral language. She now begins to view language as a living, moving force, not the fixed entity that grammar classes would have us believe. She marvels too at how appropriate these words are to their specific context. In no instance did anyone not understand what Brett or David was saying. Their linguistic creations were not randomly created but based on some sophisticated predictions about how language works. She enjoys hearing these unique variations and wants to keep alive in the children this playfulness with language.

As Chris picks up his plate to bring it to the sink, he announces to the group, "Well, I licked *that* platter clean!" Chris has taken the familiar line from the Mother Goose rhyme of "Jack Sprat," transformed it, and used it for his own particular situation. Phyllis recites poetry to the children every day after lunch. The children come to know many of the poems by heart and often recite them during their play. A line or a phrase is frequently changed by a child and used in a new context. By exposing the children to poetry Phyllis gives the children a richer and more diverse language with which to describe their own experiences.

Responding to Literature

While the children finish their lunch Phyllis reads some poems to them. She uses several editions of Mother Goose as well as a few texts from Bill Martin's *Sounds* series (1972). She then invites each child to select a story that she will read aloud to the group before nap time. The children climb down from their chairs and walk over to the bookshelf. It is filled with poetry books, folktales, and stories by such favorite authors as Maurice Sendak, Bill Peet, Arnold Lobel, Dr. Seuss, and Bill Martin. Phyllis feels it important for children to choose their books. As she puts the remainder of the food into the refrigerator she notices that some of the

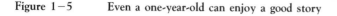

Figure 1–5   Even a one-year-old can enjoy a good story

children have already selected their story and have begun to read to themselves aloud. She sees even the youngest child involved in a story and realizes again that no time is soon enough to begin exposing children to good literature (Figure 1–5).

Phyllis waits a few more minutes before gathering the children on the couch for their stories. As Phyllis reads Becca's choice, Becca becomes more and more absorbed in the story. At one point Becca touches one of the pictures that shows men climbing high on the halyards of a ship and remarks in a worried voice, "I might fall down!" Phyllis responds, "Yes, Becca, if you were up that high you might fall down." Becca's intense personal involvement in the story causes her to reflect on the particular situation that is described. After finishing Becca's story Phyllis begins to read "Sody Sallyratus" by Richard Chase (1971), a tale from the Appalachias that was selected by Leslie. Part way through the story, after a hungry bear had eaten member after member of this family, Leslie exclaims, "He gets so fat he's like my Fat Cat." The tale of *The Fat Cat* (Kent 1971) is a Danish folktale that has been read aloud many times to the children. In this story a cat becomes increasingly fat as he eats one passerby after another. Leslie now notes the similarity between these two stories. They are both built around the pattern of successive eatings. In this way Leslie is developing a sense of how stories are put together. Phyllis trusts that children will make these connections if they are continually exposed to good literature and have the time to discuss stories and ask their own questions.

As Phyllis finishes reading aloud, the children take their story, along with several others, and begin to settle down for their afternoon nap. They each have their own separate space, set off from the others to allow them an uninterrupted time to read and sleep. After checking the children to be sure they have settled in, Phyllis fixes herself a cup of tea and sits down at the kitchen table to do some of her own reading. A few minutes pass before she hears a child's voice coming through the open door to one of the rooms. Phyllis tiptoes to the doorway and listens as Brett reads aloud some stories to himself. He reads *More Spaghetti I Say* by Rita Gelman (1977) with great alacrity. He next reads two of his favorite stories by Maurice Sendak, *Chicken Soup with Rice* and *Pierre* (1962). All these stories have a rhyme and rhythm that he enjoys. The next book he picks up is, *The Tale of Benjamin Bunny* by Beatrix Potter (1974). This book has been read aloud a few times by Phyllis but is not as popular as the perennial favorite, "Peter Rabbit." Brett begins, "Once there was a bunny..." and then his voice starts to trail off. He turns several pages, looking at the pictures and trying to recall the story language. Finally he stops turning the pages, puts the book down, and says to himself, "Phew, I haven't read this book in a long time!"

This episode is significant for a couple of reasons. First, Brett is playing the role of a successful reader. Phyllis surrounds him with good books that have a predictable rhyme and pattern, she trusts that he will read, and he does. Reading is an experience that all members of the household have come to appreciate and enjoy. Just because Brett's oral reading does not match the written words on each page it does not mean he is not reading. As he reads to himself he is using picture clues and the rhyme and pattern of stories to predict the language that is to follow. He already knows that stories ought to make sense, have a language of their own, and are to be enjoyed. The second point is that Brett is gaining an awareness of which stories he knows well and which ones he does not. He is learning more and more about himself as a reader.

The Afternoon Begins

Phyllis smiles to herself as she returns to the kitchen, feeling especially proud that the children are developing such a healthy attitude toward reading. After reading for a half hour herself she begins to wash the lunch dishes. She leaves the dishwater in the sink, knowing that the early risers often enjoy playing with the water. Shortly after she finishes the dishes the first child is up. Brett sees the

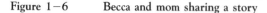

Figure 1−6   Becca and mom sharing a story

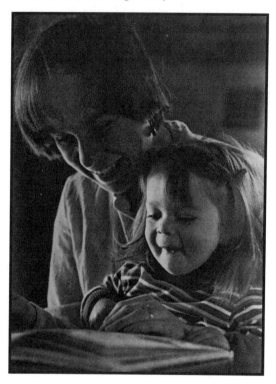

dishwater, pushes a chair over to the sink, climbs up, and begins to pour and scrub with a variety of plastic cups and utensils that Phyllis has provided. At one point he begins to swish a bottle brush around in a jar and remarks, "This is like making applesauce!" And indeed it is. Many times the children have helped Phyllis make applesauce. They were used to swishing the wooden handle in the sieve to squeeze out the sauce.

Megan is the next one to awake. After giving Megan a diaper change Phyllis relaxes in the rocker to give the youngest one her afternoon bottle. A short while later Becca totters down the stairs from her nap. Wanting Mommy's attention for herself, she tries to push Megan out of Phyllis's lap.

"Becca, go find a good book," suggests Phyllis. "When I finish with Megan, you and I can have a special story." The bottle is soon empty and Megan is placed on the floor to investigate some nesting blocks. Becca climbs up onto her mother's lap, bringing one of the children's favorite stories, *Caps for Sale* by Esther Slobodkina (1968). Becca and her mother enjoy this private time together; they laugh as the peddler awakes and finds his caps high in a tree (Figure 1−6).

Figure 1—7   Becca and the hats. A: Becca as the peddler. B: Becca shouts for her caps.

A   B

As the story ends Phyllis suggests that Becca get the hats from the box of dress-up clothes. She begins to assemble a pile of hats and starts to stack one after another on her head. As she removes some, Phyllis asks, "What do you say to those bad monkeys who stole your hats?" Becca shouts, "Give me back my caps!" (Figure 1—7, A and B).

Playing and Learning Outdoors

Once Chris and Leslie awake Phyllis asks the children if they want to help in the garden. They eagerly agree; they enjoy being outdoors and are curious about the changes that have occurred in the garden. Today some of the squash and gourds are to be harvested. Phyllis puts Megan in a backpack and the children bustle outside together. As the group gathers around the edge of the garden Phyllis begins to cut the vegetables from the vine. There are two varieties of squash and three varieties of gourds. The children notice this variety as they lug the vegetables into the cellar for winter storage. "Be sure to separate the squash from the gourds," Phyllis requests. The children talk among themselves, noting similarities and differences: "This one is skinny"; "This is a heavy one;" "It has a round top"; "These have stripes." Children observe differences in size, weight, color, patterns, and shape and are able to use mathematical terms such as "big," "heavy," "short," and "round" in a meaningful context.

As soon as all the vegetables are brought into the cellar the children begin their daily trip to the mailbox. The trek is about five hundred feet and it gives them a chance to run, chat, or play a game. Today Chris spies a nest high in a maple tree; he turns to his friends and says, "That might be a jackdaw's nest." He recalls this particular detail from *The Marvelous Land of Oz* by L. Frank Baum (1979), which Phyllis has just finished reading to the children. As they get closer to the mailbox Brett notices a clump of trees and remarks, "These are the bong trees!" The "bong trees" came from one of the children's favorite poems, "The Owl and the Pussycat" by Edward Lear. Chris and Brett's comments underscore again the role good literature can play in empowering children as literacy learners.

The Six-Year-Old Returns Home from School

As the children begin their walk back to the house, the school bus stops and lets David out. He runs ahead to join his friends. They talk together as they enter the house. David comes to the kitchen table for an after-school snack. The others, of course, join him and they continue to converse over some crackers and juice. At one point David looks to his mother and asks, "Mom, what does 'bleak' mean?" His mother is fairly certain she knows in what context he first heard this word, but to be sure she asks, "What do you mean, David?"

"You know," he says, "like he's bleak and bonio." His mother was correct in her thinking. The word "bleak" came from a favorite poem the children enjoyed entitled "Antonio" by Laura E. Richards (1935). David had heard that poem recited for several months. Only now does he inquire about a particular word from that poem. Phyllis trusts children to raise questions when something does not make sense. She knows that children's wonderings about how language works lead them in various directions. Some children act out a poem, draw a picture of it, transform a phrase, or inquire about a particular word. When the experience is kept open and the children are allowed to approach it in their own way, different interpretations and questions will arise. This diversity empowers the teacher as a learner. She knows children bring a variety of experiences and backgrounds to a given poem or story and they will live out that literary experience in their own way. Their responses provide her with new and exciting glimpses into how children transact with their world and how they continue to grow as active members of the literacy community.

As they finish their snack the children begin to engage in other activities. Leslie and Becca start to take out some of the dolls. Leslie covers one of the dolls with a quilt, feeling her head for a fever. She directs Becca to sit beside the doll while she finds the toy telephone. As she dials a few numbers she explains to Becca, "I'm the Mommy. I'm going to call the doctor. I have to give this medicine to the baby." At the other end of the living room Chris and David are using the wooden blocks to make a highway. Young Megan crawls over to investigate, pushing aside some of the blocks as she goes.

"Hey, Megan's wrecking our building. Can you get her away?" David asks his mother. The boys give her a few of the blocks they do not intend to use, hoping that these will appease her curiosity. They then return to their highway, using matchbox cars and miniature people to go on various trips. Brett comes over to join them, and the three play together for another twenty minutes. Then Brett leaves to get his writing folder and asks David if he wants to write in his journal. At Phyllis's suggestion both boys were recently encouraged to keep journals. Phyllis made the journals herself, sewing together blank sheets of paper and covering them with colorful scraps of wallpaper. Brett sits down at the kitchen table and begins to make his entry for the day as his brother looks on. He often begins by drawing and today is no exception. He draws a fire engine. David then asks him, "What are you going to say about your picture?"

Brett replies, "This is a fire engine going to David's school" (Figure 1−8). Brett is writing about an actual event, since there had been a major fire at David's school about a week ago and it had been discussed many times at home.

Brett begins to mumble "this" to himself several times. David listens and asks, "What do you hear in 'this'?"

"Z," says Brett.

"Good," says David. "Put that down."

The coaching continues as Brett begins to say "fire" aloud.

"What do you hear in 'fire'?" David asks.

"F," replies Brett.

"Good, you hear an F. Put that down," responds his brother.

Phyllis watches as David's support for Brett continues for almost a half hour. Never before has Brett persisted with his writing for that length of time. She realizes again how much children can learn from each other. David accepts Brett's spelling of "z" for "this" because he knows that is a good spelling for a beginning writer; he also realizes that spellings change over time. Phyllis has kept a folder of David's early writings, and he has noticed how he changed the spelling of his own name several times in the course of a year. By having the opportunity to reflect on his own growth as a writer, David thus gains a broader perspective on the process of writing and is able to give the necessary support to his brother as he too grows as a writer.

Figure 1–8   Brett: "This is a fire engine going to David's school."

The day begins to draw to a close as parents arrive to pick up their children. Before he leaves, Chris picks up his book of fairy tales and then shows his parents his "coat of mail." Phyllis smiles. Tomorrow will be another story, as the children continue to grow and share as language learners.

Personal Reflection

The home day care taught us many lessons. First, it taught us to trust. Although we could never predict how the children would use materials, their inventions always made sense and demonstrated how children are actively involved in constructing their own meanings. Secondly, the notion of a child's short attention span was disproved in this setting. Many times a two-year-old worked for nearly two hours with Play-Doh. We realized what a disservice is done to children when they are constantly hurried from one planned activity to the next. Third, we learned anew the power of children's literature. We constantly marveled at the intertwining of literary texts and each child's personal world of language. We realized more fully that rich and varied literary experiences provide children linguistic options in their description and reflection of their world. The day-care setting provided opportunities for all of us to grow and learn together.

References

Asbjornsen, A. J., and A. J. Moe. 1970. *East of the Sun and West of the Moon*. New York: Macmillan.

Baum, L. Frank. 1979. *The Marvelous Land of Oz*. New York: Ballantine.

Burke, Carolyn, and Kathy Short. 1987. "Creating Curriculums Which Foster Thinking." In *Critical Thinking*, ed. J. Harste. Urbana, Ill.: National Council of Teachers of English.

Chase, Richard. 1971. *The Jack Tales*. Boston: Houghton Mifflin.

Gelman, Rita. 1977. *More Spaghetti I Say*. New York: Scholastic.

Kent, Jack. 1971. *The Fat Cat*. New York: Scholastic.

Martin, Bill. 1972. *Sounds of a Storyteller*. New York: Holt, Rinehart and Winston.

Potter, Beatrix. 1974. *The Tale of Benjamin Bunny*. New York: Dover.

Richards, Laura E. 1935. *Tirra Lirra*. Boston: Little, Brown.

Rossetti, Christina. 1924. *Sing-Song*. New York: Macmillan.

Sendak, Maurice. 1962. *Chicken Soup with Rice*. New York: Harper & Row.

Sendak, Maurice. 1962. *Pierre*. New York: Harper & Row.

Slobodkina, Esther. 1968. *Caps for Sale*. New York: William R. Scott.

2

A Natural Curriculum

JEAN ANNE CLYDE

In this chapter, you will join the children and teachers of the Campus Children's Center in Bloomington, Indiana. You will see not only the variety of literacy opportunities that were available but also the way in which literacy learning was supported. While we found the daily book-sharing sessions and uninterrupted reading times crucial for the success of the program, we also discovered the importance of having the children "trip over" functional ways to use literacy. We have chosen to focus on the latter kind of experiences because of the difference they made.

These "invitations to literacy"—what we termed a "natural curriculum"—emerged through the research efforts of Laura Westberg, Denise Ogren, Susie Haigh, and myself in collaboration with the children and with one another. We wanted to create a context in which learning to read and write could be as easy and natural for these three- and four-year-olds as learning to talk. We hope you will get a sense of what Carolyn Burke and Jerry Harste referred to as the "seamlessness" of our program—a program in which there was no isolation of subject matter and no curricular fragmentation. Our natural curriculum assured that daily life at the center was an integrated experience, in which subject areas melted together and reading and writing were viewed as one of many ways to expand one's understanding of the world. While these opportunities varied from day to day, the nature of the curriculum remained consistent: it was always responsive to the needs and interests of the participants.

Evident throughout this chapter is a theme that distinguishes a natural curriculum from traditional programs: *All participants, whether tall or small, are recognized as learners.*

In large part, we tall learners attribute the success of our curriculum to our decision to become readers, writers, artists, musicians, block builders, and cleaner-uppers alongside the children. Terms such as *group*, *participants*, and *everyone* refer to the entire classroom community—the children and the teachers.

Figure 2–1   Lesson plan

Activity/Event	Time
Signing In	8:30–8:35 A.M.
Large Group Time 1 "Good Morning" (Name cards)	8:35–8:40 A.M.
Breakfast	8:40–9:00 A.M.
Large Group Time 2 Selecting a "Color Song" The teacher's plan book The arrival of *The Kids' Newspaper* The planning chart	9:00–9:40 A.M.
Self-selected activities time Lite-Brite Patrick's Happy Summer Book Singing in the block area Sending and receiving mail	9:40–10:45 A.M.
Large Group Time 3 Sharing time Cleanup	10:45–11:05 A.M.
Outdoor play/lunch	11:15 A.M.–12 Noon

Organized Flexibility: Our Daily "Lesson Plan"

The natural curriculum is flexible and learner centered; yet its thoughtfully orchestrated structure and a consistency about the daily schedule and the kinds of experiences that are offered enable children to increase their predictive power as they become more experienced as participants and language users. The lesson plan in Figure 2–1 represents this morning's events. Those events that are highlighted in boldface type—Signing In, Large Group Time 1, Large Group Time 2, Self-Selected Activities Time, Large Group Time 3, and Outdoor Play/Lunch—provide the daily structure within which experiences (many of which are created by the children themselves) are naturally tailored to the group's needs and interests.

We believe that reading and writing should be functional for learners. We believe, too, in the importance of providing all participants with frequent opportunities to shift stances from writer to reader, from action to reflection. Young children are supported as they explore the sights and sounds of written language through song lyrics, messages, notes, recipes, sign-up sheets, storybooks, personal letters, and environmental print. Additionally, the pervasive emphasis on sharing provides a natural medium through which to explore, express, and expand on ideas; sharing also ensures an audience for participants' ideas.

The Day Begins: Signing In

Each morning when children and teachers first enter the classroom, they "sign in" on the sign-in sheet just inside the door (Figure 2–2). Besides providing both an attendance count and an unofficial lunch count for the center's director, this name-writing activity also documents children's written language growth over time. It also lets participants become familiar with one another's signatures.

When children sign in, they both offer support to and receive help from one another. Today, after waiting for Jessa to sign in, Jossie stops for a moment to inspect her friend's signature. "J-E-S-S-A," she says aloud as she points to each of the letters.

Patrick makes use of environmental print that is available on a nearby wall as he watches Ryan sign in. He compares the letters that Ryan is writing to the teacher-made name cards. Although Ryan is quite competent at writing his own name, Patrick is there for support, and he reads, "A...N." as Ryan writes the last two letters of his name on the sheet.

Figure 2—2   The sign-in sheet

Large Group Time 1

 "Good Morning" (Name Cards)

After signing in, everyone gathers for a brief group time during which songs are sung while preparations for breakfast are being completed.

During this time, name cards, which participants have made for themselves, are spread out on the floor (Figure 2−3); each person finds his or hers and holds it

---

Figure 2−3   Name cards

up for Denise, our lead teacher, to read. While searching for their names, children often take time to deliver name cards to one another or provide assistance for those who have not yet found theirs. Teachers invite children to help them find their name cards as well. The identification of names constitutes an instance of reading and confirms that each person's signature is both real and readable.

Elliott, a former member of the classroom, is visiting today and is sitting next to his buddy, Gibson. Like all guests, Elliott is invited to make a name card for himself.

Children and teachers may make new name cards when they choose to do so. By reading to group members what they have written on their new cards, questions about what they "say" are answered. Cene, for instance, had been using only his first name until he made his newest name card. He then announced happily, "This says 'Cene Ketcham'!" Children do as much to support our efforts to unlock their unconventional written messages as we do to support their encounters with conventional print.

Today breakfast awaits, so Denise begins group time with the official greeting, singing "Good Morning" to group members, reading the names from the cards that they are displaying. As their names are sung, children deposit their names in the tin tray in the middle of the circle and go to the breakfast table in the common area outside the door.

Large Group Time 2

 ## Selecting a "Color Song"

After breakfast, everyone gathers once again on the large rug in the block area to sing songs; share news, ideas, and information; and plan the morning's activities. Although many songs are sung each morning, one of the highlights of Group Time 2 involves the selection of songs from a little book that everyone refers to as the "Color Song Book" (Brown 1980). Children find both its size and its colored pages, which serve as a filing system for its contents, very appealing. They especially enjoy taking turns choosing which of the songs to sing.

To determine whose turn it is, Denise directs the children's attention to the color song graph (Figure 2–4), which is posted on the message board. This simple graph provides, at a glance, a tally of the number of songs that each individual has already selected. Today, when the group looks at the graph, they see that Gibson has not picked a song in quite some time. The songbook is passed to him, and while other songs are being sung, he thumbs through it in search of a favorite.

After he has made his decision and delivered the book to Denise, Gibson

Figure 2-4   Color song graph

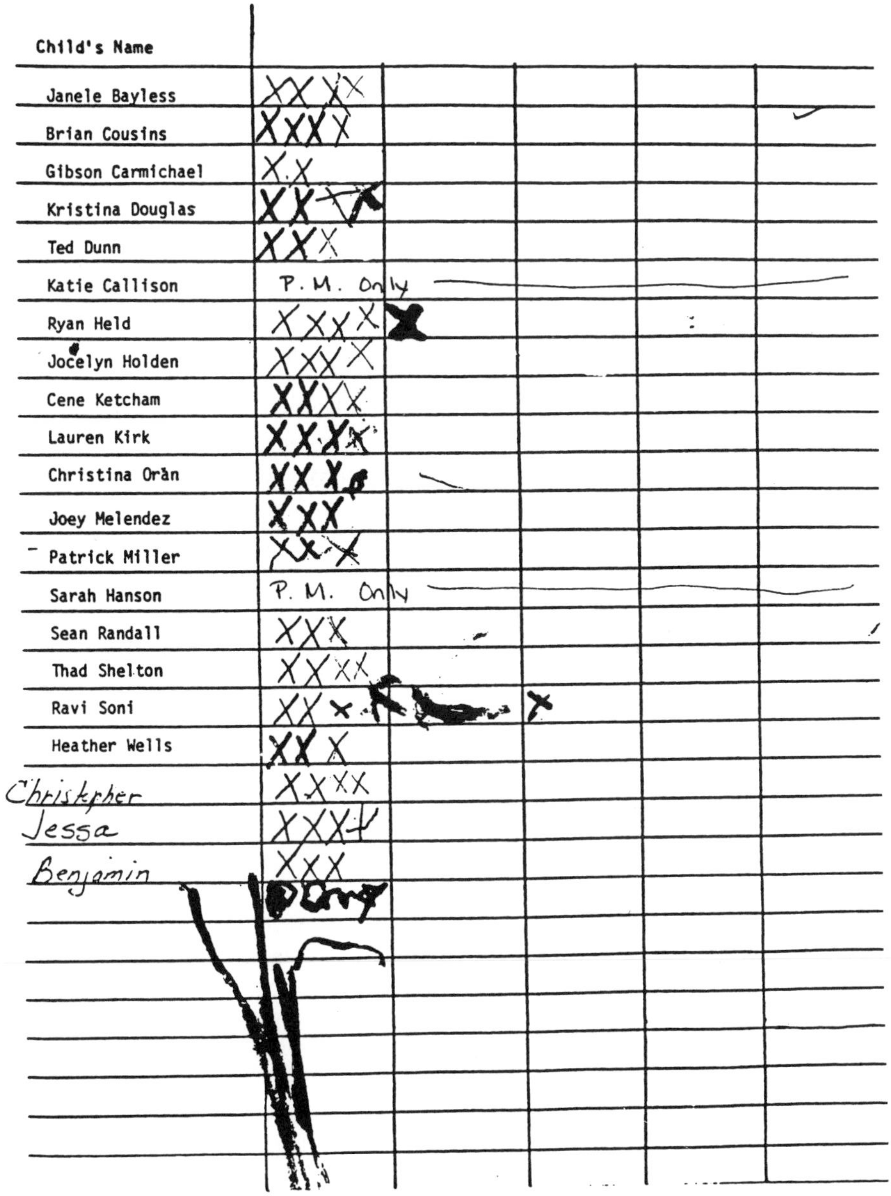

Child's Name					
Janele Bayless	XX XX				
Brian Cousins	XXX X				✓
Gibson Carmichael	X X				
Kristina Douglas	XX XX				
Ted Dunn	XX X				
Katie Callison	P. M. Only				
Ryan Held	XXX X				
Jocelyn Holden	XXX X				
Cene Ketcham	XXXX				
Lauren Kirk	X X XX				
Christina Orán	XX X				
Joey Melendez	XXX				
Patrick Miller	XX X				
Sarah Hanson	P. M. Only				
Sean Randall	XXX				/
Thad Shelton	XX XX				
Ravi Soni	XX X				
Heather Wells	XX X				
Chrishpher	X XXX				
Jessa	XXX X				
Benjamin	XXX				

signs his name on a dated piece of paper, which will be added to a book that documents the dates on which children select songs.

"Okay, this is the one that Gibson picked," Denise announces. "What color is it?"

"Green!" comes the unanimous and enthusiastic response.

"It's called 'The Wishy Washy Watermelon,' and the tune is 'John Brown's Body'...so it goes..." Denise "la la's" through the first verse for those who may be unfamiliar with the melody. Reading from the book that she holds up for all to see, she says, "But the words are, 'I'm sure a watermelon is the craziest food I've seen....'"

When the group finishes singing his song, Gibson puts an X beside his name on the graph.

Referring to the Teacher's Plan Book

Each day, teachers make a special effort to demonstrate to the group the varied functions of written language. One effective way in which Denise does this is by referring to one of her own personal resources—her daily plan book.

"Let me check and see if I've remembered to tell you everything," she says this morning, as she looks down at the book which lays open for all to see. "Oops—I've got one more thing in my plan book. This morning, you know what arrived?"

"Uh-huh," Brian nods.

"What are they, Brian?"

"The newspapers!" comes the excited response.

The Kids' Newspaper

Today marks the arrival of the third edition of a classroom document that had its origin six weeks earlier. *The Kids' Newspaper* (Figure 2–5) features news items, stories, messages, drawings, jokes, and songs created by children, teachers, and parents. This biweekly publication includes both conventional and unconventional forms of written language, providing conventional "translations" in parentheses for its adult readers.

Contributions to the newspaper are voluntary. The items that are received before the deadline are photocopied and reduced. Children are then invited to help decide the placement of pieces, to create and write headings for various sections, and to order and number pages. The "taped-up" version is then sent to the printer to be duplicated.

Because Joey has been so intimately involved in the production of this latest issue, Denise invites him to distribute the newspaper to friends. Kristy, meanwhile, leaves the group to get markers so that participants may write their names on

---

Figure 2–5   Front page of *The Kids' Newspaper*

RHELSSe BbG

(THE KID'S NEWSPAPER)

Aphille

|

NEWS FROM BENJAMIN'S FAMILY

Benjamin and his sister, Emily, are taking a trip to Chicago to go to a wedding. The kids' aunt is getting married to a young man who grew up in Russia. His name is Igor.

SUPERMAN II by SOPERMANII

Clark was Superman. Bad guys go him but he was stronger so he changed them into ordinary people. He took Lois home and went to the restaurant and then he said, "Hey! You are sitting in my favorite seat." He spinned him and pushed him over the counter. And then he went back home.

their copies. Lauren has the same idea and makes an announcement to the group: "Write your name on it in case these get lost."

As the children receive their copies, snatches of conversations can be heard. Lauren, one of the first recipients, searches for where to begin reading the paper. "Is this just starting?" she wonders aloud, until she finds something that one of her friends has contributed to the document. "Jessa! Look what I found!" she says almost breathlessly upon seeing Jessa's "coloring book," a collection of four drawings that occupies one of the pages of the newspaper entitled "All Different Kinds of Toys."

"I wanna read a joke," Ryan says, expecting to find a Joke Page like those that appeared in issues one and two. Although there is not a similar section in this edition, the teachers will later capitalize on Ryan's desire to read and share "funnies" by inviting him to contribute a joke to the next issue of *The Kids' Newspaper*.

Denise and Susie encourage the children's exploration of the document. "Open your newspaper and see what kinds of news you find in there," suggests Denise as she thumbs through her own copy of the paper. "See if you can find something from your friends."

Three-year-old Christopher spies Jessa's name in the paper and runs over to tell her. "Hey, Jessa! You made this!" His discovery, which reveals to us that he has used print to make a decision about ownership, enables us to classify our newest and youngest class member as a reader.

Also included in *The Kids' Newspaper* are "Messages from Mommies" (Figure 2–6). When Jessa finds the message from Seth (penned by her mom for her two-year-old brother), Denise uses the opportunity to help her discover that page numbers are helpful to readers. "See if you can find a page number on these so I can find the message too," she encourages.

Participants eagerly read and share for nearly twenty minutes. Noticing that several children have taken their papers to the art table in order to color portions of it, Denise and Susie draw group time to a close and begin the transition to the self-selected activities time. Attention is now directed to the planning chart.

 ## The Planning Chart

The natural curriculum is designed to promote social interactions among all participants. One of the ways in which this is accomplished is through the use of the planning chart. Children and teachers are encouraged to invite others to join them in activities during the self-selected activities time. Those interested in doing so publicly record their invitations on the chart, which remains posted on an easel in the block area all morning.

The form that the document assumes varies from day to day, from a child-dictated plan to one written by individuals who are extending the invitations. The functions of the planning chart, however, remain the same. It involves

Figure 2−6   Messages from Mommies

children with meaningful print, demonstrating its function as an aid to memory; promotes social interaction in the classroom; serves a generative function, with one individual's ideas frequently acting as a catalyst for other ideas; and informs latecomers of the invitations that have been extended to group members.

This morning children have been dictating their ideas to Susie, who records them on chart paper. Because "planning" is informal and ongoing from the time children first enter the room in the morning, the teachers reread the list to inform everyone of the choices that are available. Today, before reviewing options, Denise extends one final invitation to the group to make any last-minute additions to the list. "Anybody else have something they want to share with a friend? Elliott, do you know what you would like to do in school today?" she asks the visitor.

The arrival of *The Kids' Newspaper* has sparked in many an interest in coloring the publication, and Elliott and Gibson officially add this to the planning chart. Although individual activities such as coloring are always an option within the classroom during this time period, the activities that are listed on the planning chart are usually more social. Denise gently tries to emphasize this point as she waits for other suggestions, saying, "If there's something you want to do with a friend..." When Denise reviews the planning chart in its entirety, she will discover that this point still needs clarification (Figure 2–7).

"Okay, let me read to you what our friends said they want to do so you'll know if you want to do something with your friends," Denise begins, pointing to the chart as she reads. "We need to make Patrick's Happy Summer book, and I'll get the special paper for that; Jocelyn's going to make a Happy Easter card; Brian's going to be in the blocks; Patrick wanted to use Lite-Brite; Christina's going to be in the blocks; and Kristy's in the blocks...so Brian and Christina and Kristy—"

"I wanna play in the blocks," Heather chimes in.

"And Heather, too? You need to talk about what you're going to do in the blocks together," Denise advises, aware now of the number of children who intend to spend at least a portion of their morning in the block area. We can see yet another benefit of the planning chart—alerting teachers to potential problems that may arise because of the popularity of a particular area or set of materials.

Denise continues reading. "Cene's going to do some papers, and Lauren's going to color the newspaper, and Elliott's going to color his newspaper."

"I wanna color in my newspaper," Joey adds, and Jessa decides likewise.

"If you're doing something just like the newspaper, we really don't have to write it up here. Only if you want to invite your other friends to do it," remarks Denise in a second gentle reminder that the planning chart serves a social function for friends.

Joey, who was originally interested in coloring his paper, has now changed his mind. "I'm gonna make all kinds of kites," he informs the group. Once this final invitation has been recorded on the chart, the group is dismissed to pursue the activities of choice. Jessa remains behind for a few seconds, stopping momentarily at the planning chart to review once more her list of social options for the morning's events.

Figure 2−7   The planning chart

April 19   Friday
Patrick's Happy Summer
Book ☼

Elliott is visiting
The newspaper arrived

Jocelyn - make a Happy Easter card
Brian - blocks
Patrick - Lite-Brite
Christina - blocks - big house
Kristy - blocks
Cene - do papers by himself
Louren - make a color book in newspaper
Elliott - color in newspaper
Joey - make a kite

Self-Selected Activities Time

 **Lite-Brite**

A number of children have expressed an interest in working with Lite-Brite today. This activity involves matching colored pegs to designs on a light board. At times several children gather around and watch or assist as a friend explores the potential of this "game." Posting a sign-up sheet (Figure 2–8) in this and other popular areas enables participants to self-regulate their use and at the same time provides another real, purposeful reason for name-writing.

Figure 2–8   The sign-up sheet for using Lite-Brite

 **Patrick's Happy Summer Book**

One of the invitations that the teachers have listed on the planning chart is to make a page for a going-away book for Patrick, whose last day is today. Cene is the first contributor to the book. He is already beginning work as Susie, the assistant teacher, sits down at the table. "Happy summer," Susie reads slowly as she writes on a sign that will be placed on the table not only to designate the special book-making area, but also to provide children with some conventional spellings, should they choose to use them.

"Patrick," offers Cene, as Susie completes her "Happy Summer, Patrick" sign. Cene now turns his attention to the page that he has already begun, which will ultimately consist entirely of his friend's name and some pictures. "I writed the P. Could you write the—"

"You can write the rest of it," Susie assures him as she moves the sign in front of him. "Here are the letters so you'll know how to do it."

Cene inspects the sign, but when Susie is called away from the table for a moment, he signals an uncertainty about making an A, calling to her, "I can't write that letter. Susie, I can't write that letter." When he has her complete attention once again he insists, "I can't write 'Patrick.'" In the encounter that follows, Susie supports Cene in his efforts to write his friend's name. As they work together she makes good use of her knowledge about Cene and his interest in and love for books and print. She helps him make connections and build upon his experiences as a reader/writer. At the same time she is careful to allow Cene to direct the event and to ensure that he has complete ownership of his product.

"What's this letter?" Susie asks, pointing to the A on the sign.

"I don't know," Cene tells her.

"It's an A," she informs him. He repeats the letter name to himself as he begins exploring the making of one. "No, that's not how you make an A," he decides after examining his first effort. He makes a second attempt, and this time, satisfied with it, announces, "A" (Figure 2–9).

Figure 2–9   Writing "Patrick"

Susie does not intervene or comment on his decision to place the second letter far across the page to the left of his *P*, but she instead applauds his effort: "That's right." Then, pointing to the *T*, she asks, "Now, what's this letter?"

"I don't know," comes the response. Susie helps Cene to make connections between what she's certain he already knows and this latest effort. "It's what /T/-/ed/ [Ted] starts with," she tells him, turning his attention to the initial sound in his best friend's name.

"Tuh...," he says, stopping to think for a moment before looking at Susie and saying, "*T*."

"Right," she smiles, watching as the youngster confidently makes a *T* on his paper.

As they continue, Susie helps him keep track of where he is as Cene quickly writes *R*, *I*, and *C*. But he has questions when he encounters the final letter in Patrick's name. "And what's that?" Susie asks, pointing to the *K* on the sign.

"*K*," Cene responds without hesitation. But the making of it is not so apparent to him. "*K*? How do you make a *K*?" he asks Susie.

"Just like that," she tells him, keeping a finger on the sign at which they've been looking. Susie is aware of the importance of Cene's actual involvement in the process, so the marker remains in his hand. He begins with a straight line, to which he adds a second line by placing his marker in the middle of the first. Susie talks him through the rest of the letter. "Up, up," she says, as he makes a line to form the upper portion of the letter.

"That's right," Susie assures him. "Now make a line that goes down." With that final suggestion, Cene completes Patrick's name (Figure 2−10).

"Good! You made 'Patrick!'" she exclaims, looking nearly as excited as Cene himself. "Can you find your *P*? Find your *P*." Cene quickly locates the first letter he wrote and puts his finger on it. "Okay, there's your *P*. Now where's your *A*?" Cene continues to point to each of the letters as Susie gently reviews with him the strategy that they used to get this important meaning down on paper.

Having located his *T*, *R*, *I*, and *C*, Susie asks, "Where's your *K*?" When he puts his finger on the last of his red letters, Susie hugs him tightly, celebrating his success as a writer/reader. "'Patrick'! You wrote 'Patrick,' Cene! That's great!"

But Cene has not quite finished yet. As if to explore his independent use of this strategy, he begins asking Susie to locate letters. "What about the...uh...*R*?"

Now it's Susie's turn to do the pointing. "There's your *R*."

"And what about..." Cene's voice trails off for a second as he inspects his aborted *A*. "That's Patrick's mom," he decides, attaching significance to what was originally a "mistake."

Susie is called away from the table. Cene has completed his writing but remains at the table, where he continues to elaborate on his work, adding to it a portrait of Patrick and one of himself (Figure 2−11). After signing his name on the back of his paper he leaves it on the table for inclusion in Patrick's book and is off to another area of the room.

Figure 2–10   "Patrick" by Cene

Figure 2–11   Cene's contribution to Patrick's Happy Summer book

 ## Singing in the Block Area

While Cene and Susie are busy making a page for Patrick's Happy Summer book, Kristy and Brian have elected to sit in the wooden boat in the block area to sing songs from the "Color Song Book." Kristy, having just finished singing a song, selects one for Brian and passes the book to him to use as he sings. When he finishes, it's Kristy's turn once again, and as part of their turn-taking ritual, he returns the book to her for use as she sings.

While most of her lyrics are inaudible, when Kristy turns to a song entitled "Bend and Sway," we are able to hear snatches of the words from this favorite "yellow song." As she nears the end of her song, we hear Kristy's lyrics change to "It's Brian's turn, it's Brian's turn," before she returns the book to her young partner.

Kristy and Brian sing together for nearly eleven minutes before joining others, who are building with blocks. Later in the morning, Christopher joins them, and the singing begins once again, this time with Denise providing accompaniment on her guitar.

 ## Sending and Receiving Mail

Originally created for the delivery of valentines, mailboxes continue to be important to group members. Messages, reminders, and artwork are frequently exchanged through the classroom mail system as gestures of friendship and affection.

Because reading and writing are social events, a decision on the part of any participant to become involved with print nearly always attracts the attention of others. And more often than not, the original engagement generates new instances of literacy.

Today Jossie's announcement that she's "making mail" results in a social situation in which two friends, with differing amounts of experience, but similar intentions, work together on the making and sharing of meaning.

When I join Jossie, she creates a "picture of buildings" for me. I invite her to tell me about it and then use her description of her work when I make a thank-you card for her. The inclusion of Jossie's own words in my card will add to the predictability of the text when she later encounters it as a reader.

Unspoken "rules" govern the operation of the mail system. The most important rule is that one may not read one's mail until it has been delivered. Interestingly enough, though, it is perfectly acceptable to be present while one's mail is being created. In fact, by answering questions and making suggestions, it is even possible to assist the writer/illustrator, provided that no peeking takes place during the piece's production. Jossie promises not to peek at what I'm doing, but she remains at the table, where she soon begins working on something of her own. Both a learner and a teacher, she offers to share her expertise with me as she begins her piece.

"Do you know how I do this?"

"How do you do what?" I ask as I watch her smooth out the piece of paper that she has just folded in half.

"We cut this in half...and I'll go get some scissors and show you," she says, as she scurries off to the supply cart. Seconds later she returns. "I got the scissors. Now I straighten it out like this...I go inside of the line and...cutting it."

"Oh, is that how you know where to cut?" I ask.

"And then we cut across," she continues as she begins cutting. "See how I do this? And then you take a marker...." I pass the canister of colored felt tips to her, and she takes one and begins drawing on the page. "And then we put something..."

"Now, how do you know what to write on there?" I ask her, in a genuine attempt to understand how she is going about her decision-making process.

"Well, because I look at the bumps," she tells me, and when I ask what the bumps that she has drawn tell her, she says, "The bumps tell you what to draw."

About this time Jossie glances over at the card that I've been working on. "I can't wait for my thank-you letter!" she whispers, catching herself before she breaks the "no peeking" rule. "I'm gonna make you one, too."

When I finish the card, I deliver it to her mailbox and she quickly retrieves it. "What does it say?" she giggles.

"What does it say?" I repeat, hopeful that she will take a guess as its contents. "What do you think it—" but she's way ahead of me.

Treating the card like a letter, she opens it up and begins reading, "'Jossie.' I don't know." It occurs to me that she may not have had any prior experience with greeting cards, so I demonstrate how they are usually read.

"Well, I decided to give you a card instead of just writing you mail," I explain, folding the card once again. "So the front says," I pause, waiting to see what she will make of the print.

"'Thank you,'" she reads. Exactly. She opens the card and begins reading the message inside. In doing so, she makes good use of contextual clues, combining information about her original picture with the expertise that she has garnered during her career as a reader. "'Jossie...I love...'"

"'getting...,'" I read, to preserve the flow of language.

"'mail....'" she reads.

"'from...'"

"'you. Thanks for the...'"

"'neat...picture of...'"

"'buildings,'" she reads, as we together maintain the continuity of the message. "Yeah!" And, reading the closing, "'Love...'"

"'Jean Anne,'" she laughs and then announces, "Well, I'll make you one." "Oh, great!"

"Would you like to help me say it?" Jossie invites, as she folds her paper in half so as to look like the card she has just received.

"Sure, I'll help you," I tell her. "You just tell me what to do." I want to be sure that my role in this production is one of support, not direction.

"Um, inside it's gonna say, uh, 'Why do you give me so much mail?'" she beams.

I manage to contain a giggle at the thought of this interesting message. "Are you going to write that?" I ask, as I pass the canister of markers to my friend.

"I don't know how to write it," she confesses. Yet I know better.

"Oh," I respond encouragingly. There is a lengthy pause as Jossie waits, with pen poised, in anticipation of information from me. Aware of her familiarity with print, I also wait, giving her the opportunity to take charge of the event.

"Will you tell me?" she asks.

"Sure." Again I wait; then finally, as though I had somehow forgotten, I ask, "What are we writing?"

"'Why do you give me so much mail,'" she repeats.

"How should I help?" I ask her, again turning responsibility for the production over to her.

She now offers her message one word at a time. "'Why,'" comes the first one.

To give her another chance at independently solving the problem, I repeat the word. "'Why.'" While my intent is not to spell for her, Jossie seems to interpret my word "why" as the letter Y, and writes a Y at the top of her page. Having determined that she has captured her first word, I move to the next word in her message.

"'Do?' Is that what you said?" Again Jossie comments that she doesn't know how to write it. I repeat the letter sound, believing that she has had enough experience as a reader/writer to make a reasonable guess. "Duh...do..." After a moment's thought, Jossie quickly makes a D next to her Y.

To highlight her success so far, I point to the letters that she has written to placehold the first two words in her message: "'Why do.' What's the next word we're doing?" I ask her, again putting her in charge.

"'You,'" Jossie offers. But before I say anything, she applies the same strategy that she used in spelling "why": she writes the letter name that corresponds with the word she is working on. "You," therefore, becomes "U."

But in reading what she has just written, something suddenly clicks for Jossie, and she changes her mind about it. "Y-O-U!" she says excitedly, as she self-corrects what she's writing (Figure 2–12).

"'Give...,'" I say, prompting her.

"'Me...,'" she chimes in, somehow overlooking the writing of "give." I repeat what she has said. "I don't know," she says, as she sits, ready to write.

"'Me.' Hmmm...let's see," I say, thinking aloud. I slow down the pronunciation of the word to see what Jossie will do with it. "Mmmmm..."

Her eyes light up. "M!" She quickly jots it down.

"Beautiful," I assure her. This time I emphasize the end of the word, too. "Mmmeee...mmmeee."

"E," she says quickly, writing one next to her M.

There is a great enthusiasm building in Jossie, and decisions about what to write are suddenly becoming much easier for her. I simply continue to help her keep track of where she is in her message, occasionally rereading what she has

Figure 2–12   "Why do you…"

committed to paper thus far. In seconds, she has completed the word "so." Three Ms placehold the word "much," one immediately after "so," and two on the following line—one for each of the times that she repeated the word to herself.

Jossie has written the first letter of her last word (M for "mail") when one of the other children stops by to model a pink ballerina outfit. Seconds later, when I am able to turn my attention once again to Jossie, she has finished her original message. She has generated her own functional spelling—"mal"—for the word "mail."

I express my surprise at what she has written. "I love that message!" I tell her. But she has decided to add something else to it before sending it to me.

"I know," she smiles, and she begins spelling aloud as she writes, "I love you." About to leave the table to deliver the mail, Jossie remembers one last item. "Wait, I have to sign my name." And, following a quick signature, she is off (Figure 2–13).

Seconds later, her little girl voice sings out from across the room. "I put mail in your mailbox!"

By the time I return with my message, several children are working at our table. In celebrating Jossie's accomplishments as a writer, I engage Gibson, seated to my immediate right, as the audience. "Look, Gibson, I got mail," I tell him. "Can I read my letter to you?" He is clearly interested in its contents. This message has, by now, gained such importance that it is as though none of us has ever seen it before. And Jossie is so excited that she hops up and down as I begin reading.

"This is from Jocelyn," I say, pointing to her name. "And this says, 'Why do you give me so much mail?'"

Figure 2−13   Jossie's letter

A squeal of laughter signals Jossie's delight at her wonderful success, and we hug one another in celebration. Accepting her best effort has conveyed a strong, clear message to her: I consider her to be a writer. And sharing her writing with Gibson has demonstrated to her that her writing is readable. A simple exchange of meanings between two good friends has moved this four-year-old forward, highlighting new strategies that she can later explore as she expands her potential as a flexible language user.

Large Group Time 3

 **Sharing Time**

Sharing time demonstrates an appreciation for both the uniqueness of the individual and the social nature of the natural curriculum. It is a time when participants are encouraged to explore the many creations and experiences that friends have enjoyed during the morning. Ten to fifteen minutes are reserved at the conclusion of each morning for the group to refer back to the day's planning chart. Discussions about what each individual has done, how he or she did it, and what it is used for frequently spark follow-up projects or the generation of new ideas that are explored later that same day or sometime in the future. Also discussed are any additional activities in which group members have engaged during their free-

Figure 2—14   **The cleanup chart**

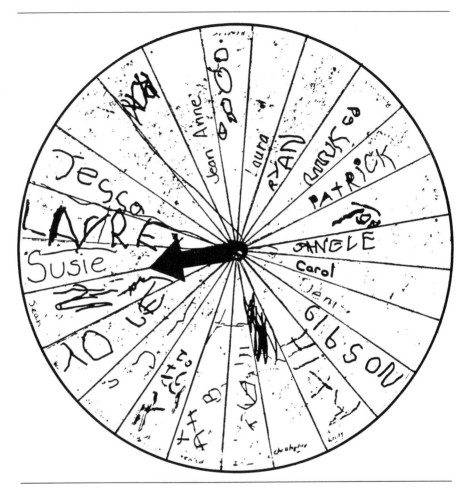

choice time that, for one reason or another, were never recorded on the chart. Sharing also provides for a nice transition into cleanup.

 **Cleanup**

Following sharing, attention turns to the cleanup chart, which has been created from a cardboard circle that once supported a frozen pizza (Figure 2—14). On it are the names of all of the members of the classroom community. Each day, the arrow is moved one space to indicate the name of the day's "cleanup teacher." This individual assigns children and teachers to clean particular areas of the room. Ordinarily, when the cleanup teacher has determined that an area is sufficiently clean, the helpers responsible for the area are dismissed to the playground. But today the group meets once more for a final, special sharing time to present Patrick with his Happy Summer book.

Special Large Group Time

 ### Sharing Patrick's Happy Summer Book

In the block area, group members present Patrick with the Happy Summer book that they have been working on all morning. As Patrick sits in Denise's lap, reading through the book, the contributors talk about the pages they made.

"Oh, look at that one," Denise says, clearly impressed with the special piece. "Who did the red one?" Cene, who is grinning from ear to ear, raises his hand. "Cene, tell us about yours."

"I wrote 'Patrick,'" he says, obviously proud of his effort.

"He wrote Patrick's name. He wrote all the letters," Denise affirms, pointing to each of them as she reads, "*P*, and an *A*, and a *T*, and an *R*, an *I*..." Denise pauses now, in search of the *C*.

Cene can barely contain his excitement. "I wrote 'Patrick'!" he nods, still beaming.

Denise, having found the remaining two letters, concludes, "a *C*, and *K*."

"And he wrote 'Patrick,'" says Joey, verifying Cene's success as a writer and supporting his efforts.

Group time has concluded, and children are dismissed to their cubbies, where they will bundle up for the outdoor play that follows. As Cene skips out of the room, we sense his satisfaction; he has just received recognition from participants— children and teachers alike— of his success as a writer. Armed with the confidence of an experienced language user, he, along with the other children in our class, will continue his pursuit of print when he wakes from his nap this afternoon.

Summary

We worked hard to guarantee that the print that littered our natural curriculum was whole, meaningful, and purposeful. Rather than focusing energies on fragments of print that, in isolation, meant nothing to any language learner, print was always embedded within the context of rich curricular experiences that grew from the interests and needs of participants.

Here children could explore the interrelationships among print, color, story, rhyme, rhythm, and other contextual features, to find multiple avenues and clues for creating meaning. They saw print function as an organizational device that engaged them in the self-regulation of what are traditionally considered to be "teacher" tasks, and sometimes time-consuming ones at that. Experiences such as signing in, signing up to use materials or to share books, or conducting surveys to vote on which of three books we should dramatize conveyed a trust in children as self-disciplinarians, capable decision makers, and successful writer/readers.

Children were helped to develop sensitivities to variations in written language use—not by presenting isolated bits of instruction designed to "teach" them, but by providing demonstrations through our own engagement as writer/readers, and by inviting them to engage in the process as well. Kids learned about newspapers, for instance—their production, the existence and purpose of page numbers, the identical nature of copies of the same published material, and so on—through participating as contributors to, and editors and readers of, their own *Kids' Newspaper*. Literacy was never dissected into little bites to be served by others to children; it was experienced by them, each and every day.

Personal Reflection

Because we understood the literacy learning process, we celebrated all engagements with print, regardless of how unconventional the surface structure of the children's efforts may have appeared. Our experiences as teacher/researchers served us well, for we were confident that with time and experience, children would develop as flexible written language users. We looked for evidence about what they already knew and understood, recognizing that their decisions as writers/readers were not random and disconnected, but instead reflected their understandings of what literacy is all about. When supporting—not directing—their growth, we used our observations to keep ourselves informed—to help us determine the kinds of experiences and demonstrations that we should provide next in order to challenge their current understandings and help them refine their current notions of literacy.

We withheld from these children the all-too-popular notions of reading and writing as mysterious and intrinsically difficult processes. Instead, we intimately wove print into the fabric of the day; we read to them and wrote with them to demonstrate how print works. We treated literacy learning as the natural, easy process that we believed it to be. We joyfully witnessed that our young collaborators were comfortably and confidently emerging as readers and writers.

References

Brown, L. 1980. *Sing a Song of Colors*. Charlotte, N.C.: Shoestring Publications.

3

Teachers and Children: Partners in Learning

HEIDI MILLS

Welcome to the Roosevelt Child Development Center, one of three such centers in the Grand Rapids Public School System created to provide an alternative to traditional preschool, readiness, kindergarten, and Montessori programs. Each center follows a cross-age grouping format and serves an integrated population of Black, Hispanic, Indian, and Caucasian children. Funded by both Head Start and Grand Rapids Public Schools, each center serves approximately 160 children in an open-space environment. The total population is split between morning and afternoon sessions. Eight professionals — four teachers and four aides — team teach together at each site. They are supported by a full-time program director and language arts teacher/consultant. A speech pathologist and consultants in physical education, music, and art visit each program one day per week.

As you visit our classroom you will see that our staff has developed a variety of complementary roles to ensure that the program runs effectively. The specific roles for staff members (coach, greeter, rover, and breakfast/lunch helper) rotate on a daily basis among the entire team. You will see how these roles get played out as the chapter unfolds. In addition to each of these positions, teachers and aides work together as partners to plan individual strategy lessons and record observations for twenty children in both the morning and afternoon sessions. Each teacher is also responsible for creating learning experiences for one of the four curricular areas: science/sensory awareness, general movement, mathematics, and language. Focusing on authentic learning experiences, each area provides a diverse range of flexible materials, activities, and strategy lessons to accommodate the varying developmental needs and interests of the four- to six-year-olds with whom the staff works.

The staff members are most concerned with providing a continuity of experience for children within and across curriculum areas. Careful staff documentation and planning meetings lead to the continual refinement of specific instructional invitations and general program goals, philosophy, and organization. The most valuable aspect of the centers' commitment to continued staff development is daily coaching. Teachers are observed by their colleagues on a daily basis. After school the staff meets to share observations. In this way, the teachers continually learn from one another by recognizing supportive teaching strategies, asking questions, telling success stories, and considering various ways to teach concepts or demonstrate strategies. Mary Lou is the coach today, so you will see how this is implemented when she observes and reflects upon Tim's interactions with five-year-old Kristina.

You will also get to know Kristina by following her through the morning. Because the center serves a tremendous number of children, it might seem overwhelming to only glance over the wide range of activities that occur simultaneously. Instead, you will play shadow to Kristina as she walks you through a typical day. It is my hope that you will come to appreciate the center's curriculum and visualize how it is organized by living it with Kristina.

The Day Begins

It's a late winter day in February. The rising sun forecasts a beautiful Michigan day. As the school buses pull up to the Child Development Center, the staff is busy inside preparing for the day's activities.

At 8:30 A.M. the two greeters walk out to meet the children as the buses unload. With smiles and hugs, the children share stories from home with their friends and teachers. Snowsuits swish and small feet stomp off snow before they enter the building. Carter, a small, sparkling-eyed four-year-old, wants to talk to Jackie, a greeter, about a message he plans to write today. "Me and my momma, we be going to K-Mart and we be going to McDonald's."

Another child, Brian, talks with a group of friends about his weekend visit with his dad. "And we watched some football on TV and we saw *Return of the Jedi* and...." Brian helps other children tie their shoes and takes a book from his backpack that he intends to read during small-group time. In this cohesive community of learners, children support and learn from one another.

Eager to start the day, the children hang up their coats, put away their belongings, and enter the center to the smells of freshly scrambled eggs, sausage, toast, apple juice, and milk. The breakfast helpers are buttering toast and pouring juice for the first arrivals. Most children choose to eat breakfast if they have not already eaten at home. Others begin selecting activities in the various learning areas.

Teachers take advantage of breakfast time to visit casually with the children. They also capitalize on opportunities to affirm children's abilities as readers, engaging them in reading the print that pervades this print-rich environment. On this particular morning, I introduce myself to Mary, a four-year-old new to our program.

"Tell me what you did in your other school."

"Played," Mary answers quickly.

"What else?"

"Nothing," Mary shrugs.

"Did you read many books?"

"I don't know how to read," she answers automatically.

"Sure, you do! Tell me what that says," I say as I point to Mary's milk carton.

Mary blushes and softly reads, "Milk." Informal experiences that highlight the functional nature of print do much to convince children that they are, indeed, readers.

At the same time Brian, who is sitting next to Mary, picks up his milk carton and reads aloud the entire "Fun Facts to Know and Tell" from the side of the milk carton. "Why is the ocean salty?..."

Such interactions further convince us that children construct meaning from print based on their individual experiences with this sign system. The social context is also important to a sound understanding of literacy learning. Like the two children having breakfast this morning, our students typically respond to print in a logical, systematic, and rule-governed fashion. With children of varying ability levels interacting throughout the day, there are many opportunities for children to demonstrate their ability to read and to support their peers' attempts.

As the last bites of breakfast are being consumed, the children begin helping the staff clean up. When they finish they move to the four major curriculum areas. During the next hour and a half, the children will visit all four areas, choosing from the many options available in each of them.

Science/Sensory Awareness Area

On any given day, children find an interesting assortment of activities and experiences available in the science/sensory awareness area: finger painting, various cooking projects (making fruit salads, yogurt, popcorn, french fries, and soup), puppet making, tie dying, and collage making are among their favorites.

The sand table also has many uses, housing everything from uncooked rice, snow, and pebbles to navy beans and a variety of measuring utensils and toys.

Today, after donning her apron, six-year-old Kristina joins her brother Jimmy and some other children at the water table where they play enthusiastically, pouring water back and forth between containers. Once Kristina has finished playing at the water table, she decides to participate in an art activity, mixing colors with eye droppers and colored water in styrofoam cups. Ellen, the art rover, encourages the children to experiment with color mixing while she supports and shares in their discoveries. There are squeals of delight from Kristina as she sees that combining two colors creates a third.

"Kristina, you've made green!" Ellen exclaims. "How did you do that?"

The youngster reflects for a moment. "Um... I took some from this water," she begins, pointing to the yellow liquid, "and some from the blue. And it made green!" Kristina's discovery has enticed other children to replicate her feat.

Meanwhile, Mike, clad in a smock, is experimenting with color in another way. As he completes a tempera painting at the easel he adds "This is a house" to his creation (Figure 3–1). Crayons, paste, colored construction paper, scissors, magazines, and colored chalk are also put out for the children's enjoyment. Other options exist for the children as well, and a quick look around provides evidence

Figure 3–1   **"This is a house."**

of their appeal. Some children are observing fish in the aquarium. Others, wearing headphones, are listening to a Hap Palmer album and experimenting with rhythm instruments.

Because the children are trusted as capable decision makers, they are free to initiate their own activities. They have just completed a unit on animals, and today many children are helping to remove drawings of birds from the bulletin boards. Four-year-old Mia suggests that they make a book about birds using those that they have constructed in the art area. Entitled *Everything You Should Know About Birds*, it reads

This bird is flying, flying, flying
I like this bird.
He is flying.
This bird is going to see his girlfriend in Texas.
Birds sit on eggs.
Birds eat snakes.
I like to see birds fly.
Birds eat worms.
The bird is flying.
I saw a dead bird.
I saw a bird.
You should leave birds alone.
If you shoot a bird it will fall.
The end.

Before leaving the sensory area, Kristina writes "klr mxen" (color mixing) on a piece of paper to share during the base group meeting. She is ready to move on to a new area of the center. Kristina notices that there one red yarn necklace left on the doorknob. This means there is room for one more child in the general movement room, and she decides to take advantage of this opportunity.

General Movement Area

Today's obstacle course, created by the collaborative efforts of children and the general movement teacher, is the most enticing option to Kristina. Written directions are posted to guide her.

Following Matt's lead (Figure 3–2), Kristina will

1. crawl through the tunnel;
2. go under the balance beam;
3. jump five times on the trampoline;
4. walk across the ladder;
5. run through all six tires;
6. start over.

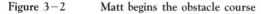

Figure 3–2   Matt begins the obstacle course

Plasticine clay and Tinker Toys are the choices available at the fine motor table. Dwain, one of the teachers, is on the floor working with Jerwarn, who is making a space station. "Look!" cries Jerwarn, excited about his creation. "I made a space station! Want me to show you how to make one?" he asks Dwain. After a quick double check of the obstacle course, Dwain accepts Jerwarn's invitation and begins working on a space station of his own. Dwain carefully follows Jerwarn's lead, casting himself as learner in this child-initiated experience.

"What should I do first?" he asks his five-year-old friend.

"See, it goes like this," explains the youngster, demonstrating how to make a space station. As Jerwarn continues, Dwain makes a mental note of what this demonstration might suggest that the child knows and understands. These informal observations will be the basis of future instructional decisions regarding Jerwarn.

When their stations are complete, they begin improvising an elaborate space story, using the Tinker Toys as props. "Hey, you sure know how to tell exciting stories," compliments Dwain. "I'll bet your friends would love to hear this one. Would you like to write it down to share with them during gathering?"

Jerwarn nods his head, grinning from ear to ear, and off he goes to get supplies to record his story.

By now Kristina has completed her journey through the obstacle course. She skips out of the room in time to the music that is playing.

As she is leaving the general movement room her friend, Amy, sees her and invites her to work with her in the "grocery store" in the language area. Delighted that Kristina is interested, Amy asks, "Do you want to be the customer or the cashier?"

"The customer," Kristina decides, adding, "We can switch later, maybe."

She looks through the prepared shopping lists that consist of product labels the children have collected from home, pasted on tagboard, and then laminated. She selects the one in Figure 3–3 to use as she shops. With grocery bag in hand, Kristina begins, finding the product containers that match the labels on her list. Because she is one of many children who initially helped to create the grocery store, she finds the items easily. Like the real thing, the center's grocery store is logically organized and divided up by types of food. Kristina knows to look for the milk, eggs, and butter in the dairy section.

While Amy is anxiously waiting at the cash register for Kristina to finish her shopping trip, she entertains herself by counting on an abacus and then hitting the number on the cash register that corresponds to the beads. Once Kristina fills her list, she proceeds to the checkout station. Amy's eyes light up as she finally has a chance to act out her role.

Figure 3–3   **Grocery list**

"Did you find everything?" Amy asks.

"I think so," says Kristina as both girls compare the product containers in the bag with the list.

"You forgot the peanuts," says Amy matter-of-factly. "They are in the vegetable section."

"I know it, but I hate peanuts," Kristina confesses, wrinkling up her nose.

Both girls giggle as Amy begins adding the prices on the abacus while Kristina reads them. "Cereal, $1.00; lemonade, $2.00; potato chips, $1.00..."

"Wait! You're going too fast," Amy tells Kristina, and her friend adjusts her reading so that Amy can accurately move the beads on her abacus. When Amy has totaled the prices, she hits number 4 on the cash register with glee. As the money drawer pops open, the two exchange pretend money.

In the meantime, Tim, one of the teachers, is informed by his aide, Jackie, that she has finished working with most of her ten children. She is now free to relieve Tim of his responsibilities in the math/cognitive area. He has been monitoring and supporting the ongoing math activities throughout the morning. Picking up his clipboard and daily plans, he begins to search for his base-group children. He notes their activities. He has a checklist that is representative of the materials typically available in each area so he can efficiently record his observations. He notices Kristina in the grocery store. After observing her for a moment, he decides to invite her to work with him once she has finished her shopping. Kristina agrees immediately, as do most children, who value the daily individual attention they receive from their base-group teachers.

Math/Cognitive Area

"I'm ready now," Kristina tells Tim, tugging at his pant leg. They exchange smiles as Kristina hands him the math book they have been working on. "I want to call it *My Spring Book*," she tells him.

Kristina wiggles a bit as she makes herself comfortable on the floor next to Tim. She proudly shows him each illustration in the book that they began several days earlier. It was inspired by the reading of *One Bright Monday Morning* (Baum and Baum 1962). "The cover looks like spring to me, too, and many of your pictures remind me of spring," he tells her, focusing on her developing awareness of the relationship between book titles and their contents.

Unlike an earlier math book Kristina made in which she had simply named objects and the number of times she had represented each on a particular page ("5 stars," "2 squares," and so on), today she is interested in dictating a story. Believing that Kristina should have complete ownership of this text, Tim is careful not to dominate Kristina's efforts. He reaches for a marker and asks, "Okay, what do you want to say on the first page?"

Kristina carefully counts the objects in the picture and begins her predictable storybook.

> One spring day, on my way to school I saw 1 tree, 1 flower, 1 sun, 3 birds, and 8 blades of grass.
> One spring day, on my way to school I saw a beach with 13 birds and mountains.
> One spring day, on my way to school I saw 5 pools and 1 flower.
> One spring day, on my way to school I saw 1 girl playing with a red ball.

Kristina doesn't need much encouragement to share her book. She uses the pictures for support as she meticulously reads each page to Tim. He listens attentively. She pauses momentarily when she encounters difficulty. She counts and names the objects she has designated to each picture and begins the page anew.

Meanwhile, Tim is writing "three pluses and a wish" for Kristina:

+ Kristina creates and counts pictures of objects to 17.
+ She has combined experiences from her first math book and *One Bright Monday Morning* to create her own unique, predictable story.
+ When experiencing difficulty rereading her story, Kristina turned to her illustrations for support.

WISH: That Kristina would write her next book on her own and not rely on my taking dictation.

This record-keeping system points out children's capabilities, while at the same time encourages teachers to generate appropriate goals for individual children. In doing so, the teachers reflect upon their role in the teaching-learning process. The teachers make curricular decisions to promote quality experiences for each child. The opportunity to act on these insights also allows the teachers to grow.

While Tim is working with Kristina, Mary Lou, the coach for the day, is recording observations of the two of them. She is seated at an appropriate distance so that she may hear their conversation and yet remain as unobtrusive as possible. Her notes will be converted into three pluses and a wish once she has completed all of her observations for the day. She will then return to the office where she will sketch what she has seen. This indicates the staff members' appreciation of art as a communication system not only for children, but for their own use as well.

Kristina has now successfully finished reading her book and looks quite pleased and somewhat relieved that she has read it from cover to cover. Tim hugs her. "I think this book is my favorite of all the books you've written," he tells her. He suggests that she read it to her little brother, Jimmy, and take it home to share with her family.

"Do I have to take it back to school?" she asks.

"You don't have to. But it would sure be nice if some of the other kids had a chance to read it," Tim tells her. Kristina tries to look disappointed, yet beneath the facade one can tell that she is looking forward to sharing her book with her friends.

There are many other options available in the math/cognitive area besides writing a book. Some children are making a picture graph representing their favorite storybooks, drawing pictures of their favorites, labeling and pasting them at the top of a column on a large graph. Others are voting on which of those represented is their favorite. They add the reasons for their decisions to the graph so that others may read them. The coach, who is in charge of leading the large group time, will review the results with the entire group during gathering.

Bianca and Kevin ask the teacher to put out their favorite dice, spinner, and card games. Several children are playing with the large unit blocks, making a town for the wooden cars and trains to run through. Others are working with friends or independently with the balance scales, puzzles, geoboards, parquetry blocks, large styrofoam numerals, and sorting trays containing buttons and seeds.

Amy notices that Tim is finished working with Kristina and invites him to "talk about time" with her. She proudly announces her new competence by stating, "I bet you didn't know that I know how to tell time now."

Tim reacts warmly, "No, Amy, I didn't know you could tell time, but I'm not surprised."

Their conversation continues (Figure 3–4). Tim takes brief notes to capture her current hypotheses about time.

Teachers also plan structured activities for the math/cognitive area. On any given day, children may be invited to make and label patterns featuring a variety of materials (red square, red square, yellow circle, red square, red square, yellow circle...); take surveys (What is your favorite color? Figure 3–5); make a graph (How many boys? How many girls?); try their hand at weighing, measuring, and estimating (How many scoops of sand will fill this container?); make number books (1 red house, 2 moons in the sky...); walk on enormous number lines; and the like.

Kristina is ready to move on now. She looks around for her brother, Jimmy, so that she can share her book with him. Unable to spot him, she shrugs her shoulders, deciding, "Oh well, I'll show him later." She looks around the center as a quick reminder of what she has left to do this morning. The language area is her final destination.

The Language Area

As Kristina makes her way back into the area, she passes by many children who are busy at work at the writing table preparing messages to share at gathering: "I love my Mom"; "I love my Dad." A few are listening to Bill Martin tapes while reading along in his books. Two children are making a tape of their own that will

Figure 3—4   Amy and Tim talk about time

Figure 3—5   Color survey

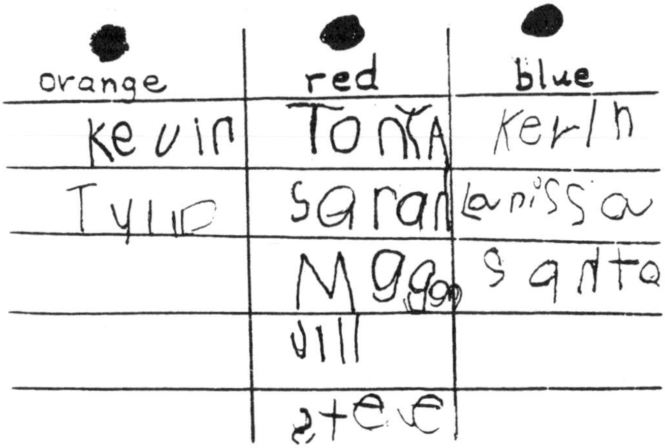

orange	red	blue
kevin	Tonya	kevin
Tylie	saran	lanissa
	Maggy	santa
	Jill	
	steve	

Figure 3—6   "I want to type."

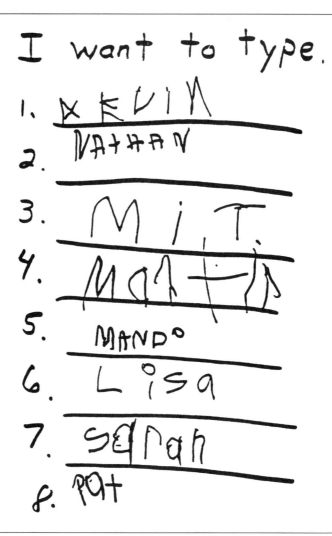

I want to type.

1. KEVIN
2. NATHAN
3. M i T.
4. Matti
5. MANDO
6. Lisa
7. Sarah
8. Pat

accompany the original books that are in our collection. The typewriter, as always, is being used. There is a sign-up sheet next to it so the children may regulate its use on their own (Figure 3—6).

Sitting on the floor working at a long row of shelves constructed from bricks and boards are children involved in a variety of writing experiences. Some are

Figure 3—7   Brian: "I'm reading a book to Amy. The book is *One Bright Monday Morning*."

I M rIADING
A BooKToAMy.
T HE BooK iS o No B riT MONDAy
MorNiNG.

BriAN

making books, some are writing about art projects, some are composing letters and stories. The large selection of materials — from crayons, pencils, pens, markers, blank premade books, and magazines to staplers, paper punches, and an assortment of paper — enable the children to create uniquely personal texts.

The huge, overstuffed chair is a popular reading place. Children are free to select from class books, books made by individual children, and published children's literature and magazines (Figure 3—7).

Several children have decided to play in the housekeeping area, which is often converted into various dramatic play settings. Today Matt has established the "Kit Cat Club" — an exclusive restaurant — in this area. He ventures around the room, advertising spaghetti as the featured special on each of the chalkboards. He draws arrows that point toward the housekeeping area. His "Yes, we're open" and "Sorry, we're closed" signs notify customers of the status of this special dining establishment (Figure 3—8, A, B, C).

Matt uses written language to generate, organize, and share with others information about his newly established restaurant. His young colleagues respond meaningfully to his written invitations. They become regular customers until the "Sorry, we're closed" sign is posted.

Kristina finally notices that I have written her name on my chalkboard. As the language arts teacher, this is my way of informing her that I want to work with her today. When she joins me, I thank her for the letter that she sent home

Figure 3−8   Matt's signs. A: "Kit Cat Club." B: "Yes, we're open." C: "Sorry, we're closed."

A   B   C

Figure 3−9   Kristina's letter to Heidi: "To Heidi. From Kristina. Dear Heidi: I love Heidi. I am
                    going to bring my jump rope Monday."

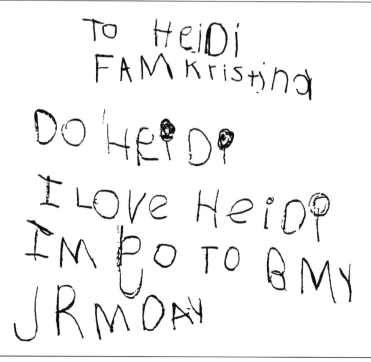

for me yesterday with my husband, Tim (Figure 3−9).

"Your letter made my day, Kristina!" I tell her. And it really had! In response to it, I have done what all conscientious receivers of mail do: I have written back.

"Will you read it to me?" Kristina asks as I hand her an envelope with her name on it.

"Let's read it together," I suggest, confident that much of what I have written will be readable for her. As we read, other children in the area are busy reading, writing, and conversing.

José has selected a task card that instructs him to write a funny story. There are many topics listed on cards for children to choose if they want writing ideas. He elects to draw a picture and then writes, "Clown that sneezes" (Figure 3−10). Danny, who has been waiting quite a while for his turn at the typewriter, is typing emphatically. Christie is writing a story. When she shares it during gathering, we will find out that it says, "Mom, I love you but I am sad. I am going to Tennessee. I am sad 'cause my mom's gone. She's in Tennessee. That's how

Figure 3−10   **"Clown that sneezes."**

Figure 3–11   **Christie's story about her mom in Tennessee**

come I go to Tennessee to see her" (Figure 3–11).

José decides he wants to write about a photograph I recently took while he was making a word pattern. Kristina and I are completing our discussion and he attempts to interrupt. "I'll be right with you, José," I tell him. "Kristina and I are almost finished."

José appears frustrated, but he returns to his spot at the table and begins writing fast and furiously all over his paper. After working with Kristina, I sit down next to him. He looks quite disgusted and points to a series of S's and O's that he has dashed off. "SOS means 'I need help!'" he states in an exasperated, yet very stern, voice (Figure 3–12).

I can't help but laugh. But I'm quite pleased that José has used writing to satisfy a personal need, to express his meaning. "Well, let's look at this picture," I say, slipping an arm around him. "What are you doing here?"

"Making a pattern," he informs me. He goes on to elaborate. "It's 'dog, bear, dog, bear.' And that's Jason working with Mrs. Weaver," he adds, after looking again at the photo.

"What do you want to write first?" I ask. My question simply helps him

Figure 3–12   José: "SOS means 'I need help!'"

organize his own thinking. "About the dog!" he exclaims as he puts pen to paper.

A quick glance at the various pieces published this morning in the language area leads to the discovery that although the children's products are not yet conventional, they are quite sophisticated. A closer examination of the children's writing files uncovers logical growth patterns within and across writers. Because the children are encouraged to take risks to convey meaning, their writing is valued for the process. All rough draft efforts are accepted and celebrated. The children never cease to amaze us as they make new connections between current writing opportunities and previous encounters with print. These children are quite efficiently moving forward as accomplished readers and writers.

Cleanup and Gathering

Music signals "cleanup/gathering" time. The children and staff help put away toys and materials used during the morning. Then, all assemble at the stage where the coach leads gathering. Today Mary Lou leads the children and staff in an aerobic dance to a popular song. Almost everyone sings along.

Next the children read their messages to the group. Amy is first. "I love my

Mom," she reads in a quiet, yet confident voice (Figure 3–13). Carter is next. He has recorded the news that he had to share when he arrived at school early this morning. "Me and my Momma, we be goin' to K-Mart and we be goin' to McDonald's." And so it goes.

After message board, the coach typically introduces new materials or activities, invites children to act out or read stories to the group, or directs the group in songs, finger plays, and so on. Today, Mary Lou invites a group of children down to present a newly written story to the group. Five children have worked collaboratively in creating a story line to an old Peter Pan story that I made into a wordless picture book by covering up the original print. The children have created a new text that corresponds to the illustrations. After completing the story, we decided to act it out for the whole class. The children organized the event by assigning character parts and creating costumes and props in the science/sensory area. The group decided that I should read the story while they act it out.

> Peter Pan is flying to open the window. He is in the house window and Tinker Bell is following him. Crystal, Robert, and Alex are jumping up and down and playing ring-around-the rosy. Then they all start flying out the window to follow Tinker Bell and Peter Pan. They are going to Little Kids' Land. When they get there all the people in Little Kid's Land say, "Hello." After they have a little chat, they all start marching away. They are singing "Jingle Bells."...

Figure 3–13   **Amy: "I love my mom."**

When the performance is over, the children and staff applaud and the actors bow. Mary Lou thanks them and suggests that they put their costumes away while we complete gathering.

"Before we go outside, I want to show you our latest class graph." Mary Lou asks for some help. With Laura's assistance, she holds the graph so everyone can see it, and the children are invited to read it. Mary Lou guides the discussion by asking questions like:

"Which story was the most popular?"

"How many children chose this one?"

"How many more children liked *The Giving Tree* better than *The Cat in the Hat?*"

"Why did so many kids choose *The Giving Tree?*"

"What did they say about the book?"

Mary Lou announces that she will hang the graph in the math area and encourages the children to make some more observations. Now it is time to go outdoors.

"If you are wearing green, you may get your coat, boots, hat, and mittens," says Mary Lou, as she weaves a review of colors together with an organized dismissal procedure. Most of the children choose to go outside where they enjoy pulling each other on sleds, writing their names on the brick wall with snow, and playing on the equipment. Some decide to remain indoors and continue working in the center.

Base-Group Time

Music is played again to signal that outside time is over and that it is base-group time. The children return to their respective groups where they share projects completed during free-choice time. The base-group teachers conclude the morning by reading to the children.

With the announcement of their buses' arrival, children gather their belongings and join the greeters, who are waiting to escort them to their buses. Once the children have left, the staff meets to relax and enjoy lunch and to share stories about the morning group. Soon buses will return with children who are enrolled in the afternoon session.

Coaching

Immediately after the second session, the staff meets for coaching. Today Mary Lou presents illustrations that communicate the observations that she has made. Her observations of Tim's interaction with Kristina are interpreted as follows:

+ You supported rather than directed the lesson.
+ When Kristina was reading and encountered problems, you refrained from jumping in and allowed her to work them out herself.
+ You encouraged her to share her book with others.

WISH: Encourage Kristina to write more herself instead of letting you take dictation for her.

This staff development strategy fosters collaborative learning among teachers and aides. They work together to fine-tune the general curriculum as well as specific teaching strategies. They have daily opportunities to learn from each other.

The remaining part of the day involves planning and record keeping for individual children.

It has been a good day for teachers and children alike.

Summary

The learning community that was established in this center reflects a whole language philosophy of instruction. Parents who enroll their children in the program are guaranteed that their children will frequently encounter authentic literacy experiences. Children have daily opportunities to read signs, books, and personal messages; to sign in; to respond to a graph or survey; or to contribute to a class book or the class calendar. Children learn to read and write while using reading and writing to learn. The open-ended structure of the activities allows all students to participate successfully regardless of their prior experiences with print.

Children understand early on that the teachers value their ideas and all attempts to communicate them. They are supported as learners; that is, it is safe for them to take risks to test new strategies. Teachers trust children enough as learners to allow them to determine which reading and writing projects they will find most valuable. And they find that it is much more effective to create activities for children so that they can experience, see demonstrated and come to value literacy (Harste and Short with Burke 1988, 11) than to force-feed language instruction upon them.

The teachers, however, do not value the activities as ends in themselves; instead they are concerned with the processing strategies children use in particular experiences. The teachers identify characteristics common to accomplished literacy learners and then demonstrate strategies for children who need support.

In addition to celebrating the children's accomplishments, the teachers learn from the children's errors. They recognize that children's "miscues" are natural and necessary for growth and learning, and they view errors as rich sources of information to be used to guide their curricular decisions.

Personal Reflection

This morning's visit to the Roosevelt Child Development Center represents a typical day in February. The center's whole language curriculum continues to evolve to meet the needs and interests of all participants. Teachers and children collaborate to support one another's growth. Like the teachers, children are guides in this classroom; and like the children, teachers are also learners. Working together, the teachers and children continually shape and reshape this powerful learning environment.

References

Baum, Arline, and Joseph Baum. 1962. *One Bright Monday Morning.* New York: Random House.

Dr. Seuss. 1957. *The Cat in the Hat.* New York: Random House.

Harste, Jerome C., and Kathy E. Short, with Carolyn Burke. 1988. *Creating Classrooms for Authors: The Reading—Writing Connection.* Portsmouth, NH: Heinemann.

Silverstein, Shel. 1964. *The Giving Tree.* New York: Harper & Row.

4

A Day with Dinosaurs

TIMOTHY O'KEEFE

This was my first year as a transition classroom teacher. The children in my class had been identified through a screening test as not being ready for first grade. The transition rooms in our district have been recently established to give some children an extra year before entering a traditional first-grade classroom setting. Most of the children in the transition classrooms go into first grade. A few will be promoted to second grade if they show the potential of being successful there.

I have been a classroom teacher for nine years in three different states and have worked in every grade level from four-year-old Head Start programs through sixth grade. These experiences have given me a clear perspective not only on language arts, but on every area of the curriculum. Having been fortunate enough as an undergraduate to have studied with Dr. Jerome Harste, I have been a whole language teacher from the beginning.

My classroom looks and feels different each year because the children in my classes bring their diverse backgrounds and experiences to school, and their interests and needs significantly affect our curriculum. I continue to grow and change as I learn from the children in my classes.

Our tutor, Sandra, is a thoughtful and patient person whom the children easily grew to love and respect. Her observations and insights have been extremely helpful throughout the year.

While this class was supposed to be homogeneous, in a group this size the children were actually very different. I valued their diverse experiences, interests, and learning strategies. Each year I teach, I learn more. This was particularly true this year.

The Day Begins

Today the children burst into the room with unusual enthusiasm. Before dropping off their belongings, they sign the attendance notebook and go off to select an activity or project.

"Good morning, my friends!" is my usual greeting as I look up from mixing paints for the easel. I can see Rashaun, who usually needs to be reminded to sign in, make his way to the front of the classroom and the large chalkboard. On his way he unfastens the suspenders of his snowpants and they fall down around his waist and then to his knees. He picks up a piece of colored chalk and begins to draw a large dinosaur, either brontosaurus or diplodocus by the looks of it. As he puts on the finishing touches he turns around to greet me with a dinosaur growl and a beautiful grin, his snowpants now around his ankles. April follows Rashaun's lead and draws a dinosaur too (Figure 4–1).

Other children are busy with different activities during this free-choice time. Jermaine has his own private book on dinosaurs out and is engaged in a heated discussion with Chris about who would win between triceratops and tyrannosaurus rex, the King.

"The King can take anyone, y'all. Look here!" Jermaine points to a picture in his book of a fight between the two dinosaurs in question. Raphael quickly goes to the science area, picks up another book on dinosaurs, and brings it over to join in the debate (Figure 4–2).

"Look at this one!" Raphael chimes in. His book is open to a page with a picture remarkably similar to Jermaine's. "Triceratops poked his nose horn right into the King!"

"That couldn't be the King, y'all; he would win any fight," says Jermaine. "Anyway, he's smaller than the King. Look here." Jermaine points back to his book and compares the relative size of the two-legged dinosaur in his book to the unfortunate two-legged creature in Raphael's book.

As I look around the room I can see the children busily engaged in projects, each having been lured to an area of interest without any prompting from Sandra or me. Dinosaur pictures and paraphernalia have filled the room. There are dinosaur posters on the walls, including a time line on dinosaurs, which we refer to constantly in an effort to determine which dinosaurs lived around the same time. The children are busy putting together a 250-piece dinosaur puzzle. On the class calendar, where each day a different child records important school events, I

Figure 4−1   April draws her version of a brontosaurus

Figure 4−2   Ricky and Raphael compare dinosaur literature

can see the various times when they have decided to write about dinosaurs. The chalkboard is constantly covered with stylized drawings of dinosaurs. Each child's own unique style has already become apparent to the rest of the class. Children are making and battling with clay dinosaurs at the clay table. Three children are at the easel using the different art supplies. April is drawing a mama brontosaurus and several babies with large markers. Shamarla is painting a colorful pterodactyl with water color paints, and Amanda is using the temperas to paint her favorite animal, a horse. Rashaun has moved to the listening center with Raphael and Katie to listen to a tape called "Dynamic Dynosaurs." They are singing aloud, completely oblivious to each other, in their own keys since they can't really hear themselves: "Tyrannosaurus, King of the reptiles, teeth sharp like steak knives, fights all to live or die." Five children are playing a class-made dinosaur game (Figure 4–3). This time of the day has become my favorite because I can see children teaching and learning from each other in an environment set up to allow just that.

Figure 4–3   Some children playing the dinosaur game

The unit on dinosaurs has taken off more than I could have hoped for. It has almost developed a life of its own. The children and I have learned an incredible amount, but our new understandings have extended beyond the topic of dinosaurs. Together we have learned how to go about investigating a topic. In the process I have learned even more about how to capitalize on children's interests, how to let go and let them take charge of their own learning, how to focus on their strengths, and how to allow them to teach each other.

Planning with Children

Little did I know that my decision three weeks ago to involve children in deciding what to study would create such enthusiasm about learning. After a successful unit on animals—an area I know a great deal about and had used for several years while teaching second grade—I decided to allow the class to choose the next topic for science and social studies. Our topic went far beyond our afternoon science/social studies period and, for a while, became the focus of our whole curriculum.

After lunch one day, I listed several themes I was interested in on the chalkboard. The list included outer space, plants, the weather, and (my personal choice) the human body. I then opened up the list to their suggestions, which I recorded along with my own.

Chris offered sharks, which brought out an enthusiastic murmur. But when Rashaun suggested dinosaurs and growled it out in a dinosaurlike fashion, it was obvious that his energy for this topic was contagious. Dinosaurs were the clear choice when our secret votes were tallied.

"Now I'm in for it," I thought. I knew as much about dinosaurs as the average adult—next to nothing. We generated lists of things we knew about dinosaurs and what we wanted to find out. This seemed a good place to start.

By using art and writing April was able to use her personal theme—babies—to explain what she knew about dinosaurs. By including cracking dinosaur eggs in her first drawing, April cleverly included this theme. She was able to use this theme in almost every topic or discussion. April quickly found out that "brontosaurus rex" is not the name of a dinosaur, but two different names combined (Figure 4–4).

While Jesse doesn't use letter sounds in most of his writing, he feels free to approach this activity using what he does know about written language. When making the sound coming from the dinosaur's mouth, Jesse intently made the sound to himself while writing a series of r's. He knows that there should be some punctuation mark to show the importance or force of the utterance. Jesse chooses a question mark. Although the placement of the punctuation at the

Figure 4—4   April: "They eat meat and plants. I don't know about brontosaurus rex."

Figure 4—5   Jesse: "I know they have sharp teeth. I want to know how big feet they have."

Figure 4—6   Ernie: "The dinosaurs lived long before the Pilgrims. Why did they die?"

end of the sound is not conventional, it certainly is logical (Figure 4—5).

Ernie's question brings up an important concept for very young children. We knew that the Pilgrims and the first Thanksgiving happened a long time ago. For Ernie to reason that dinosaurs existed long before them was perceptive, and it added to the class's concept of history and the relative passing of time. His astute question, which was also asked by many others on this small project, is still debated by scientists today (Figure 4—6).

Independent Choices

Today, after April completes her brontosaurus with babies at the easel, she takes her painting and lays it down on the counter to dry. She knows how important it is to sign her artwork. She goes to the science area, picks up a postcard with a picture of a brontosaurus on it, brings it over to her painting, and copies the dinosaur's name onto her paper. She pauses for a moment and finishes by writing "and babies."

One job children are often invited to do before our gathering time is to participate in a graph or survey. I ask Raymond to help me come up with this morning's survey idea, and he suggests finding out which dinosaur is the class favorite. With Raymond's help I write out the question for our survey: "Which dinosaur do you like?"

As others see what we're making, they also want to be involved. April wants to draw tyrannosaurus, Jesse offers to draw stegosaurus, Ernie volunteers for brontosaurus, and Raymond wants triceratops. The survey is posted early in the morning so each person can vote. Raymond stations himself close to the graph so he can answer any questions or explain what the children need to do.

The value of graphs and surveys is already clear to the class. Graphs have been used for a variety of purposes: to find out about class preferences (Which book do you like best? Which color is your favorite? Which version of Pinocchio do you prefer?); to make class decisions (What should we have to eat at the party Friday? What should we name the turtle? What color should we paint the puppet theater?); and simply to learn more about our world (Do you like to handle worms? Which one do you think runs the fastest, a horse or a rabbit?).

The graphs and surveys we have created are tools for learning. In the process of creating and analyzing our graphs and surveys children not only learned *about* them, but *through* them. The children see graphs as an efficient and interesting way to record and interpret information. Today's graph is no exception. As soon as the graph is posted children come, a few at a time, to sign under their favorite dinosaur. We usually save discussion and interpretation of the graph for gathering time, which follows independent choices.

Ernie, Chris, Shamarla, and Katie choose to create their own games on the theme of dinosaurs. I'm continually delighted at the way these children can work together on class projects. As I monitor the centers I pick up some of their dialogue and observe the process of their creations. Several of the games never make it to the playing stage and are simply a wonderful open-ended opportunity to work cooperatively, share ideas, and engage in authentic math and language experiences. Many children create rich stories and characters to go along with their games. Other games do make it to complete products with precise, complicated rules. One game, simply called "The Kids' Game," became one of the most popular free-choice time activities in the class.

Today Ernie and Chris are making a dice game using four small plastic dinosaurs as the moving pieces. After gathering the needed supplies they start to work. Chris starts by drawing a snakelike path across the tagboard. Carefully, he and Ernie divide it into squares of different sizes and colors.

"Be careful Chris," cautions Ernie. "Make it nice and good." Chris makes a large blue circular shape in the lower left quadrant of the game board and proceeds to fill it in.

"What's that for?" Ernie inquires.

"I'm making an ocean. If somebody gets in the water they got to wait down here."

"When do they get out?" asks Ernie, needing clarification.

"Only when it's their turn again," answers Chris.

Then Ernie extends the blue of Chris's ocean to the lower right corner and reaches for a brown marker. Ernie draws a rickety bridge over the water. When asked about the bridge Ernie states matter-of-factly, "It has holes in it and when brachiosaurus walks on it he would break the bridge and fall down and his long neck would stick out of the water."

Shamarla and Katie's game is different in that the players draw cards to determine the action. Their arms intertwine as they color their game board.

"What do your cards say?" I ask. They sit up and reach for their pile of cards.

As Katie reaches for one, I can see a series of letterlike marks. She is comfortable as a risk taker and rarely hesitates to read her writing for me when I ask. She looks at the card, pauses, and says, "That's not the one." Then she grabs another card from her deck, also covered with letterlike marks, and reads, "Don't go where the red line is or you will be in big trouble!"

"This one says, 'Watch out for the birds,'" Shamarla reports, and she points to some large birds she has drawn close to the path on her board.

"Extra turn," Katie reads from another card.

"Go twelve," Shamarla reads for her turn. She turns to Jermaine, who is walking by, and asks, "How do you make a twelve, is it a one and a two or a two and a one?"

"A one and a two," Jermaine answers.

Shamarla picks up one more card with the letters I FSH written on it next to a bright yellow sun. "It is finished," she reads. "That means you won!"

Gathering

We usually have two gatherings each morning. The first is to take care of class business and assign the rotating class jobs. We have about half as many jobs as there are children so each person has a formal job every other week or so.

As I reach for my guitar to play the cleanup/gathering music, I marvel at how much these children have grown since coming into our class last fall. These people are empowered learners wonderfully willing to expand their understanding of the world, simply needing the opportunity to share what they know and to risk going beyond what they know in a nonthreatening atmosphere. They are my most powerful teachers in my quest to become a better teacher and learner.

As I play a soft instrumental on the guitar the children finish up projects, put away materials, and join the class in a circle in the front of the room. Two children are "gathering helpers" and it is their job to help others clean up and remind them when it is time to come up to the front of the room.

When the whole class has assembled I take suggestions for songs we can sing together. We always start with "Good Morning." Jason suggests "Tools," which is sung with gusto. Everyone wants to sing it through again since it is so short and by far the most popular song in our repertoire. Finally James suggests "This Land Is Your Land," a new one for us.

Next we go on to business. One person each day illustrates the menu. Today is Ricky's turn and he accepts the job. If he did not want to do it, the menu job would have gone on to the next child on the alphabetized class roster.

It is Jermaine's turn to do the class calendar. He also has a right to turn down the task, but few children ever do. He gladly accepts the responsibility this morning. One child each day gets to record events on the large calendar bulletin board. For school days, the child must record something about school. Each day is represented by a four-by-five-inch card. Jermaine takes down the card for yesterday and begins thinking about something to write and draw about.

Four children have signed up to share their journals this morning: James, Joyce, B. J., and Jason. I am particularly pleased that B. J. has decided to share since she is a very quiet child and often unwilling to speak in front of the group. I make a mental note to be sure to offer to do a written conversation with anyone who has signed up for journal sharing. Reading back and forth for the class is often easier than reading alone for shy children.

"I put out some new dinosaur shapes for tracing in the writing area," I announce. I demonstrate with the pterodactyl shape for the class. "There is one condition for using these," I continue. "If you'd like to hang it up in the room for others to see, you need to write about your picture."

"Can we just write the dinosaur's name?" asks Ernie.

"It would be nice if you could write something about the dinosaur. You could write something you know about it or make up a story about what it could be doing."

"Can we add other characters?" Jermaine inquires.

"Sure, that's a great idea. I'm anxious to see what you come up with."

The last order of business before quiet writing time is to share what we've observed about this morning's graph. I've learned that a very effective way to start these discussions is with an open-ended question so as not to get them started thinking in a particular direction.

"What do you notice about the graph, Raphael?"

"Most people like the King," is his immediate reply.

"Anyone else?" I ask.

"Four people voted for stegosaurus and two people voted for triceratops," adds Crystal.

"That's six!" Ricky puts in.

"How do you know?" I challenge.

"I just know, two and four is six, that's all."

Next I ask a few children why they made certain choices. This allows them to share information they may have about the specific dinosaurs.

"Why did you vote for the King, Raphael?"

"'Cause I like him. He eats a lot."

"Jesse, how about you? Why did you choose stegosaurus?"

"'Cause he gots a big bump on the back of his tail."

"Why do you think its tail is like that?" I ask.

Jesse answers, "It looks like a big bat with spikes."

"He has it to protect himself from the meat-eaters," Jermaine adds. Jermaine has a fantastic memory for the dinosaur names and specific information about their relative sizes and which ones lived in the same time period. It does not surprise me that he comes up with such a good observation.

This morning's graph has highlighted math that is both functional and meaningful. Our discussion was open ended and invited individual interpretation. The children were using the language of mathematics easily and naturally. Each child had the chance to teach and learn from everyone else.

Quiet Writing

After our first gathering the class begins quiet writing time. Most children write in their journals, spiral notebooks kept in their desks. Jermaine goes to the calendar on the bulletin board and pulls down the card for today. He comes back to the writing table where Ricky is already at work on his task of illustrating the day's menu. I have offered to do written conversations with the children who have signed up to share journals. B. J. and Shamarla gladly accept and we join the others at the writing table. I find that written conversations are valuable in that they bring the reading and writing processes together. The children enjoy this form of "talking on paper." Jason and James want to write and draw in their journals and share those.

Looking around the room, I can see Sandra, our tutor, moving from desk to desk, giving encouragement and helping the children to develop their ideas. She is also engaging in some written conversations in journals. Some children are drawing, and Amanda is giving an impromptu art lesson at her desk to Rashaun. The sound is a wonderful murmuring of children helping others with ideas and conventions—whispering, laughing, a dinosaur noise or two, and April singing "Have you ever seen an ankylosaurus, he reminds you of an army tank" while writing and drawing in her journal. Her song comes from a tape in the listening center. Daehoon has already written numerals up to fifty and is now making up addition and subtraction problems for himself. Chris is writing out the words for the song "Tools" by John Denver in his journal in his own invented spelling, and Joyce gives Jermaine feedback on his ideas (Figure 4–7).

Joyce, B. J., and I begin written conversations about dinosaurs (Figure 4–8, A and B). These two have made so much progress and they are so comfortable writing this way that neither one asks how to spell any words. Both write with confidence and are not self-conscious in the least when I ask them to read what

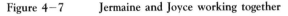

Figure 4—7   Jermaine and Joyce working together

they have written so I can write appropriate responses.

Joyce uses a combination of words she knows, words in the classroom that she can see, and her own invented spelling, sometimes putting letter/sounds together and sometimes not. I also notice that Joyce uses two punctuation marks, both appropriately. I had only noticed her using punctuation a couple of times before. This signifies another landmark. Although I'm pleased with her growth in understanding language conventions, the important thing to me is that she writes for meaning.

I had noticed B. J. using letter/sound relationships for a few months and I am very pleased at the level of sophistication she has developed. She communicates her thoughts and ideas clearly and succinctly. I am very excited that she has decided to share this with the class.

At the second gathering Jermaine reads the calendar card for the day and places it on the bulletin board in the proper space (Figure 4—9). At the end of the month these will be taken down and assembled into a book. These books are placed in the class library and are read often. Children like them as a record of major events for the class and as a way of documenting their own

Figure 4—8   Written conversations. A: Joyce. B: B. J.

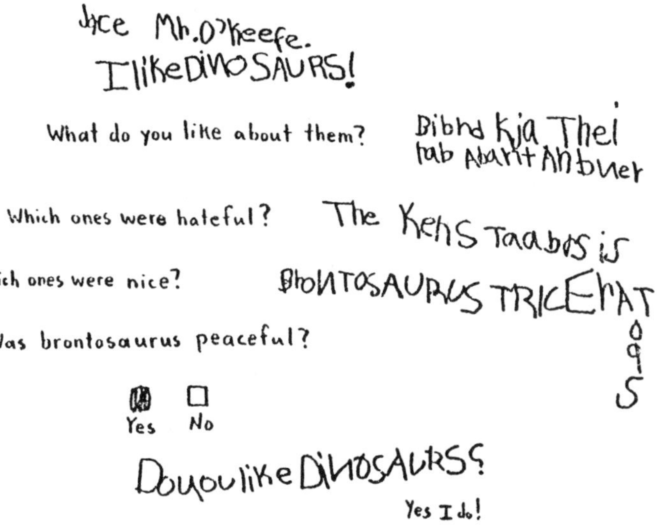

Jce Mh. O'Keefe.
I like DINOSAURS!

What do you like about them?   Bibhd kja Thei
tab Alarit Ahbuer

Which ones were hateful?   The Kehs Taabes is

Which ones were nice?   BroNTosAuRus TRICENAT

Was brontosaurus peaceful?

☒ ☐
Yes No

DoyouLike DiNosAuRsS?

Yes I do!

A

A
I like dinosaurs!
What do you like about them?
Because some are hateful and some
are nice.
Which ones were hateful?
The King, stegosaurus.
Which ones were nice?
Brontosaurus, triceratops.
Was brontosaurus peaceful?
Yes.
Do you like dinosaurs?
Yes, I do!

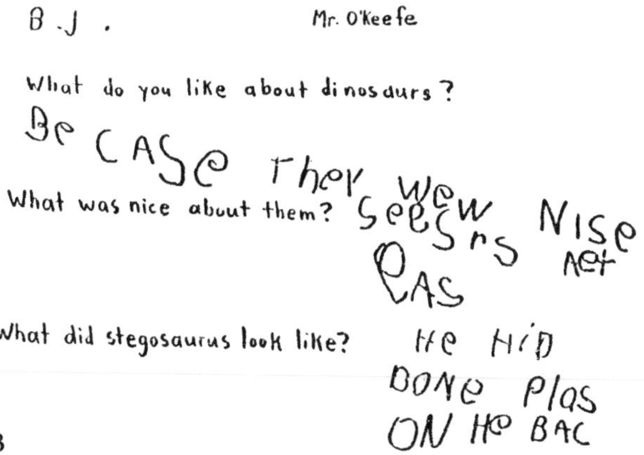

B. J.   Mr. O'Keefe

What do you like about dinosaurs?
Be CASe They wew Nise
What was nice about them? SeeJrs Net
RAS
What did stegosaurus look like?   He HiD
DoNe Plas
ON He BAC

B

B
What do you like about
dinosaurs?
Because they were nice.
What was nice about them?
Stegosaurus ate grass.
What did stegosaurus look like?
He had bony plates on his back.

---

progress as writers and artists.

Ricky has the yardstick now and is using it as a pointer. The menu has been taped on the chalkboard and he reads what we're having for lunch, one item at a time. These are also bound monthly into books for the class library.

Figure 4—9   Calendar card: "We played the dinosaur game."

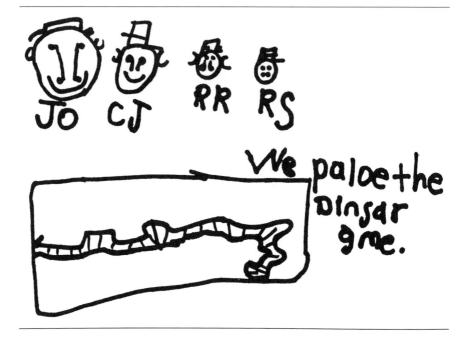

Sharing Time

Now it is journal-sharing time and, as is our convention, the children come up alphabetically to share. B. J. is first and she and I take turns reading our conversation on paper. She reads so quietly that she is barely audible. Everyone is so excited that B. J. has decided to share that the class listens attentively and breaks into applause.

James is next, and he sits in the chair in front of the group. He waits for the class to quiet down before reading his journal entry, "Dinosaurs lay eggs" (Figure 4—10).

April says spontaneously, "I like your picture, James!"

While James is not writing conventionally, he has come a long way this school year. Last fall, James would rarely write at all without having a model to copy. The fact that he has assigned meaning to his writing and that he is reading it aloud shows that he sees himself as a reader and writer.

Figure 4—10   James: "Dinosaurs lay eggs."

Joyce and I are up next and we read our written conversation. The children giggle at the idea of hateful dinosaurs. I point out to the class that Joyce used two punctuation marks. I write Joyce's first sentence on the chalkboard and ask the class about the punctuation mark.

"It means she really, really means it," says Jesse.

"How about this mark?" I ask, after writing her last sentence on the board.

Figure 4−11   Jason: "Tyrannosaurus eats plant eaters."

Daehoon offers, "That means she wants to know about something."

Finally it's Jason's turn to share his journal entry, "Tyrannosaurus eats plant eaters" (Figure 4−11).

Jason's writing and drawing demonstrate his understanding of the relationship between the carnivores and the large but vulnerable plant eaters.

Literature Study

For this morning's story I have chosen to read *Danny and the Dinosaur* by Syd Hoff (1958). The children really enjoy listening to stories and become very involved with the text, predicting what will happen next, commenting about the story line, laughing at the appropriate times. At one point in the story the dinosaur gives all of Danny's friends a ride. Joyce asks, "How do they all stay on?"

"They grab the fur," answers Jesse.

"Dinosaurs don't have fur!" exclaims April.

Later the children in the story applaud the dinosaur because he wins at a game of hide and seek. Jermaine asks, "Is that a brachiosaurus?" April says it is, but James thinks the dinosaur is a diplodocus. These children are not interrupting the story but rather are actively interacting with it.

In our follow-up discussion we focus on the story's mood, considering whether it is happy or sad.

Shamarla argues for happy: "I like it when they rode on his back."

Jason agrees: "They were happy when they played all them games."

Crystal thinks the story was sad because "Danny had to let the dinosaur go back to the museum."

The children's next task is to write and draw about the story. The assignment is purposely vague and open ended to allow them to express their ideas freely. As the "passers" put the materials out, the children start chattering about the story and what they're going to do. Crystal starts by drawing the dinosaur and asking Rashaun what color he was. Jesse begins with a stylized house with the dinosaur far in the background. When I ask Ernie about his picture he says, "The Dukes of Hazard car is jumping over the dinosaur and the sheriff is after them."

"And this car's name is General Lee," Daehoon clarifies, pointing to the car on Ernie's drawing.

Next I come up to Shamarla, who has finished her picture of Danny on the dinosaur's back and is busy sounding aloud the words she wants to write. When she puts the period at the end of her sentence I ask her to read what she has written. "I like big... I like big... Just a minute." I watch Shamarla as she finds the syntactic error in her writing and am fascinated by the clever way she corrects it; writing the omitted word below the line, she indicates with an arrow its proper placement in the sentence (Figure 4–12).

Shamarla is clearly not only a thoughtful writer, wanting to connect written text with her picture, but she is also self-monitoring: she writes the best she can and comes up with a strategy to correct herself. She did not ask me how to fix her sentence, nor did she hesitate to act when she found that she had omitted a word. What pleases me most is that she makes a syntactic change in her text to ensure semantic coherence. I make a mental note to share Shamarla's strategy with the class when we get back together.

I am puzzled by what Jermaine writes on his paper: "He changed back and forth into a different dinosaur."

"What do you mean by that?" I ask. He picks up a copy of the book and flips to a page showing a very large dinosaur compared to the houses and buildings.

"See there," he says, pointing. "And watch, he changes back into a little dinosaur." Jermaine flips to another page that shows the dinosaur trying to hide behind a lamppost. In this second picture, the dinosaur was drawn only to be about twice as large as Danny. He went on to show other discrepancies in the drawings: "See, he was on two legs," pointing to one page; and then, flipping to

Figure 4—12   Shamarla: "Danny and the dinosaur. I like [how] big he is."

another, "Now he was on four legs. He trying to trick us!"

I am impressed by how perceptive Jermaine is as he points out the anomalies in the illustrations. I have read the story many times and the fact that the artist changes perspectives so drastically never really occurred to me. Whether a dinosaur walked on two legs or four was critical for us in classifying dinosaurs. Jermaine knows that, with exceptions, two-legged dinosaurs were predators. The four-legged dinosaurs were generally the more peaceful herbivores. For Jermaine to draw on that knowledge and apply it to this story is a sign of his strategic thinking.

Daehoon is anxious to share his project with me and is obviously proud of his efforts. Daehoon has been a great risk taker from the beginning of the year and as a result has grown tremendously as a reader and writer. He is a great asset to the class in that he is confident and not at all self-conscious about taking risks (Figure 4—13, A and B).

Figure 4—13   Daehoon's story. A: "Danny and the Dinosaur" [by] Daehoon Rie. B: "The dinosaur hid behind the house and the children find him. The dinosaur hid behind the gas tank, the children find him. Then they made a plan, and the dinosaur won."

A   B

Like Shamarla, Daehoon corrects his text as he reads it to me. Daehoon's writing about the story reveals the predictable nature of the original text. The four small drawings at the top of his page of writing go along well with his story and extend its meaning.

It is almost recess time. The children gather with their finished projects and most are anxious to share what they've done. In this way they are writing for a larger audience than just me. Writing goes beyond mere task completion and truly becomes communication.

I invite the children to share their papers with the rest of the class. They may read their own work or let me read it.

I also consider this a good opportunity to highlight the strategies children use as they construct meaning. After Shamarla has read her paper, I write her original sentence on the board, just as she wrote it. I explain how Shamarla cleverly inserted the word she forgot. I point out that she corrected for meaning, that when she reread her paper it didn't make sense to her, so she fixed it. Sharing children's strategies validates my belief in them as competent thinkers and problem solvers; it also encourages the notion that children can learn from each other and that they should look to their peers as resources of information and ideas.

Recess

I invite Jesse to call out categories for children to get ready to go outside. We do this to avoid the chaos of everyone getting up at once and rushing to the door. "Everyone with blue jeans on may line up," he says, making sure his friend Raymond is in the first category. "Everyone with writing on their shirts may line up." He continues with the categories until everyone is in line. I join the children outside at recess time, turning the jump rope, pushing children on the swings, and initiating a game of tag.

Quiet Reading Time

The morning's activities have run a little longer than expected so by the time we return from recess, we have about fifteen minutes for quiet reading and washing for lunch. Several children select books about dinosaurs from the science area (Figure 4–14). Katie and Joyce select a *Curious George* book from the class library and find a quiet area to read together. April has chosen to read the same magazine for several days, an old *National Geographic* with several pictures of baby dinosaurs. Chris and Ernie are looking through an old calendar book, while Amanda and Crystal look through an old class-made book from the beginning of the year about "Our Favorite Things." "I can't believe I used to make my S's backwards!" exclaims Crystal upon viewing her old work. Rashaun has the Disney version of *Pinocchio* (1973) and is reciting the story from memory as he looks at the pictures. Daehoon has a copy of *Danny and the Dinosaur* and is carefully reading the written print. James and Jermaine have selected some Bill Martin books from the listening center and are sitting at James's desk reading in unison. I am reading ahead in *Lost in Dinosaur World* (Williams 1987), a short children's novel, so that when I read to the children later on this afternoon I will be familiar with the story. The children wash their hands and then get ready for lunch.

Figure 4–14   Rashaun and Jason reading quietly

Lunch

Lunch time is another good opportunity for me to visit with the children. They must line up alphabetically to go through the lunch line and are seated alphabetically in the cafeteria. I sit at a different place each day so that by the end of the week I will have been close to everyone.

When we return to the room we play "Simon Says" and sing a couple of songs. Today Raymond suggests "I Know an Old Lady" and April, "Hush Little Baby." I read a chapter from *Lost in Dinosaur World* (Williams 1987). To date we have read *Charlotte's Web* (White 1945a), *Stuart Little* (White 1945b), *The Wizard of Oz* (Baum 1956), and a few other long stories. Longer stories offer rich character and plot development along with descriptive language. By reading them over several weeks we really have a chance to explore and discuss the story.

Dinosaur Mathematics

This afternoon we're planning a math and language activity that I'm sure will actively engage the children. I have taken some small pictures of dinosaurs and run off copies for each child. On the page are four small pictures of four different kinds of dinosaurs—tyrannosaurus, brachiosaurus, triceratops, and stegosaurus. The open-ended instructions are simply these: to use the pictures, scissors, glue, crayons, and construction paper to create a number story. While my intent clearly is to highlight math during this period, science, social studies, art, and language experiences are easily and naturally incorporated.

The children enjoy these open-ended activities because they can create their own language-rich stories drawing on their knowledge and experiences. Additionally, by creating their own mathematical situations and sharing them with others the children are exposed to far more than a single mathematical concept in this one activity. I want the curriculum in our class to reflect authentic learning situations as much as possible; therefore I strive to plan for invitations that incorporate as many meaning systems as possible.

Each child by now has a lot of content knowledge about dinosaurs from which to draw, and they have each other as potential resources and editors. Matt makes a simple two-part pattern with tyrannosaurus and triceratops. The triceratopses' tails are dangling dangerously close to the mouths of the kings. In a bubble coming from the mouth of the middle tyrannosaurus are the letters "KGMDTL." I ask him to read it to me.

"The King said, 'Triceratops, give me that tail!'" Matt shows his patterning skill and his knowledge of the relationship between carnivores and plant eaters.

Rashaun uses simple one-to-one correspondence to show this same relationship by pairing three tyrannosauruses with three brachiosauruses. With red crayon, Rashaun puts blood on the backs of the large herbivores and on the mouths of the vicious kings. On his paper he writes a series of letters and letterlike marks and the numerals 3 and 6. He reads, "There were six dinosaurs. One dinosaur was eating off a tree. The King ate him and left his bones. He ate some more. Three were left."

Daehoon shows his knowledge of simple addition and subtraction in his stories (Figure 4–15, A). He then flips his paper over to create his subtraction problem, indicating the two unfortunate deceased dinosaurs with black X's (Figure 4–15, B).

Shamarla shows her knowledge of content and simply uses numbers to help tell her story. I watch her cut out five dinosaurs and glue them onto her sheet of construction paper. Then she walks over to the sink and collects two paper towels.

"What are you going to do with those?" I ask.

"You'll see," she answers.

Figure 4−15   Daehoon's story. A: "3 + 2 = 5. There was three. Two came. There was five."
                 B: "There was three and two died. There was one. 3 − 2 = 1."

A $3 + 2 = 5$

tar was
3 2 cam
tar was 5

$3 - 2 = 1$ tar was
                3 and 2 was
                did tar was 1

B

Figure 4–16   Shamarla: "Three died. Two came back now."

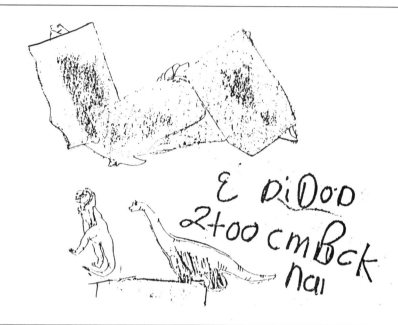

After tearing the paper towels, she puts glue on the back of some small pieces and covers three of the dinosaurs on her paper (Figure 4–16).

Shamarla proceeds to write her story using numerals very naturally. She points to the dinosaurs covered by the brown paper towel and says, "These three died. These are the stones, like fossils!" Shamarla is beaming, obviously proud of the originality of her work.

While Raphael does not use plus and equal signs in his stories, he clearly shows his understanding of addition with three addends. After gluing down his dinosaurs, he carefully counts each type, records the number, then counts all of the dinosaurs and records the sum.

Raphael easily explains his stories using the numerals he recorded for reference. "These two came and then these two came and then these three came and this was seven." He turns his paper over and reads, "I said these three came in and I said these four came in, and this was one; that makes eight."

Because the children are allowed to approach this task any way they want, at sharing time I expect to see an amazing diversity of connections. The popularity of this type of experience has long since convinced me of the need for it.

Workbooks and worksheets with single right answers may fill the need for a very limited type of practice; however, allowing children to create their own scenarios, to evaluate and reflect upon their own and others' problems, provides a more accurate introduction to the uses of mathematics in our lives.

After sharing our dinosaur number stories the children go to special classes. As Sandra and I walk back to class after walking the children to the library, we reflect on the day's activities and share "kid-watching" stories.

Small Group Activities: Dinosaur Choices

When the children return to class for our final forty minutes before bus group, there is a sign-up sheet for activities for the rest of the day. The children have shown a strong interest in puppets. We have just created a puppet theater from a large carton and I thought that the children needed a formal activity involving it, so dinosaur puppets is one of the choices I provide.

A colleague has suggested dioramas, and the choice seems like a good one since it's clear that the children would be interested in creating miniature landscapes for the small plastic dinosaurs.

The third choice on the sign-up sheet is making clay dinosaurs. Again, this is following an interest the children have shown during their free-choice time.

Children selecting puppets have paper bags and a variety of other art supplies at their disposal. As usual their individuality is reflected in their creations. "I have an idea!" Crystal says to herself cheerfully and proceeds to cut a long jagged green piece to put on her dinosaur's back. "These are his bony plates!"

April and B. J. are busy sketching the dinosaurs they are planning to make into puppets. They have dinosaur books and pictures as their models, along with the posters and other dinosaur paraphernalia around the room. The children in the group decide to perform a puppet show at the end of the day before the buses come. Knowledge of the upcoming performance provides further motivation to cooperate and do a good job. Jason and Raymond are drawing parts on construction paper and cutting them out to glue onto their paper bags. B. J. is simply using the markers to draw on the bag. Sandra stations herself in this area and provides assistance and inspiration.

At the clay table the children have already drawn sketches of the dinosaurs they intend to make and are engaged in a rich discussion about dinosaurs. "Why don't the dinosaurs have any ears?" Amanda asks after examining her own clay sculpture of a tyrannosaurus head.

"They have to have ears or they couldn't hear!" remarks Jermaine confidently. James reaches for a book on dinosaurs. "Look!" he says excitedly. "They just have holes!" He and Chris are both making the King, helping each other with hints on how best to make the mouth and roll out the tail on the table before attaching it.

When I ask Jesse and Jermaine which dinosaurs they're working on, they answer in unison, "Brontosaurus."

"You should be able to tell, Mr. O'Keefe," says Jesse, almost scolding. "They have long tails and long necks." It becomes clear that the medium causes children to think about the physical characteristics of dinosaurs in a different way.

"I'm making a palm tree," says Ernie as he works on his diorama. Using green yarn and a stick he collected from outside, Ernie fastens his tree down with a small piece of clay. Raphael has cut a piece of blue construction paper to put in his box as a swamp. Joyce is already finished with her diorama and is playing out a scene between dimetrodon and triceratops. The children look through books and pictures and continually add ideas to the list of things that may have been in the dinosaurs' world. Rashaun dampens the sand in his box and is fascinated with making realistic dinosaur footprints. Items included in the shoe-box environments are mountains, volcanos, eggs, trees, rocks, swamps, and sand.

As I look across the room and all three centers, I sense the spirit of cooperation and enjoyment. Jermaine is helping James roll out the clay teeth for his tyrannosaurus. "In real life, the King's teeth were six inches long," Jermaine says matter-of-factly. Jesse and Amanda are comparing their clay creations and are helping each other with hints to make them more realistic. The puppet group is practicing their play, and Raymond is insisting that an announcement be made that this is "a pretend play." He wants everyone to know that they are aware that dinosaurs didn't really talk or play hide and seek. Joyce is drawing the sky on her shoe box and is helping Ernie to do the same (Figure 4-17). Soon other children notice what they are doing and, following Joyce's lead, add a blue sky to their dioramas.

As I play the cleanup music on the guitar, there is genuine disappointment that we don't have more time. "If we hurry and get ready, we can watch a play by our friends who made puppets," I announce. This encouragement hastens our cleanup, and soon all are seated with their belongings.

The announcement is made that the puppet story is a pretend one, per Raymond's suggestion: "The children in the play would like you to know that this is a pretend story and that the dinosaurs in the story have assumed the children's names." The children's names are announced and the play begins. "Many years ago there were many dinosaurs. One day one of the meat eaters ate some grass and died. Suddenly, he received some special power and came back alive..."

The children applaud when they hear that "the dinosaurs lived happily ever after." I invite the children in the audience to tell what they liked about the play. The children in the play take turns calling on members of the audience.

"I liked the puppets," says James.

"I'm glad it had a happy ending," adds Crystal, who is always looking for the happy parts of stories. The audience offers several thoughtful, positive comments about the story and the puppets. We are interrupted by the announcement of the buses on the loudspeaker. As the children leave I can tell they have had a great day and are anxious to return to school for another day with dinosaurs.

Figure 4–17   **Ernie and Joyce work intently on their dioramas**

Summary

Whole language is not a set of activities. While the experiences described here were wonderfully educative and generative for this class of "transition" children, they are not meant to be taken as part of a formula for a "whole language look at dinosaurs." The activities fit into a larger curricular frame in which meaning is the focus: children learn language arts, mathematics, science, and social studies by using them in a way that is clearly meaningful and functional.

Being flexible and following the children's lead are a big part of what whole language is about. I often find that activities I plan are not as successful as I had hoped they would be, but I'm coming to realize that when ideas do fall short of expectations, it is often because the ideas are mine rather than the children's. Critical to the success of this classroom is confidence in the children, in their ability not only to make decisions about what to do in the classroom but also to learn from and to teach each other.

Personal Reflection

Next year our class may not do a unit on dinosaurs. Each individual and class has a unique set of experiences and interests. I have learned how valuable it is to follow the children's lead in creating a learning environment that is exciting and interesting. This, of course, does not imply throwing up my hands and allowing the children to do whatever they want. By planning open-ended invitations and questions, using strategy-sharing sessions, allowing meaningful choices, and instilling in children the notion that they are competent learners with much to share, we can help children go easily and confidently beyond what they currently know.

By looking past the children's products into their process and intentions I am much more able to see their strengths as strategic thinkers. Thus I am able to focus and build on these strengths and encourage children to share their strategies with each other.

Had the children chosen a topic from the choices I had presented to them, I may have taught more but certainly would have learned less. Not only have I learned about dinosaurs but, more importantly, I have seen how children learn language and learn about language while learning through language.

References

Baum, L. Frank. 1956. *The Wizard of Oz*. New York: Grosset.

Cramer, Pam Tims. 1985. *Dynamic Dinosaurs* (record and book). Oklahoma City, Okla.: Melody House.

Disney, Walt. 1973. *Pinocchio and His Puppet Show Adventure*. New York: Random House.

Hoff, Syd. 1958. *Danny and the Dinosaur*. New York: Harper & Row.

White, E. B. 1945a. *Charlotte's Web*. New York: Harper.

———. 1945b. *Stuart Little*. New York: Harper.

Williams, Geoffrey T. 1987. *Lost in Dinosaur World*. Los Angeles, Calif.: Price, Stern, and Sloan.

5

Supporting Literacy Development: On the First Day in First Grade and Throughout the Year

VERA E. MILZ

Today is the first day of a new school year! "Welcome to Room 28" reads the sign on the classroom door. Another chart, from which a large felt-tip marker hangs on a piece of rug yarn, reads "We are in First Grade" and has a large space for children to write their names. On a table, name tags are ready for children to pick up and use to claim a coat hook for the rest of the year. Shelves filled with hundreds of books define a reading corner that is complete with child-sized chairs and stools. A wire book rack holds many of the books by Marc Brown, who will be visiting the school in late October.

Across the room, a mailbox labeled with each child's name holds a brief note for every child. A wooden bookcase has a sign: "Put your lunches here." A set of plastic toy dinosaurs sits on the science table. Most of the bulletin board space is empty, but one board is titled "Find a Friend in a Book." Beneath the words, several colorful posters from publishers of children's books have been stapled. One poster tells that Marc Brown's Arthur is celebrating his tenth birthday. A large book, *Mrs. Wishy-Washy* (Cowley 1980), sits on an easel waiting for readers. Paper, cardboard, notebooks, crayons, pencils, and other writing implements are in the writing center. A few copies of books written by children in previous first grades line the shelves. The room is ready for the children and teacher who will learn and live together during the coming school year.

This chapter will take you to a first-grade classroom at the Way Elementary School in Bloomfield Hills, Michigan. I have been teaching in the district for more than twenty years and have gradually developed what is now called a "whole language" approach to the teaching of the language arts.

For more than ten years, I have used books by professional children's authors/ illustrators as the foundation of the reading program. As a beginning teacher, I was given a basal reading series to help children learn to read. After one year, I realized that the materials were inadequate for helping children, and I turned to reading aloud books that I loved as a child, such as *The Little House* (Burton 1942) and *Make Way for Ducklings* (McCloskey 1941). I wanted to make the books easily accessible to my students to read on their own, so a classroom library collection was started using paperback book clubs, discards from children who had outgrown the books in their home libraries, some hardback purchases, and books that the children authored themselves. Instead of filling in workbooks, children began to keep journals, make advertisements for favorite books, and create their own stories to be published in the classroom.

Ken Goodman later defined what had happened in my classroom: "Whole language is an attempt to get back to basics in the real sense of the word—to set aside basals, workbooks, and tests, and to return to inviting kids to learn to read and write by reading and writing real stuff" (1986, 38). The basal reader framework used in 90 percent of American classrooms is not present in this room. Instead, children learn to read—as well as to write, speak, and listen—as they engage in functional activities while they interact with one another.

As the teacher in Room 28, I am a participant as well as a facilitator. Rather than acting as a manager or director responsible for the learning in this classroom, I gather materials and create an environment that I believe will support my young language learners. Each year brings a new and unique group of children. Though the school district has been described as an affluent upper middle-class neighborhood, the children are members of a rapidly changing society and come from a variety of cultures and backgrounds. This diversity makes the classroom an exciting place to develop new insights into how language works, yet the children need support and help, just as children do in any school setting.

Starting Out

The 9:00 bell rings. Footsteps and voices are heard in the hallway. Some parents accompany their children to the classroom and, with hugs and kisses, they say their good-byes. Some children come alone, and they grin widely as they recognize me. The children look around for familiar points of interest; most had visited their classroom yesterday, on teacher preparation day. A few go to look for their name tags. Julie heads right to my mailbox and puts a note inside (Figure 5–1, A

Figure 5—1   Julie's note. A: Julie puts her note in the teacher's mailbox. B: The note.

A   B

and B). She then comes over to me and tells me, "There's mail in your box." Other children find chairs and claim desks. Several read the sign on the board and sign their names. Kelly and Stephanie look at the collection of Marc Brown books. They each choose one and sit down to look at it. Finally, all twenty-three six- and seven-year-olds are present and ready to start this year's adventure.

This day is not a beginning in the true sense of the word. It is a day of continuation—an extension of the language learning that began at birth. By the time they enter first grade, all the children are able to communicate with the adults and caretakers they encounter each day. I know that they will continue this same kind of interaction with me. As I listen I want to discover their home language, and if they can all communicate in English. In recent years, several have had a first language other than English. I quickly realize that in this particular class each child, except for Tomo (who comes from Japan), is proficient in English.

Just a short week ago, all of the children had been merely names on a list, but already I am beginning to notice their individual strengths and needs, particular interests, and unique personalities. When Heath asks me if he can put his lunch on the wooden bookcase tomorrow, I realize that he has read the sign that is posted on it. Even before I read her note, I am pleased that Julie has chosen to use written language to communicate with me when she placed an envelope in my mailbox. Even though I do not know my new students well, I believe that each is already a reader and a writer. In the coming days, I will discover what they know as we engage in "real" reading and writing activities.

Getting Together

I ask the children to join me in an open area of the classroom. We introduce ourselves and talk informally for a few minutes. Then I write my name on the front chalkboard. I invite Adrienne and Sujeet to do the same. Then I demonstrate how they will sign up as a "buyer" or a "carrier" for lunch on the next day. Heath shows everyone where to put their lunches if they carry them. Our discussion addresses the many problems that will face the children on the next day of school, which, unlike today's half-day session, will be a full one.

I then tell the children I would like to read a story with them. "Every day, we will read lots of stories together and later, if you like, you can read them by yourselves," I say.

"But I can't read," exclaims Reed. I reassure him.

"Don't worry. I'll bet you can. As we read together, you help me, and I'll help you. I think you will be surprised at how much you are already reading."

I start to read *Mrs. Wishy-Washy* (Cowley 1980) (Figure 5–2). The whole class can easily see the words and pictures, and the children can enjoy the book just as if they were sitting with someone who was reading it just to them. When Don Holdaway (1979) noticed the benefits of lap reading between parent and child, he suggested the use of a large-format book for teachers with a classroom of children. When I finish the book, the children say, "Read it again!" So we do, and this time, I notice that voices chime in as I read: "And she paddled in it....Oh, what lovely mud!...and he rolled in it...wishy-washy...wishy-washy...Away went the cow." By the time I reach the last page, nearly every voice can be heard, along with lots of giggles.

Figure 5–2   Reading *Mrs. Wishy-Washy* together

"I like that story. It's so funny!" exclaims Reed.

"I knew they were gonna go back in the mud."

"Me, too! Me, too!" is heard across the group. A lively discussion continues for several minutes. Some children relate their experiences at a farm, and one child tells how his dog wouldn't let him bathe him. As they talk, they relate to the story, making connections to their own lives. Their understanding and enjoyment of the story grows as they talk together.

Now that we know each other a bit more, the children relax, and we begin to talk about what we will do in Room 28 this year. Together we start to establish procedures that will help us use, enjoy, and care for our classroom. We move to the reading corner. "Look at all the books," says David.

"Yes, and they are standing on the shelves in a special way," I reply. "All the books by one author are together. In this place are all the books by Tomie de Paola, and here are all the ones by Steven Kellogg." I pull a book out.

"I like *A Rose for Pinkerton*," (Kellogg 1981) says Alyce. "I have that one at my house."

"That's great!" I tell her. "Maybe you would like to read our copy. Here's how to get it and be able to put it away." In our shelf marker system, the children place a two-by-twelve-inch card with their name on it in the place where they find a book they want to read; then they read the book and return it. Because books by the same author are grouped together, children can easily find other books by an author they enjoy.

"Why are those books there?" says Kelly, pointing to the Marc Brown collection.

I explain, "Sometimes, we will take all the books by one author and put them in a special author's book rack, just like I did with Marc Brown's books. Every day we will read one or two of our special author's books together, and maybe later, if you really like the books, we could write letters to tell the special authors what we think is great about their books. Also, I have a surprise about Marc Brown. He's coming to visit our school next month." I then pick up Marc Brown's book *D. W. Flips!* (1987). After talking briefly about the author, we read it. The book is new to the children, but they quickly relate to D. W.'s difficulty when she tries a somersault for the first time. They are pleased when she finally accomplishes the task after she tries and tries again. Judging by the response to the book, I believe they will pick it up independently and also head to the library to search for it or other Marc Brown titles. Then I hand out the shelf markers with each child's name at one end. I ask each child to choose a book and place it on their desks. The book will then be available if the child chooses to read later.

I then ask the children to come to the front of the room for a few minutes. We talk about reading to ourselves and how it differs from when I read *D. W. Flips!* Matthew shows how I held up the book so the class could see the pictures, and how he would hold his book to look at it when he reads it himself. "When I read to myself, I keep my mouth shut," says Heath.

"My Dad reads the paper that way," says Sam, "but sometimes he reads me about the Tigers [our area baseball team]."

"I hope that you will enjoy reading by yourselves," I tell them, "but I also hope that you will read me many stories that you like, or even parts of one." Later, we will have reading conferences during which the children will share books they love, and I will encourage them to try some that I enjoy.

Recess Time

The morning is passing quickly, and it is time for an outside recess, so the children line up to go to the playground. Once outside, before they run off, I take pictures of each child to be used for a class book later in the week. After I return to the room, I quickly answer Julie's note and place it in her mailbox.

Work Time

The bell rings, and it is time to come in. Next, we enjoy a few finger rhymes that Marc Brown has collected in another of his books, *Finger Rhymes* (1980b). The children are familiar with "The Squirrel" and "The Eensy, Weensy Spider." Their voices join in and their hands perform the accompanying actions. I know they will later search out this book and begin to read those pages by themselves. The pictures will help them to read rhymes like "This Little Pig" or "There Was a Little Turtle."

Then I hold up a stack of eight-and-a-half-by-eleven-inch white paper. I tell them that we are going to have "work time": I ask them to make a picture of themselves, perhaps doing something they like. I also invite them to write about their illustrations. Before dismissing the group, I note on the board: "THINGS TO DO." The list begins with "Make my picture" and "Read a book," and I ask the children for more suggestions. Many are given: "Play with the dinosaurs," "Write a letter," "Write my name," "Chalk on the board." The children scurry to places they want to be.

Now I walk around the room and assist children as needed. Many return to their desks to make their pictures, with crayons and pencils from the Writing Center. When the first child, Julie, finishes, I hold her picture up and ask that children bring their pictures to me when they finish. Julie tells me about her picture, and I write her name on the bottom along with the word "and" (Figure 5–3). I want to make a long sentence that begins on the first page: "We are... Julie and Kelsie and Jihan and Jenny and..." Then I place the children's pictures in two piles—one for girls and one for boys. The children quickly realize what I am doing. I then make a summary sentence for each stack: "We Are the Girls in Room 28" and "We Are the Boys in Room 28." I will put covers on each stack, and the Room 28 children will have written two books on their first day in school.

After the children finish their pictures, they turn to other materials in the classroom. Leigh adds her name to the list on the chalkboard, and several follow. Sam writes his name on the chalkboard to show where he will sign if he buys his lunch. In both places, children begin to look for each other's names, and they ask missing children to "sign in." Leigh, Adrienne, and Nedda put *Mrs. Wishy-Washy* (Cowley 1980) on the floor and read it together (Figure 5–4). Julie goes to her mailbox and realizes that I answered her note when I slipped back into the room during the recess. She brings it over for me to read. Three other children then settle down to write me a note. Matthew and Reed create a junglelike scene with the dinosaurs, by taking cardboard, drawing trees and bushes, and placing them with the dinosaurs.

Figure 5–3   Julie's page from the *Guess Who* book

Figure 5–4   Leigh, Adrienne, and Nedda read *Mrs. Wishy-Washy* together

Sharing Time

Suddenly, it is almost time to go home. Many of the children have looked at their books and returned them to the bookshelves. Others place their books in their desks. Chairs are stacked in the front of the room. We gather together again in the front of the room. I hold up the finished class books and read them to the class. "Can we read *Mrs. Wishy-Washy?*" asks Reed. "Yes, yes!!" comes a chorus of voices. So we do. Then I read *Arthur's Tooth* (Brown 1985) as our final story of the day. We talk briefly about bringing lunches tomorrow, I remind them to take home the notes for their parents, and they are on their way home.

After the First Day

As the year progresses, the children become more proficient in their use of language. They learn to read while actually reading, just as they learn how to write while they are writing. Yet each year, different children bring their ideas and knowledge into the classroom, and new paths are taken. This year is no exception.

The daily time spent reading aloud, reading to others, and reading silently leads children to a variety of books and introduces them to many authors. When a particular author speaks to a child through a special book, the child is usually quick to go to the library and ask for other books written by that person.

After several days, I read the first chapter book, *The Beast in Ms. Rooney's Room* (Giff 1985) to the class. Less than halfway through, the class is already captivated and urges me to read more. They are eager to move into the next book in this series, which features a fictional class and its adventures through a school year. Each book in the series focuses on one month of that year, and though I want to read each book during the month it is set in, this does not stop the children from finding out what happens next. Even though the majority of the children cannot read the books themselves, they are able to find parents and other readers who will read ahead with them. Reading is a valued and significant part of each school day and beyond, well into the evening hours.

Children grow and change as writers. They write notes, journal entries, and stories. The pieces grow longer, their spelling moves from a few conventional words to invented spellings and conventional forms, and they are able to communicate more proficiently. Soon Kelsie is able to move far beyond the few correctly spelled words she produced in September (Figure 5−5, A) to being able to record a shared experience with her dad (Figure 5−5, B). As Valentine's Day gets closer, I find a note from my secret admirer — a direct link to *Arthur's Valentine*

Figure 5—5   Kelsie. A: September. B: May: "Yesterday I went down to my lake with my dad. And we brought some bread to feed the baby geese. They were very cute. I liked them a lot. They were very funny, too."

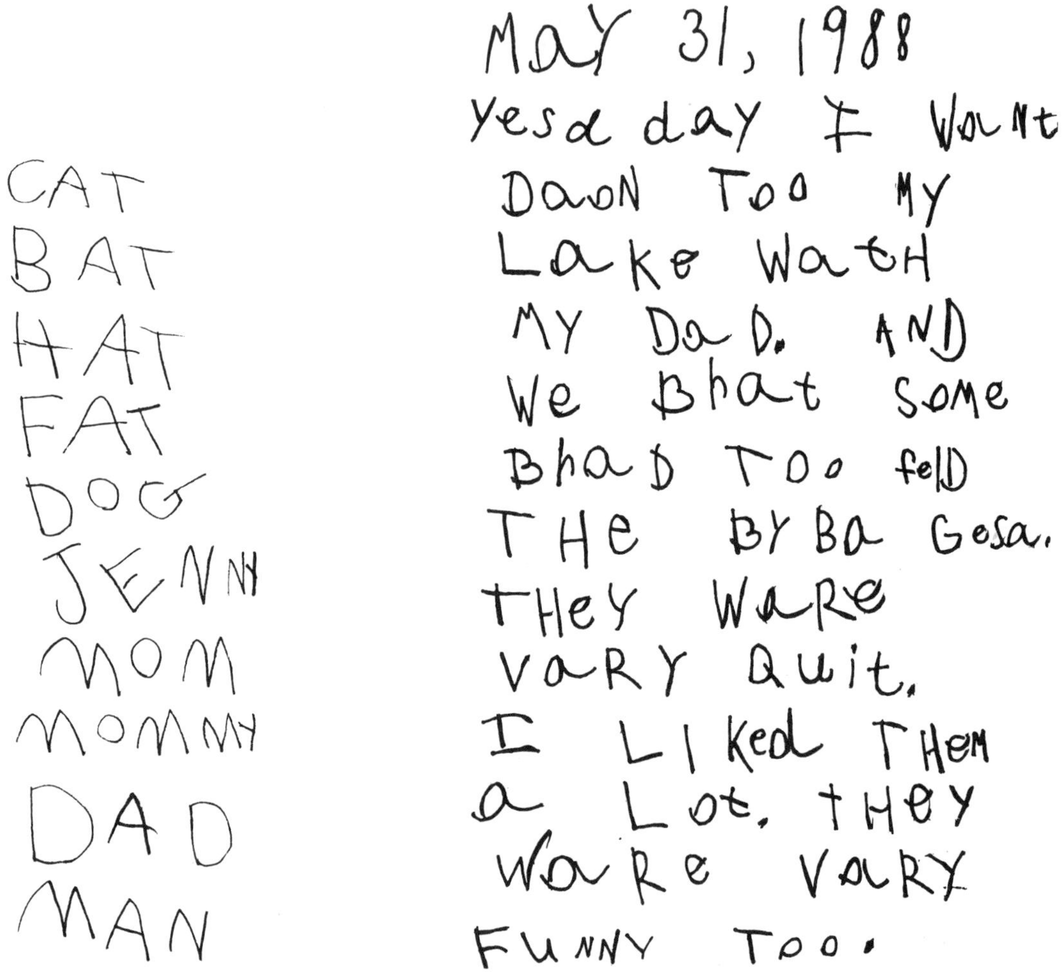

CAT
BAT
HAT
FAT
DOG
JENNY
MOM
MOMMY
DAD
MAN

A

MaY 31, 1988
Yesa day I Want
DaoN Too MY
Lake Watch
MY Da D. AND
We Bhat some
Bha D Too felD
THE BY Ba Gesa.
tHey WaRe
vaRY Quit.
I LI keD THeM
a Lot. tHey
WaRe vaRY
FuNNY Too.

B

Figure 5—6   Sean's secret note to his teacher: "I like you. You are the best teacher. From your secret admirer."

(Brown 1980a), which we had read and enjoyed together earlier in the year and again by request as the holiday drew near (Figure 5—6).

During the year we write many class books together. Sometimes, the books are a collection of birthday notes to help a classmate celebrate the happy occasion. Often they are extensions of books that the children had become familiar with as they were learning to read.

Figure 5−7   "Who do you see?"

ParisParis
Who do you see?
I see Matthew
looking at me.

One of the first books that the children enjoyed reading and listening to on a tape recorder is Bill Martin's *Brown Bear, Brown Bear, What Do You See?* (1967). The book begins with "Brown Bear, Brown Bear, what do you see?" and the response, "I see a Redbird looking at me," indicates the next colorful animal in the book. Using the photographs that I had taken on the first day of school, the children invent a book in a similar pattern: "————, ————, who do you see?" They write their names in the blanks and make pictures of themselves looking at the child in the photograph. Their friends' names supply the answer: "I see ———— looking at me" (Figure 5—7). The finished pages are collected into a class book for the children to read. In the process of making this book, many of the children learn to read the names of their classmates. In making and reading these books, the children grow as readers and writers.

Each year, our school is fortunate to schedule a noted children's author for a visit. When I introduced Marc Brown as this year's author, I knew it would be a special opportunity to make his books seem even more real to my students.

An author's visit often inspires in children new ideas for exploring reading and writing. In his slide presentation, Marc Brown demonstrates how his stories and illustrations are based on his personal experiences. For example, the theater in *Arthur's Valentine* is the movie theater in his hometown of Hingham, Massachusetts. The children begin to understand how their own writing could come from happenings in their own lives. Later in this school year, the children decide to make a Birthday Book for Arthur, which is mailed to Marc Brown. Both in the classroom and in the school library, Marc Brown's books are continually read and enjoyed by the children. No one ever needs to "assign" his books to them.

Personal Reflection

Since this chapter was written, a new group of children has entered the room. Just as last year, I am confident they will grow as language users, but, best of all, I can't wait to see the paths they will take as we learn together during this school year. I have learned to trust the children as learners. By listening to their ideas, providing support and materials, and interacting with them, I am constantly pleased and amazed at what they can do. Children write to tell they are present in the classroom, to remind themselves of something important to them, to communicate an idea, and to order a lunch. They read to find out which hook to place a coat on, to enjoy a story, and to learn about the world around them. Each time, as they interact with each other and with me, and participate in classroom happenings, they are "wholly" and "naturally" involved in learning. The spontaneity and joy that come from discovering and creating language make Room 28 an exciting place to be.

References

Brown, Marc. 1980a. *Arthur's Valentine*. Boston: Little, Brown.

———. 1980b. *Finger Rhymes*. New York: E. P. Dutton.

———. 1985. *Arthur's Tooth*. Boston: Little, Brown.

———. 1987. *D. W. Flips!* Boston: Little, Brown.

Burton, Virginia Lee. 1942. *The Little House*. Boston: Houghton Mifflin.

Cowley, Joy. 1980. *Mrs. Wishy-Washy*. San Diego, Calif.: The Wright Group.

Giff, Patricia Reilly. 1985. *The Beast in Ms. Rooney's Room*. New York: Dell.

Goodman, Kenneth. 1986. *What's Whole in Whole Language?* Portsmouth, N.H.: Heinemann.

Holdaway, Don. 1979. *The Foundations of Literacy*. Portsmouth, N.H.: Heinemann.

Kellogg, Steven. 1981. *A Rose for Pinkerton*. New York: Dial.

Martin, Bill. 1967. *Brown Bear, Brown Bear, What Do You See?* New York: Holt, Rinehart and Winston.

McCloskey, Robert. 1941. *Make Way for Ducklings*. New York: Viking.

6

Teachers and Students as Decision Makers: Creating a Classroom for Authors

GLORIA KAUFFMAN   KATHY G. SHORT

In the last five years, my curriculum has undergone major changes. When I began teaching ten years ago, the curriculum was fairly traditional, based on the various textbooks in our school. While I never completely depended on textbooks, they were still the core of the program. I supplemented the textbooks by bringing in literature to read aloud to my students and for them to read independently. Children wrote daily on topics that I developed. I was in charge at all times, telling the children what to read and write and when and how to do it.

As the years went by, I became increasingly frustrated with the textbook curricula. The children's writing sounded like the reading basal text. The English textbook concentrated on grammar and spelling and had little impact on their writing. The creativity in their creative writing came from me. The daily time limits set for completing a piece of short writing did not give the children enough time to really think through a story. They were concerned with how long and how perfect their writing should be, and not with how to better express and explore their thinking.

In reading, I was bored with the reading groups and the basal stories. Since I was the most active person in the group, the children had to be even more bored.

Throughout the chapter, "I" refers to Gloria and "we" to Gloria and Kathy.

They seemed unable to get beyond superficial, literal answers to the basal reader questions. The skills that were to be taught with each basal story did not connect with the story or with the children's needs. I felt as if I was "covering" material to make sure it was mentioned, yet the children were not learning or using those skills. Students were often uncomfortable in the groups, afraid of reading aloud and making mistakes. The children in the "low" reading group thought they were failures and could not read. When I looked at my own habits as an adult, I realized that I enjoyed reading and often read for pleasure as well as to learn new ideas. While I read for purposes I saw as important to me, my students did not.

Exploring a New Curricular Framework

When Kathy Short approached me about working together on a research project to develop a curriculum that was process centered and collaborative, I believed that this was the opportunity I needed to explore a different approach to teaching and learning. I was excited and apprehensive about the changes that might take place both for me and my students. Kathy and I developed a joint project where we worked together closely as coteachers and coresearchers for a year in first grade. We were excited by the understandings about curriculum and learning that came from that project. Since that time, I have been teaching in third grade and I'm continuing to think about and develop curriculum with my students and other educators.

One of our frustrations was our need for a new curriculum framework. Kathy and I both knew that we wanted to move away from "scope and sequence" charts and teachers' guides, but we did not know what we were moving toward. We thought for a while that we had a "grab bag" curriculum. We had gathered together all kinds of neat "whole language" teaching ideas that we could randomly pull out of the bag and use, but there was no curricular framework that tied these activities together. We needed a framework that was both theoretical and practical and that would allow us to generate and evaluate curricular experiences with our students.

The framework that became the basis of our learning environment was the authoring cycle, as illustrated in Figure 6−1. The authoring cycle stresses the importance of building from life experiences, engaging in many uninterrupted experiences with communication, collaborating on and exploring ideas with others, revising ideas, presenting those ideas later in a more public form, reflecting on our learning, and offering new invitations for learning.

Initially we defined *authoring* as writing and saw the authoring cycle only as a way to organize the writing curriculum. In time, however, we realized that authoring is a general process of constructing a chunk of meaning that we can share with others. When we read a book, we construct, or author, our own

Figure 6–1   The authoring cycle as a framework for curriculum (Burke and Short 1988)

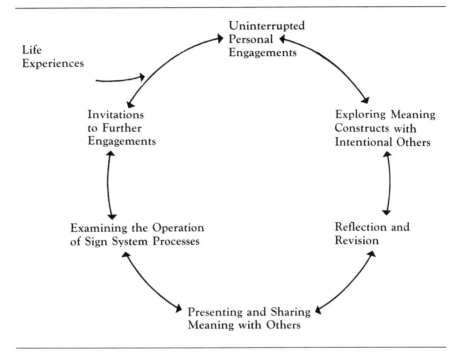

understandings about that book. In addition to using written language we can author meaning through other communication systems such as art, music, drama, and movement. As we worked with the cycle, observed the responses of the students, and talked with Jerry Harste and Carolyn Burke, we gradually came to see the authoring cycle as the broader framework for which we were searching.

Introducing the School Context

My third-grade classroom is situated in Millersburg, in northern Indiana. Millersburg Elementary School serves students from small-town and rural backgrounds and is located in a working-class community where most parents work on trailer factory assembly lines. About a third of the children come from Amish and Mennonite families, with the other children coming from a wide variety of backgrounds. The school curriculum is fairly traditional, and most teachers use textbook approaches.

The administration, however, does allow teachers to try new approaches as long as they have thought through their curricula carefully.

Because my classroom is organized around the authoring cycle, the day is set up fairly flexibly. Although we will describe a particular schedule in this chapter, the children and I often change the schedule to give more time to particular projects. The day usually begins with journals and a group meeting, and then the children spend the rest of the morning focusing on authoring through reading and writing. Afternoons are devoted to children exploring understandings in math, science, and social studies. In the afternoon the children also leave the classroom for art and music classes. We end the day by coming together as a class for read-aloud time with a chapter book, and to talk about the book and the day. Throughout the day, I look for opportunities to build our sense of the class as a community. Ending the day by thinking and reflecting as a group helps to build our sense of togetherness.

While this chapter is organized around one particular day, we will also be moving back and forth in time to give readers a sense of how decisions about curriculum change over time and how children move through authoring cycles. It is important to understand that planning does not focus on individual days or even weeks. Instead, the authoring cycle provides a continuous curricular framework for supporting children over time in their growth as authors of their own lives.

Establishing a Working Atmosphere: Journals

It is a cold rainy day in April as third graders enter the room in small groups, a reflection of the bus schedule. Chris, Lynn, and Phillip begin handing out personal journals to the other students, while Harry and David take down orange chairs from the six round tables. Once the room is set up, Chris, Lynn, and Harry informally chat about their baseball cards and the events of the previous evening before they settle down to write in their journals.

Since there are no assigned seats, as other children enter the room, they decide where they will be sitting for their morning work. This flexible seating arrangement provides opportunities for children to become comfortable working with everyone in the room. Throughout the day, children can change seats according to what they are working on and the group they perceive to be most supportive for them in completing that work. As Chris will tell you, "If you want to concentrate and get some serious work done, you don't choose to sit with your best friends."

Within twenty minutes, all twenty-one children have arrived, greeted each other, given me lunch money, and settled down to informal conversations and journal writing. Starting the day in this quiet informal way is important: what happens when children first enter the classroom establishes the working atmosphere for the day. I want a mood of sharing and reflecting to be immediately present.

During journal time, children write personal entries about what happened the night before or what will be happening in school that day. For example, today Josh writes

> Last night I took my flashlight and read a book. Sunday we went to our cousin's church. Then we went to their house. We had turkey sandwiches. My dad got Buster Bars and we ate them. I felt happy. I ran around the house. The dog chased me. Then I laughed. When I'm happy, I do not get mad easily.

When we began journals at the beginning of the year, it was difficult for the children to write effectively about their personal lives. They were used to writing for others rather than for themselves. As the year continued, the children began to experience the benefits of expressing and reflecting on their actions, feelings, and thoughts, and now they value journal time.

Sharing with Others: Group Meeting Time

As the children complete their journal entries, they move to the corner of the room for group sharing time. Children who are finished early grab a book to read or talk quietly with others.

The corner of the room where they are gathering for group time contains several old choir risers arranged in a U-shape. Because the risers are of different heights, we can have many options for the use of our space and can arrange the risers in different ways to accommodate group meetings, stages for plays, or work areas for anyone who wants to work alone. Children place pillows on them for more comfortable seating as they spread out to write, read, or talk with others.

At 8:20 I ask everyone to come to the meeting. Children who are not finished with their entries can complete them during the morning work time. As we gather on the risers, Tara says, "Let's share our journals out loud today." The others agree and bring their journals to the meeting. Anyone who wants to share reads a journal entry aloud to the group. The children do not raise their hands or look to me for permission to read. They simply wait for each other and jump in to read whenever there is silence. If two children begin reading at the same time, one child stops and waits until the first child has finished. I am part of the group and sit quietly listening, sharing when my turn comes.

When there is a long period of silence, signaling that everyone who wants to share has done so, we talk briefly about the reading work time and the progress different literature discussion groups are making. Karen, who is in the group discussing *Julie of the Wolves* (George 1972), reports, "Our group has compared

Julie with Karana from *Island of the Blue Dolphins* (O'Dell 1960), and today we want to make a chart showing how they are the same and different." After the other groups report, the meeting ends and the children move off to get their books and literature logs.

Throughout the week and the year, our group meeting and planning times are flexible and responsive to the needs of the children. For example, at the beginning of the year, we spend more time organizing our daily work plans and setting goals for the work period. Children actually wrote out their plans for the morning. By this time of the year, they can organize their time without writing out a plan, so we are able to discuss the morning schedule briefly and go on our way.

Other kinds of sharing also occur during our group meeting. Sometimes I read a picture book to the class and invite them to have a class discussion on the book. Other times I use storytelling techniques to share literature and then leave the materials out for them to use during reading time. Sometimes we discuss filmstrips that introduce a particular author or style of illustrating; these are then placed into a listening center to view during work time. We might also reflect as a group on strategies that children are using in reading or in their discussions. Children share from their literature response logs or from the ideas they have listed or charted in their literature discussion groups as strategies others can use to organize their thoughts. Sharing these strategies is often helpful for children who are having trouble. One group meeting each week is devoted to interviewing a child from the classroom, an experience that enables us to know each other better as people and as learners. Group meetings are times when children have an opportunity to share their ideas and accomplishments with each other.

Authoring Through Reading: Reading Work Time

Immediately after the group meeting, children gather books and literature logs and begin moving into their literature discussion groups. Today, there are five groups of children meeting. The five groups have each read a book centering on the theme of survival—*Sign of the Beaver* (Speare 1983); *Julie of the Wolves* (George 1972); *Babe: The Gallant Pig* (King-Smith 1983); *Robinson Crusoe* (Dolch 1958); or *The Door in the Wall* (de Angeli 1949). The theme of survival had emerged several weeks earlier from our discussion of *Island of the Blue Dolphins* by Scott O'Dell (1960), which I was reading aloud to the class. As we shared our thoughts about this book, the class had focused on how Karana survived with her dog Rontu on an island alone for twenty-eight years. The children were intrigued with the topic of survival so we decided to explore that theme through our next set of literature circles. I began searching for books we could use with that theme. I introduced the books with a book talk so the children had a general idea of what each was about. Afterwards, they were given time to browse through the selections and make their decisions about which book to read and discuss. I put a large piece of paper on the board with the five titles and with the numbers 1–4 below each title so that the children knew how many participants could be in each group. Because the literature circles were not grouped according to ability, children could choose which group they wanted to join. As they made their decisions, they signed up for that circle, took a book, and began reading (Figure 6–2). Sometimes, I use a ballot system instead, in which the children write down their first and second choices, and I put them into groups based on their choices.

The five groups spent last week reading their books and writing several entries in their literature logs in preparation for this week's circles. Log entries reflect their responses to what they read, including parts they liked or did not like, questions about things they did not understand, comments on what they think the book means, and connections to characters from other books and to their own lives. This week they are meeting to talk and think together about their interpretations of their books.

At the beginning of the year, children needed to meet and talk as they were reading their books rather than waiting until they had finished them. They met briefly each day at the beginning of the reading work time to discuss quickly what

Figure 6–2   **Reading time**

they had read the previous day and to contract with each other on how far they would read for the next day. Once they had finished the book, they met in literature circles during the next week to explore various issues in depth. Although they now wait to begin discussion groups formally until after reading their books, they still often have informal discussions with each other as they read.

At this point in the year, the children can easily conduct their groups without my being a member. As I walk around today, I hear the *Sign of the Beaver* group retelling parts of the story to clear up some questions and misunderstandings. The *Babe* group is sharing literature log entries with each other. The *Robinson Crusoe* and the *Door in the Wall* groups are each brainstorming a list of possible ideas they could discuss in relation to their book. They organize their ideas by making a web, a diagram of ideas, on a large sheet of paper. Children in the *Julie* group are further along in their discussion and are making a chart comparing their book to *Island of the Blue Dolphins*. I overhear Miranda arguing, "Karana was lonelier than Julie because she only had a dog to talk to, but Julie had a wolf and a pen pal."

At the beginning of the year, I stagger the groups so that I can be part of each group to demonstrate how the discussions function and to set up positive interaction patterns. This morning, however, I choose not to join any of the groups. Instead I listen to the discussions and take notes on how well the groups are functioning. On other days I might join a particular group to help them get their discussion started, focus their discussion, or talk through an issue.

After about thirty minutes, each group decides on what they want to talk about the next day, and children begin moving into other reading-related activities. Some write in their literature logs. Others reread parts of their book or do some research in other materials to prepare for their next day's discussion. Some go immediately to other independent reading.

In the *Julie* group, Melissa announces, "Tomorrow I want to talk about how Karana and Julie dressed." Karen disagrees, saying, "I think we should talk about how the girls hunted." "Well, we could talk about dress tomorrow and hunting the next day," suggests Miranda. "I agree," remarks Jamie. "Let's talk about dress tomorrow." "Okay," replies Karen, "but I think we should look at some books on Eskimos before we talk tomorrow so we can compare Eskimos and Indians." "You can look at Eskimo books," responds Jamie. "But I'll look in *Julie* for ideas." Karen goes to the library to look for books on Eskimos while Jamie goes to the risers and rereads several sections of *Julie of the Wolves* (George 1972). Melissa and Miranda decide to reread some parts of *Island of the Blue Dolphins* (O'Dell 1960) to find out what Karana wore.

Gradually the children move into what they call "free reading," meaning they choose what they want to read from the variety of materials in the classroom. The classroom library and display areas are filled with all kinds of reading materials including fiction, information books, folklore, and poetry. I provide many picture books and chapter books that are related to their literature circle books and to our science and social studies units. Today I have many books out that are related to the nature study we are doing in science. There are also displays of books by particular authors whom we are featuring in the classroom. As they read, children record the titles on sheets of paper in their reading folders.

During free reading, children can choose to read alone or with others. Lynn is reading alone in a corner while Chris and Jason are "partner reading": Chris reads one page and then Jason reads the next. Melissa and Miranda are using the strategy "Say Something" (Harste and Short with Burke 1988); they take turns each reading a section of the story aloud to the other person. After each section, they stop and talk briefly about the connections and predictions they are making. Jamie, Valerie, Josh, and Harry are "popcorn reading" their chapter book: one person reads aloud, stopping suddenly, and whoever pops in first continues reading and then pops out again so someone else can pop in.

As the children read, I walk around, giving support to any group or individual who might need it. Today, I partner read and do "Say Something" with Harry on a book about deserts, as well as talk informally with several other children about what they are currently reading. By the time recess draws near, all of the children have had a chance to consider a piece of literature closely as well as an opportunity to read widely for enjoyment and information.

At 10:15 all of the children are sitting in various groups around the room reading books of their choice. Karen goes over and turns out the lights to signal that there is an announcement. The class freezes, waiting to hear what the message will be. Karen announces: "Time for recess. Remember to clean up your spaces and get out your writing folders so you'll be ready to start writing after recess."

The children share in the control and responsibility for classroom routines and schedules. Each week, a secretary is assigned and is responsible for announcing recess, lunch, and pull-outs (such as for art and music classes) and for getting the class lined up. The children have learned to listen to each other and to respect the process of shared control.

 ## Moving Through an Authoring Cycle in Reading: Children as Critics

While the children are at morning recess, let's take some time to understand the authoring cycle that underlies our reading work time. This cycle emphasizes that all authoring must begin in children's own life experiences. For us, this means giving children choices in what they read and encouraging them to respond personally to their reading. They also need large chunks of uninterrupted time during which they learn by engaging in many different reading and writing experiences with a wide variety of materials. Some of their reading experiences, however, should involve in-depth explorations of literature as readers make connections and reflect on their reading with each other. Literature circles encourage this more intensive and collaborative exploration of ideas.

The kind of exploration that occurs in literature circles varies depending on whether the children are reading the same book or reading from a set of related, but different, books. If all of the children in a group have read the same book, the discussions will focus in depth on issues and themes in that book. In contrast, discussions of a text set, a group of related books, focus on retellings and connections across books. Each person in these groups reads different books from the set. When the group meets, they share brief retellings of their books with each other and then look for comparisons across their books. Among the text sets we have enjoyed are Cinderella variants, books about dragons and dinosaurs, "magic pot" variants, books by Arnold Lobel, books dealing with the theme of "friend or foe," and different versions of *I Know an Old Lady Who Swallowed a Fly*.

After readers have had a chance to explore with others, they present some of their understandings more formally through sharing or presentations. The cycle continues with strategy lessons, which are classroom activities designed by the teacher to highlight some aspect of reading seen as important for a particular group of students. Students are encouraged to reflect on both the content and process of reading and to offer new invitations to class members for future reading experiences.

Before the children return from recess, let's take an in-depth look at one literature group moving through this cycle over a three-week period. We will follow the group that read and discussed *Babe: The Gallant Pig* (King-Smith 1983) from the point where they chose their book to their presentation of the book to the class.

When the five survival books were introduced to the class, Chris, Kim, David, Matthew, and Nicole all signed up to read *Babe: The Gallant Pig*. The story is about a pig who is raised on a sheep farm and becomes a champion sheepherder by politely asking the sheep to move, instead of barking loudly as the sheepdogs do. I talked with the children about why they chose the book. "I want to read it because I like *Charlotte's Web*," (White 1952) Chris informed me. "I want to see how Babe escapes from being butchered," responded Kim. "I want to know how Babe is going to be gallant," explained David. Nicole smiled: "I like books where animals talk"; Matthew added, "I like books about pigs."

The *Babe* group decided to begin their reading of the book as a group (Figure 6–3). They met together on the rug and used the strategy "Say Something." For example, Kim would read a section aloud and predict what would happen next, and then Chris would read and make some comments about what he thought the passage meant. After several days, the group decided to continue reading alone, but all read on the risers so that they could still comment to each other about the book. Chris told me, "Exciting parts would come up and I would tell the group to look on page such and such. I would give my opinion and then we would continue reading."

During the week they were reading the book, the children made several literature log entries about their responses to the book. David wrote: "The spider

Figure 6—3   Literature circle on *Babe*

in *Charlotte's Web* is like the dog in *Babe*. Babe and Wilbur have to face the same life." Kim wrote: "Today I read the part where Babe meets a sheep named Ma. I don't think Fly [the dog] realizes that not all sheep are dumb." Chris wrote: "I would like to know why Farmer Hogget almost shot Babe? I wonder why the dogs thought sheep were dumb? I think the sheep respect Babe more than Fly." These entries helped the children reflect on the story as they read and raised questions and issues they wanted to discuss with the group during their circles.

At the beginning of the following week, everyone had finished the book, so the group met for their first discussion. They began by talking about various parts of the book, particularly one section that several had found confusing. "At first I didn't understand the part where Babe almost got shot," said Kim. "Yes," agreed David. "It confused me when the author wrote about the gun having two nostrils."

After talking briefly about the book, the group decided to make a web of all the possible topics they could discuss. Webbing or making a list of ideas is a strategy groups often use to help focus their discussions. The webs or lists usually include characters, favorite sections of the book, the messages from the book, the author's style of writing, exciting or confusing events, related books or topics, and the connections between the book and their personal lives. The *Babe* group decided to web their ideas for several reasons. Matthew explained, "I like webbing

Figure 6-4   Web of issues to discuss for *Babe: The Gallant Pig* (Chris, grade 3)

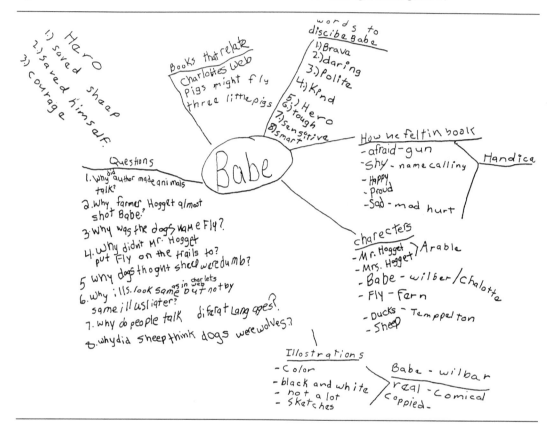

because everyone in the group can write on the same large sheet of paper and it is easier to get all the ideas down." David added, "I think webbing helps us organize our thoughts into categories we can discuss. We can write down more ideas where they fit." Chris's web is shown in Figure 6-4.

Once the group had webbed their ideas, they chose one topic and began their discussion. The topic they chose was why the sheep thought that the dogs were wolves. They talked about how wolves and dogs belonged to the same family and compared this story to others such as "The Three Little Pigs," in which wolves use trickery.

The group then moved on to discuss the feelings of the pig and the other animals. They were intrigued with how the sheepdogs looked down on the sheep and thought they were stupid. This conversation led them into talking about how we treat people who we think are not smart. David pointed out: "We talk loudly and slowly when we talk to people who are foreigners. We think they look weird and so they must be stupid." "Yeah," said Chris. "You know that kid in third grade who flunked? He was in an accident and acts weird." "Kids say he's stupid," responded Kim in a worried voice. "He hangs out with all the mean guys. I'm kind of afraid of him." "We talk to handicapped kids like him loudly and slowly, too," commented David. "We don't really try to talk to them nice." "It's just like when the dogs yelled at the sheep and scared them," replied Kim. "But Babe asked nicely and said please so the sheep listened to him," added Chris. At that point, David remarked, "*The Door in the Wall* group is reading a story about a boy named Robin who was handicapped with polio and still ended up being a hero." His comment led the group back to their web, and they decided that the next day they would discuss heroes in *Babe*.

The following day, Nicole began the discussion by asking, "Could Babe have found another way to be a hero other than getting rid of the rustlers? I wonder why the author decided to write about the rustlers?" "Stories about sheep always have rustlers in them and so Babe had to be the hero and get rid of them," explained David. The group spent some time talking about sheep rustling and the other ways in which Babe was a hero in the story. They ended their discussion by looking back at their web and deciding to discuss the illustrations.

David began the discussion the following day because he was upset about the illustrations. "I think they look exactly like those in *Charlotte's Web* and I think that the illustrator copied off of E. B. White's work." The group compared the two books and could not decide if the illustrations were copied or not. Nicole said, "Wilbur looks more cuddly." Kim continued, "And Babe looks more like a real pig." "I wish that the illustrations would be in color instead of pencil so I could see more details," remarked Matthew. Kim disagreed: "All chapter books have black-and-white pictures." "But the covers need to be a colored picture," David pointed out, "or you wouldn't be interested and pick up the book."

Over the next several days, the conversations continued as the group discussed the author's choice of names for characters and the relationships of the characters to each other and to Charlotte and Wilbur from *Charlotte's Web* (White 1952).

After discussing themes and characters in *Babe* for a week, the group decided they wanted to do a presentation on the book to the class. They knew that their presentation had to reflect the most important issues they had discussed, so they made a list of their main ideas and what they wanted the class to understand. Kim said, "We should show how brave and gallant Babe was even if he was an ordinary pig." "I think the class should realize that everyone needs a chance to show what they can do and that they should not feel sorry for people who look like they can't do things," suggested Chris. "I agree," responded David. "They should respect each other's abilities and not give an opinion before getting to know that person." Matthew added, "I want our class to work together and depend on each other and share our feelings."

Based on these goals and issues, the group made a list of possible extension ideas for the book. Kim began by commenting, "A play wouldn't work because the book has too many characters and a play wouldn't get at their feelings." "A puppet show would be fun and comical and would show the humor of the book," suggested David. Chris offered another idea: "We could do a mural showing a barn with doors that open and have different scenes in Babe's life." "I think a comic book would be fun to show that Babe was brave," Kim remarked. The others were excited about this idea and added that the comic book could also show that Babe was strong, kind, sensitive, intelligent, and tough. David announced: "It could be *A Hero's Greatest Moments*. We can show that anyone can be a hero."

The group began working on the comic book (Figure 6–5). Chris drew a scene of a wolf in a helicopter rustling sheep, and the others created four different personalities of Babe to come to the rescue. The group decided they would let the class choose which of their characters would actually rescue the sheep—Rambo Pig, Karate Pig, Pigyver, or Lincoln Pig. As they worked on their book, other groups became interested in their idea and asked to see the different characters.

When the group finished their comic book, the class gathered on the risers to share and celebrate their presentation. The group began by briefly retelling the main plot of the book and by making connections to *Charlotte's Web*. David told the group, "Wilbur and Babe both faced the same crisis of staying alive." Chris pointed out, "Wilbur had Charlotte to save him, while Babe was a true hero because he had to deal with the problem himself." The group talked about some of the issues they had discussed. They then shared their comic strip and told how the different Babe personalities might save the day.

The class responded with comments and questions. Jason remarked, "I think the comic strip was a good idea because there's a lot of humor in pigs." Jeff asked, "Why did you choose pig characters for the comic book?" "Well," answered Chris, "the book had a pig and Babe was not just a pig, he was a hero." Jamie asked, "Why did you choose those four kinds of pigs?" David explained, "Rambo Pig is the tough side of Babe's personality, Karate Pig is the disciplined side, Pig Lincoln is the diplomatic side that talks things over, and Pigyver is the inventive side that frees the sheep." "But why did you use Rambo?" asked Miranda. "Bad guys don't always listen to pigs in suits so Rambo was needed to make things right," answered Chris. At the end of the sharing, the class commented on how much they enjoyed the comic strip, and the group agreed to put it in the class library and to write more adventures.

After the other groups had given their presentations, we talked as a class about what we had found out about survival. I then decided to plan a reflection time later that week to encourage the children to reflect about how they felt they were changing as learners during the year, and about what they were learning through their participation in literature circles. I was excited by the changes I had observed in the children and in the range and depth of ideas being explored in the groups. Having the children reflect on their growth with me would give all of us a chance to stand back and evaluate our learning and the role of literature circles in our classroom.

Figure 6–5   Cartoon drawings for *Babe* presentation

The children's comments indicated that the circles allowed them to think more deeply about what they read and to explore new ideas with others. For example, Lynn remarked, "I have grown as a reader from just sitting there and reading a book and getting nothing out of it to really thinking about the book." "Me, too," said Jason. "Literature circles help bring out more ideas. You can say what you think and then other people can either agree or disagree. As a learner, it makes me get all excited."

Authoring Through Writing: Writing Work Time

The hallway is suddenly filled with the voices of children returning from morning recess. It is 10:30, so we quickly hurry back to the classroom. Morning work time continues as children enter the room and open their writing folders. They talk quietly with each other as they gather their writing supplies and plan what they will work on during writing time today. Corey tells Valerie, "Come and sit by me so I can read my story to you." Philip asks Josh, "Would you help me draw an alien for my space invader book?" SuEllen looks for a quiet place where she can work on the second draft of her story.

Earlier in the year, we would have begun with a group meeting to find out what each person was working on and to develop plans for the writing time. Children are now so familiar with the process and the organizational structure of the writing work time that they plan on their own.

As in reading, writing work time is organized around the authoring cycle. Authoring in writing is rooted in children's life experiences, particularly as they choose their own topics for writing. They engage in many different kinds of writing experiences including journals, literature logs, pen pal letters, messages, science logs, and stories and reports in their authors' folders. The pieces children are considering publishing for a wider audience are taken to an authors' circle. There, they can talk with others about what is and is not working and what, if anything, they might do next with their pieces. After the circle, authors make decisions on revisions and then either edit their pieces themselves or give them to outside editors from the classroom. Once the pieces have been edited, they are typed by a parent volunteer and published in newspaper or book form. These publications are shared with the class, and each person's authorship is celebrated publicly through "receiving" that author's work. The cycle continues with new invitations for writing and with strategy lessons and reflections on the writing process.

Today children are engaged in all different aspects of the writing cycle. They are starting rough drafts, rereading drafts, and having informal conferences with others to get ideas for continuing a draft. Some are talking in authors' circles, while others have finished a circle and are revising the meaning of their piece.

Others are editing for conventions, such as spelling and punctuation, and still others are gluing their books together and beginning their illustrations.

Jeff is working on illustrations. I encourage him to join Lynn and Jason at the table so he can share their crayons as he illustrates his book. Karen, David, and SuEllen are sharing the wallpaper books and glue at another table. Melissa is beginning a new rough draft, while Miranda is rereading her partially finished rough draft. Harry is reading his own rough draft and revising it. Josh is illustrating his science book on milkweed, and Chris is doing research on his nature report.

Tara turns out the light momentarily and announces, "I want two people for authors' circle." Nicole and Kim accept her invitation and take their drafts to meet with Tara on the risers. A little later, Jason checks the revision box and sees that Lynn and Chris have drafts in the box. He knows that he works well with them in discussing revisions, so he turns out the light and says, "Chris and Lynn for authors' circle."

During this time I am circulating around the room helping wherever I can. I spend a great deal of time informally sharing ideas with children. I offer ideas on new ways to illustrate their books by showing them examples of professionally published books, slides from books written by children in previous years, and examples of books from this year. I make suggestions to help children overcome writer's block, and listen to many stories to see if they make sense. I help glue pages together in published books and send children to classmates who are experts in spelling, drawing, or story ideas. I have a parent who comes in once a week to help with typing the stories, but sometimes I quickly type up a special poem or short story during this time for a child who wants to begin illustrating immediately.

We spend the last ten to fifteen minutes of writing time either sharing informally or receiving published books. Today, children are discussing ideas from their reading, writing, and illustrating. Ben shows the crayon scratch designs he is using to illustrate his poems. Nicole shares part of her family story about her grandfather being the iceman. "You should publish that story," encourages Tara. "It's really interesting to hear about how people got ice long ago." Josh and Matthew tell the class: "Be sure to read Bill Martin's book, *Knots on a Counting Rope* [Martin and Archambault 1987]. We read it and beat on the drum to make it sound like an Indian chant."

Karen, the class secretary, has been watching the clock. "It's 11:30. Time to clean up and get ready for lunch." As soon as Karen feels that the room is organized and the class is ready, she dismisses them for lunch. She checks to make sure that the students have placed their math books out on the tables so they are ready to switch for math class right after lunch.

Moving Through an Authoring Cycle in Writing: Children as Composers

While the children are at lunch, let's again take an in-depth look at the authoring cycle, this time at one child moving a piece of writing through the

Figure 6–6   First draft of Jason's story

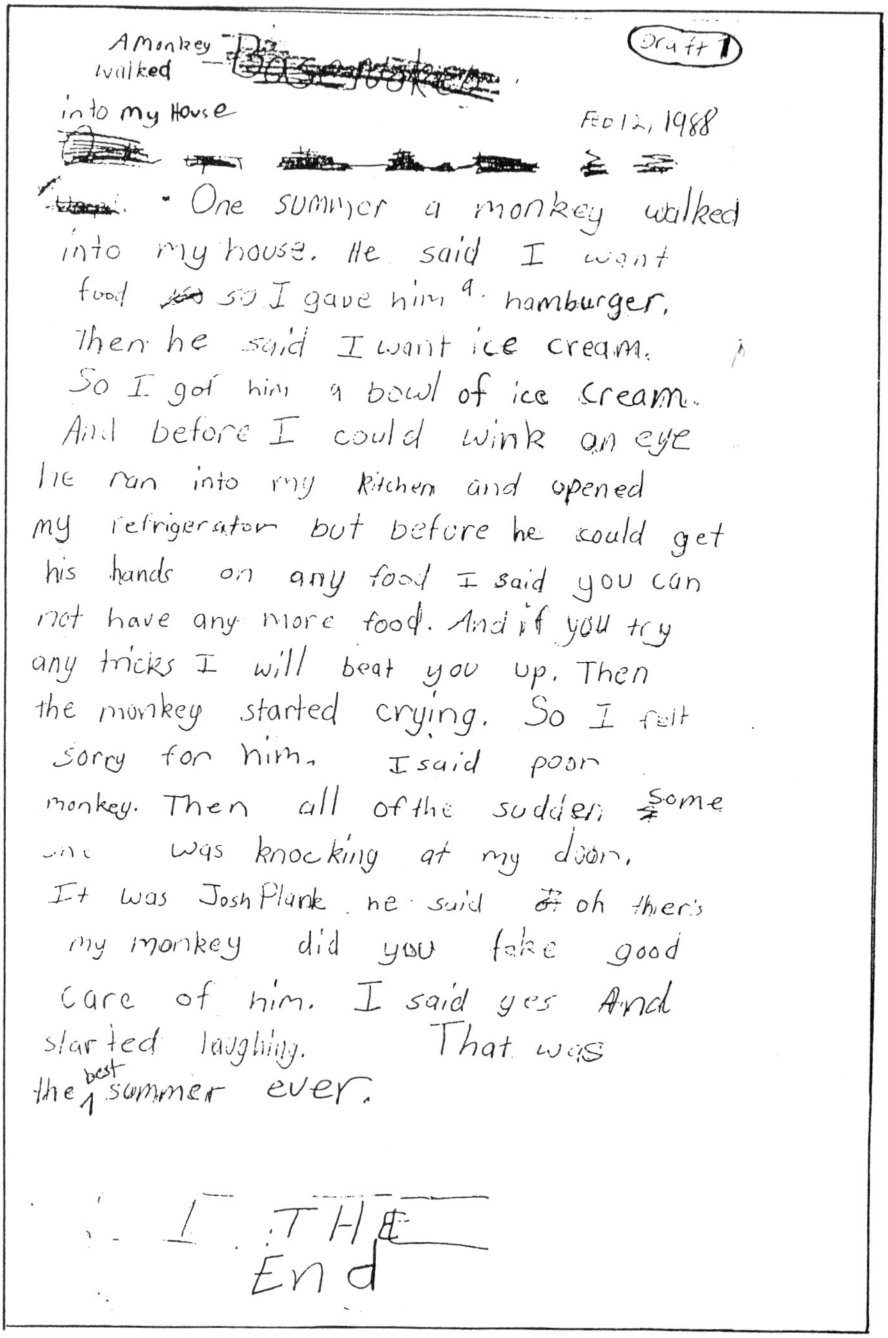

A Monkey ~~walked~~ walked ~~into my House~~   Draft 1

into my House   Feb 12, 1988

~~ ~~ · One summer a monkey walked
into my house. He said I want
food ~~so~~ so I gave him a hamburger,
Then he said I want ice cream.
So I got him a bowl of ice cream.
And before I could wink an eye
he ran into my kitchen and opened
my refrigerator but before he could get
his hands on any food I said you can
not have any more food. And if you try
any tricks I will beat you up. Then
the monkey started crying. So I felt
sorry for him.   I said poor
monkey. Then all of the sudden some
one was knocking at my door.
It was Josh Plank. he said oh thier's
my monkey did you take good
care of him. I said yes And
started laughing.   That was
the best summer ever.

             I THE
             End

cycle. We will follow Jason as he writes, revises, and publishes his story, "The Monkey's Revolt."

Jason is a third grader who enjoys writing. He chooses his own topics and usually has specific goals for particular pieces of writing. In February, Jason began the first of four drafts titled "The Monkey's Revolt." When I asked him what his goals for his new piece of writing were, Jason replied: "I want a story that is an action-packed adventure and that has funny characters. I want it to be a monkey story because several other kids wrote about monkeys and the class liked their stories. I want the class to relate to my story so I'm going to put Josh in it. I just finished reading about survival in *The Pet's Revolt* [Greenwald 1972], so I want my story to have something about survival in it."

Jason quickly produced a first draft (Figure 6–6). As he reread this draft, he commented, "I've been rough on the monkey by wanting to beat it up. It doesn't make sense to have the monkey come in the door and start talking about food." He thought that the ending was poor and stated, "I need to do some rereading in *Pet's Revolt*."

Before he made any revisions on his own, Jason shared his story with Harry (Figure 6–7). Harry gave Jason some suggestions: "I think there isn't an ending and more action is needed in the story. I don't think the story really says anything."

Figure 6–7   **Jason's conference**

Jason agreed with Harry's comments and decided to go through an authors' circle with Lynn and Chris to get more ideas. They gave him the same advice. Lynn told him, "You need more action. The story is boring." Chris added, "The beginning is too short and the middle too long." "And there wasn't an ending," Lynn informed him. Jason agreed with them, "I guess my story doesn't fit together very well."

After leaving the circle, Jason began to revise his story. When he completed his second draft, he shared it with Chris and Josh. Chris inquired, "Why didn't you tell Josh over the phone what the problem was?" Josh asked, "How did the monkeys get lost?" Even with all of these questions, Jason felt good about his story and his revisions. While everyone gave him honest feedback about what was not working, they also told him that they liked the story and wanted him to

Figure 6—8   Fourth draft of Jason's story

The Monkey's Revolt

One hot and icky summer, Josh called me on the phone. He said he had a big problem and he sounded upset. I rushed over with some lemonade to calm his nerves. When I got to Josh's house, he sounded more furious that he did before. I went into the kitchen to get ice for our drinks.

I shut the freezer and turned around only to find the lemonade was gone. Since I saw some pop I went ahead and put ice in the glasses. I reached to pour the pop and again it was gone.

I rushed into Josh's room to tell him that someone was stealing the lemonade and the pop. But when I got to Josh's room, he was disappearing under his bed.

I raced over to the bed and grabbed his ankles. I found myself being pulled under the bed. Now I was getting furious and worried.

Then Josh and I started laughing because we were both laying under the bed with more hairy arms and feet than we could count.

I told Josh to try and claw him way to the phone. When he finally got to the phone, he called the monkey alert. He dialed 911 M.O.N.K.E.Y. He told the monkey team that his 60 monkeys were out of control.

When the monkey team got to Josh's house, Josh took them to his room. By the time they got to Josh's room, I was getting kicked by all of the monkeys. One of the monkeys grabbed one of the monkey team and threw him out of the window. But this was good because it gave the monkey team more time to set up a better trap.

The way they were going to make the trap was to put a netful of bananas on the ground and all the monkeys would jump on it.

The plan worked. All the monkeys had to go to the zoo. Josh told the monkeys he would come and visit them every Thursday and Saturday. The monkeys started to get a little bit happier. Then Josh and I finally enjoyed some pop and sandwiches.

continue writing it. Josh remarked, "I like being a character in your story." Lynn added with a smile, "Monkeys are really fun to read about."

As Jason began to revise for the third time, he added more descriptive words. He felt that his sentences were getting better and that he was adding more adventure. He reread some of the Curious George books for more ideas about naughty monkeys. Jason took this third draft to a second authors' circle. This circle went much better and only a few details still seemed to be needed. Harry asked, "Why was he making lemonade?" Josh wanted to know, "How did he call the monkey alert team?"

After he left the circle, Jason revised for the fourth and last time (Figure 6–8). He again reread sections of *The Pet's Revolt* and added a section to his story about setting a trap to catch the monkey. Jason felt good about his story, so he reread it for editing and then put it into the box for typing. After the story was typed, he cut it apart, glued it into a book, and illustrated it.

Finally the story was published and Jason was ready to share and celebrate with his classmates. At the end of our writing time, Jason read his story aloud (Figure 6–9). After the reading, Jeff said, "I really enjoyed the part where the monkey team is called." Lynn chimed in, "I like the part where he threw the monkey team member out the window." Class members continued naming sections of the story they particularly liked. Philip then asked, "Why was Josh in the book?" Jason replied, "Because he likes monkeys." Other students asked additional questions about the story and about Jason as a writer. David informed the group,

Figure 6–9   **Jason reads his story**

"I've read some other books that relate to this book. They were *The Summer of the Monkeys* [Rawls 1976] and the Curious George books." Chris pointed out, "This would be a frightening story if it really happened to Jason." Everyone agreed and the discussion drew to a close.

Over the next several days, the children read Jason's book and commented on how he used suspense to keep his readers interested. Because they wanted to know more about suspense, Jason offered an invitation for anyone who wanted to talk to him about how he put suspense into his story. Several children accepted his invitation and, after talking with him, tried to make their stories more suspenseful.

Authoring Through Mathematics: Math Work Time

The children's voices alert us to the end of the noon break. Time to return once more to the classroom. As the children come into the room, they pick up their math books and line up at the doorway. (In the third grade, children are grouped by ability for math, so they need to get ready to move to the other third-grade rooms.) This time period is our chance to get to know the children in the other third-grade classrooms. We rotate sections each year, and I have the "average" math group.

This year, I have really focused on making math meaningful and on emphasizing the group process and working together. The children all have math logs where they work problems and keep notes about important math concepts. They are thus able to review previous work to see their progress. They also write comments about their successes and frustrations as well as the strategies they use to solve problems. As I read the math logs, I can comment and deal individually with their areas of difficulty.

Today we are reviewing multiplication facts. We have been working on webbing with multiplication. I put the number 12 with a circle around it on the board and the children write as many ways as they can think of to get 12 into their logs. Children are invited randomly to come to the board and share their findings with the class. Emily puts up $(3 \times 2) + (2 + 2 + 2)$ and Jeremy puts up 4×3. We continue brainstorming and writing down as many ideas as we can.

We then move into solving problems through computation. I write problems such as 439×2, 439×3, 439×4 on the board and children begin working on the problems in their math logs. These problems reflect our class focus on the process of carrying and on searching for patterns during problem solving.

Veronica is not sure how to solve one of the problems. I invite her to come to the board and work her problem, asking for assistance when she needs it.

When she gets stuck, she exclaims, "I need help!" Emily comes to her rescue and tells her, "You need to multiply the tens first and then add what was carried." The rest of the class continues to work in their logs as volunteers come to the board and teach others who are stuck on how to solve the problems. We then talk about the different ways they solved the problems and why their attempts did or did not work, and the children write about their strategies in their math logs. Kristi writes how she solved the problem 58×2. "I used place value and I did $8 \times 2 = 16$ and then I carried the 1 and then I did $5 \times 2 = 10$ and then $5 \times 2 + 1 = 11$ and then you use the 6 from 16. Then the answer is 116."

During the rest of the period, the children work at their own pace in doing problems from the textbook. We decide as a class how many days we will take to work on a particular chapter, and children have that entire time period to work on the problems rather than having a specific assignment each day. We decide by browsing through the chapter and trying some problems at the beginning and the end to see how difficult the work will be. The children then set their own goals for how much they each want to get done in a day. Some children work alone, but many of the children work as partners. At some tables, children work alone and then check their work with each other. If they get stuck, they ask others at their table or their partner for help. If they still need more help, they flip the lights to ask for an expert from the room. If no one can help, then I provide support.

Throughout the math class, I try to help the children focus on strategies for solving problems rather than on having right answers. I want children to understand the process and the concepts of mathematics. If they only memorize a list of facts or procedures, they will not have a chance to become authors in mathematics.

Authoring in Fields of Study:
Science and Social Studies Units

At the end of the math period, the children move back to their homerooms and we use the next block of time for a variety of activities related to our social studies and science curricula. I focus on many hands-on activities during the afternoon part of our unit studies. The reading, writing, and research areas of science and social studies are included in the morning reading and writing times.

Today, we are continuing a science study on nature that connects with the survival theme that children are discussing in their literature circles. Our third grade will be going to an environmental center to do a soil and geological study, so we have been reading and doing experiments to prepare for our field trip. I have set up four experiments for the children. Along with doing the actual experiments, each group will make a web of their findings and ideas from the experiments and will add any information they have discovered in their morning readings. These experiments will continue all week with groups rotating and sharing ideas.

Group one is examining soil erosion. Harry informs the group of their task: "We have three tilted cookie sheets of dirt and we have to plow them in two different ways. We won't plow the third field." "First, we're supposed to web our predictions for what will happen when it rains," says Kim. After writing predictions, the group uses a watering can to bring rain to their fields and observe the erosion of the soil. As they observe, they add their findings to the web and compare them to their predictions. Later in the week, they will brainstorm ways to protect the land with trees, rocks, and grassy areas to catch the run-off soil.

Group two is examining an assortment of plants that have been grown in milk cartons. Their focus is on observing, predicting, and recording how plants and trees crack rocks. Jeff exclaims, "Look at how the beans expand and are bursting the milk cartons." The group adds the information to their science observation logs.

Group three is continuing to observe, web, predict, and record how rocks are weathered by rain and flowing water in rivers. Lynn suggests, "Let's put vinegar on the limestone and see what happens." "Wow, it's fizzing," yells Karen. "Next we are supposed to shake these rocks in a tin can five hundred times to see what happens to the rocks," Melissa reads from the group directions.

Group four has become acquainted with glaciers. They have milk cartons of frozen water with gravel, water with sand, water with soil and grass, and just water. They have observed the cartons all day. "Look at how the soil and rocks are carried as the ice melts. It looks just like small hills and sandy rivers," says Jason excitedly.

Amid the hubbub of the four groups, Karen, the class secretary, announces, "It's time for recess. Clean up." The groups quickly clean up and head outside.

Ending the Day Together: Class Read-Aloud

When the class returns from recess, they have music, one of their pull-out programs. They have thirty minutes of art, music, and library with other teachers each week. I teach physical education twice a week during this time.

Upon returning from music, we spend the last half hour reading aloud from our current chapter book, *The Secret Garden* (Burnett 1987). After I read several chapters to the children, we compare the moor in England with the prairie we will see on our field trip. Harry talks about his report on the desert. We discuss the survival themes and the characters that are in this book and compare them to the books we are reading in literature circles. The discussion then moves to their own lives, and the children make connections with how they overcome fears.

Karen signals us that it is time to get ready for going home so we quickly begin gathering up books and papers. The children head out the door talking about what they will do tomorrow.

Personal Reflection

The children have taught us a great deal about teaching and learning as a result of experiences such as the ones we have described in this chapter. We have learned to trust children as learners. Children can be responsible and independent learners if they are involved in a curriculum that supports them in making choices, setting goals, and being self-motivated learners. We have not turned the classroom over to children. Instead, we have learned how to collaborate with the children in sharing the classroom.

We have learned from the children how important it is to establish a classroom atmosphere that is personal and social. When we asked the third graders how they had changed over the year, the first thing they said was that they knew each other well. Both we and the children learn about each other as individuals with something unique to offer to the classroom community. Children's individual voices can be heard in their stories based on their own experiences and in the connections and responses they make to the literature they read. Because they are aware of, and value, their own voices and the voices of others in the classroom, they collaborate well. We are continually impressed with how much children learn to care about and support each other. They are able to help each other move forward in their thinking. This feeling of support allows the children to be risk takers. They know they can make mistakes without fear of ridicule, and they have come to see mistakes as part of learning.

Through these experiences with children, we have regained a sense of ourselves as learners. Because we join literature circles as participants, not leaders, we have gained from these discussions along with the children. They have helped us see new ways of thinking about books and new connections between our experiences and the literature we read. Their presentations have helped us better understand the importance of communicating through a variety of systems such as music and art, rather than only through language.

We used the authoring cycle as a curricular framework to help us construct a learning-centered curriculum with students. The important issue, however, is not the specific organizational structure we used but whether that structure has empowered all learners. The excitement we have felt in the classroom is the excitement of becoming authors, authors of curriculum and authors of our own lives.

References

Burnett, F. H. 1987. *The Secret Garden*. New York: Scholastic.

de Angeli, M. 1949. *The Door in the Wall*. New York: Scholastic.

Burke, C., and K. G. Short. 1988. "Creating Curricula That Foster Thinking." Unpublished paper.

Dolch, E. [reteller] 1958. *Robinson Crusoe*. New York: Scholastic.

George, J. C. 1972. *Julie of the Wolves*. New York: Dell.

Greenwald, S. 1972. *The Pets' Revolt*. New York: Scholastic.

Harste, J. C., and K. G. Short, with C. Burke. 1988. *Creating Classrooms for Authors: The Reading—Writing Connection*. Portsmouth, N. H.: Heinemann.

King-Smith, D. 1983. *Babe: The Gallant Pig*. New York: Dell.

Martin, B., and J. Archambault. 1987. *Knots on a Counting Rope*. New York: Holt.

O'Dell, S. 1960. *Island of the Blue Dolphins*. New York: Dell.

Rawls, W. 1976. *The Summer of the Monkeys*. New York: Dell.

Short, K. G. 1986. "Literacy as a Collaborative Experience." Ph.D. diss., Indiana University.

Speare, E. G. 1983. *The Sign of the Beaver*. New York: Dell.

White, E. B. 1952. *Charlotte's Web*. New York: Scholastic.

7

Mind Games: Discovering Poetry Through Art

MARGARET GRANT

P oets and artists. The classroom is filled with them.
   Let me tell you the story of a learning sequence in my third-grade classroom through which we witnessed the poet and the artist come alive within ourselves. It is a story told at two levels: the account of the actual classroom events and the record of my thoughts, feelings, and decisions in the course of the learning sequence.

This story is one example of what I have come to call a *language event*: shared, active learning in which artificial boundaries—such as those separating reading from writing and language arts from content areas—melt away. The story describes how one particular language event unfolded, beginning with the moment the idea first came to me and continuing all the way through the changing scenes of the event itself.

The Idea

It was an uncomfortable, scattered feeling: so many questions flipping around in my head. Or was it that they were all interrelated and I didn't know how to address one without addressing them all?

☐ How can I continue the momentum of our current unit, "Planting Seeds of Greatness?"

☐ I know I need to give the kids another experience with poetic language. How can I use this "seeds of greatness" theme as a purpose for reading and writing poetry?

☐ What material can I use that will allow us—the students and me—to draw out our own personal purposes for learning?

☐ How can we avoid that feeling of having learning imposed on us from outside our own actual needs?

☐ How can I ensure that the learning will have that quality of being genuinely, urgently needed by kids?

☐ How can I make all these connections?

These questions were not new ones. They were reflecting the classic concerns that are with me whenever I am planning. Actually, I look forward to this time of creative discomfort that goes with lesson planning. Because it is the time in which I face directly the uncharted days ahead, it reminds me once again of the responsibility for learning that goes with teaching. There is no way, I reminded myself, that I would want to think of myself as a passive teacher. Decisions and risks go with an active teaching style; it is okay to experience the anxiety that goes along with the art of teaching.

And so the key questions were with me once again this early February afternoon. With my students in gym class, I had been using the quiet to thumb through the pages of a book and look for poems. The book in my lap was a basal reader text that I use as a resource book for planning language experiences. Looking now for material that I could use for shared reading on the "Planting Seeds of Greatness" theme, I suddenly felt everything connect for me.

I was looking at a familiar page, a collection of four poems for children written in response to the painting *Children's Games*, by the sixteenth-century Flemish artist, Pieter Brueghel (Figure 7–1).

The first page of poetry featured one poem alongside Brueghel's painting of a courtyard scene, reminiscent of our own playground, in which people were playing dozens of familiar games. The second page focused in on close-ups of specific games in the painting, each accompanied by a poem. I remembered the poems well; they were wonderful. But it was Brueghel's painting that brought all my concerns into focus. As I studied closely the games the children were playing, I was filled with thoughts to share with my class. Here in this exciting piece of art was the reading/writing/poetry idea I was searching for.

As my thoughts started to flow, I began to visualize the general framework for a whole language process that would use these pieces of literature and art as its base. First, we would "walk through" the picture; then, once we had put ourselves into the scene, we would be ready to hear with an inner ear the poems in the book, thinking of them as reflections of how others had walked through the same

Figure 7−1   *Children's Games* by Pieter Brueghel (Kunsthistorisches Museum, Vienna)

scene. These experiences of art and poetry could naturally lead into creating poetry and art of our own. I would need to trust the exact structure to evolve in its own unique way, depending upon the interaction of the kids with the art, the poetry, each other, and me. I would need to trust myself to guide the evolution from poetry reading to poetry writing. I knew I would need to take seriously the connections the children would make with the poems and use these connections to lead them into creating with their own words.

My thoughts returned to my original questions. How would this art/poetry experience fit into the larger theme we were currently using? I had chosen "Planting Seeds of Greatness" as a vehicle for teaching biographical and autobiographical literature and writing. I had also wanted to give kids reason to dig into corners of history, geography, math, and science as they naturally appeared through the lives of great people. It was exciting to me to think up ways of connecting our third-grade units of study in content areas to the lives of such people as Martin Luther King, Helen Keller, the Wright brothers, Harriet Tubman, Louis Pasteur, and Christa McAuliffe.

I had another goal for the unit also: to help the children make connections between each of these biographies and their own lives. Something special had been happening as the children searched for the words to describe the qualities of greatness they were discovering in each of these lives — compassion, inventiveness, curiosity, courage, imagination. It was exciting to watch the children compare these attributes to the seeds of greatness they were planting in their own lives every day in our classroom, on the playground, with their friends, and at home. Everyone had been catching classmates in the act of demonstrating that they had seeds of greatness sprouting in them. As a class we had also been trying out some of the ideas and skills represented by these "seeds": sign language, designing and measuring the flight of paper airplanes, making up suspenseful plays about the Underground Railroad.

Now, through the life of Pieter Brueghel we would be able to integrate art appreciation into the unit. By learning from Brueghel and the poems about his art and by trying our own combinations of art and poetry, we could experience these two dimensions of self-expression as ways to plant more seeds of greatness.

On the heels of my excitement, however, came a new feeling of uneasiness. Time. It was always the beast that I had to control. And so now I focused very deliberately on time structures. I began to leaf through my lesson plan book, blocking out possible time frames within which I could fit this art/poetry experience. Part of me wished to begin *now*; the other part knew to wait until the beginning of the week. The weekend must not fall at a time that would interrupt the focus. Our need to write must be immediate, concrete, urgent. Also, I wanted to take a slide of the painting so that we could see it greatly enlarged and discuss it easily as a whole group.

As I looked again at the painting's title, *Children's Games*, I could see that using the slide to explore the painting together, building one discovery upon another, would give us our own game to play — a *mind* game. It was occurring to me that playing games with your mind has always been a favorite kind of children's game. Now I knew how I was going to think of this whole poetry experience — as mind games. How much more fun, how much less threatening, to say "We're going to play some mind games that you've never played before" than to say "I'm going to teach you how to write poetry."

Titling a page "Mind Games with Art and Poetry" and taking swift notes of my projections for this language experiment, I clipped it into the log section of my planbook. Then, realizing my prep period was almost over, I hurried down to the library to look through the large reproductions on file there. It seemed to me that these art reproductions, which I had used for a dozen other purposes through the years, were simply shouting to be used as subjects for children's poetic language; they would provide the perfect follow-up to the experience with Brueghel's painting and the poems written in response to it.

My arms full of prints, I met the children at the gym door. They could tell I was excited.

Matt's eyes discovered the big laminated rolls. "All right, Mrs. Grant—confess! What have you got up your sleeve?"

"Well, Matt, I'll give you a hint: they're 'mind games.' Have you ever heard of mind games?"

Matt shook his head, mystified.

"No? Has *anybody* heard of mind games?"

Everybody looked around, shaking their heads.

"Nobody at all? Well, I'm going to show you how to play them. But we've got to wait till Monday, when I'll have them ready."

"But tell us *now* what they're like!"

"*Please*, just tell us a *little* bit!"

"Can't you just show us *one* of the mind games?"

I made a face. "I can't stand waiting any better than you can. But we'll just have to anyway!"

I could already tell this lesson was going somewhere.

The Event

 ## Phase One: Using Art and Oral Language

Monday morning came. How could I connect the lives of my third graders with the life of a sixteenth-century artist? "Are you ready to play mind games? I'm about to connect your mind to the mind of a man who lived over four hundred years ago. You've probably never ever heard of him, but he was very real. His name was Pieter Brueghel, he lived in a country called Flanders, and he painted wonderful pictures. . . ."

As I told them the story of this man, we subtracted dates at the chalkboard to get a feeling for how long ago Brueghel lived (1529–65) and how his life span compared to those of the other great figures we had studied. Then we added his "life line" to the time line we had been keeping of them all. Next we turned to the globe to find the modern countries that occupy the geographical space of medieval Flanders, and we compared maps of modern and medieval Europe to see that Flanders was located where northern France and western Belgium are today. In the process, the historical person of Pieter Brueghel began to come to life: a favored artist of the royal family of Hapsburgs and a risk taker who broke away from the traditional idea that art was used to represent only special people and special events. Pieter Brueghel was the first artist of his time to use paint to tell the story of everyday life. His art was a way of declaring that ordinary people and events are also important.

Now that we had established a context for the painting, we were ready to start exploring it. "Let's play our first mind game: we're going to walk into a world that is over four hundred years old. How are we going to get there? Through one of Brueghel's paintings. There were no photographs or movies four hundred years ago. So this painting gives us a peek into this ancient world that we can't see any other way. Let's pretend that we can walk right into the painting, actually walk around in it and see what people are doing. Ask yourself where you would be if you were really there. What would you be doing?"

I flipped the slide representation of *Children's Games* on the screen. There was a quiet moment in which everyone's eyes were searching through the maze of its many figures. One by one, individual students began to get their bearings in the context of the painting, and voices began to pop up: "I'd be on those barrels!" "I'd be playing king of the mountain!" "I'd be camel fighting. That's 'cause it's not allowed on our playground. Hey—it *was* allowed way back then!"

"I see you'd know just what to do if you were there," I concluded. "Isn't it amazing to find so many things in this picture that you already know how to do, even though the time is so long ago? How many different games do you suppose we can name before I say 'stop'? In order for us to know where you are, give us directions like you use on a map as you name your game. You know, like north, south, south-central, northwest. Okay, begin...now!"

For five minutes the names of games came pouring forth: leapfrog, blind man's buff, king of the mountain, follow the leader, London bridge, stilts, somersaults, crack the whip, hoops, swimming, climbing up the cellar door, flying kites, standing on your head, spinning skirts, hide-and-go-seek, and on and on.

"We've already played two mind games with this painting," I observed. "'Where Would I Be?' and 'Name the Games.'" Here's the next game: think of all the titles that would be good for this picture."

Titles began to tumble on top of each other: *The Playground, Fun Times, Friends and Games, Our Favorite Games, In the Days of No TV.* That led us to an interesting conclusion: except for TV, medieval kids were doing a lot of the same things we like to do today. People of long ago must not be all that different from people today. Everybody likes to play games.

"Okay," I said. "Let's change the rules. There are many different kinds of actions in this picture. Let's name all the actions we can find, and I'll try to keep up with you by writing the words down on the overhead projector."

As our eyes raced once again through the courtyard scene, any signs of hesitancy were gone and in their place were signs of power and authority. Often, each child's word built on the one before until the children couldn't think of any more: tug, pull, yank, heave. Then someone would think of a new trail to follow. First came obvious words (sit, hit, jump, run, spin, twist, jerk, follow, hop, skip, twirl, race, balance, teeter). Then the less obvious (dodge, dart, copy, challenge). Later came the feeling words (laugh, cry, pout, fear, worry, panic) and words for invisible actions (think, wonder, imagine, create, discover). In a few minutes we had about a hundred words on our list. Power. We knew so much. We had so much ability to express human actions and emotions with precision and intricacy. We were beginning to feel a new kind of authority over the picture.

It was time for a harder challenge. I wanted the children to discover their own mind games.

"It's your turn!" I said. "*You* think up a mind game and tell us what to do."

Now there was a sudden proliferation of short mind teasers: find all the running games, find all the jumping games, name your favorite game, name a game you've never played before, name a game you are planning to play this recess, get into small groups and tell funny stories about yourselves playing one of the games.

Feeling the need for more exploration of descriptive language, I called the whole group back together again. "Try this! Find a game and think of the one word that best *describes* the game so that we can picture it in our minds and tell where you are in the picture. Your describing word may describe the game or it may describe the feeling that you have when you play the game. Don't be surprised if your word goes with another game just as well as the one you are thinking about!"

Now we were getting words like dizzy, perched, balanced, teetering, cool, breezy, slippery. I showed them how they could add phrases with "like" or "as" to any of our words to build a word picture. From my examples, "as balanced as a tightrope walker" and "teetering like a toddler on the stairs," the children began to build word pictures of their own. I taught them the name "simile" for this new word game. Then I showed them how much more interesting the simile is if it does *not* sound familiar. We figured out that "slippery as the snow under my skis" is more interesting than "slippery as an eel" because we had invented the phrase ourselves rather than copying a common phrase that everyone has heard.

By now it was time for recess. We had started with the story of Brueghel first thing this morning; in the hour and a half since, we had worked with the time line, the globe, the maps, the subtracting problems, the slide of the painting, and all our mind games. As we lined up I noticed the camaraderie among the children as word experiments continued informally in small groups. Even though we were glad to be taking a break, the word play was going to continue all the way to the playground. Glad to be together as we headed down the hall, we were savoring this comfortable feeling of strength, satisfaction, and anticipation.

 ## Phase Two: Experiencing Poetry as a Response to Art

Freshened by running, shouting, and the crisp winter air, everyone eagerly flipped through the books on their tables until the page with the now-familiar medieval playground scene fell open. The page was arranged with a long, skinny poem beside the picture.

Hoopla

hOOp
hOOp
hOOp
OOps

hOOp
hOOp
whOOps

hOOp
hOOp
hOOpety

hOOpety
hOOpety
lOOps

<small>LORENCA ROSAL</small>

I prefaced reading the poem with a few thoughts. "We've been making up our own mind games in response to the painting. Now let's look at four poems that use other people's mind games. Some of them will be the same as ours; some will be new ones. Look at the title of this first poem. Can you guess where this writer is in the painting?" I asked.

Everyone wanted to answer. The hoops! At the bottom of the picture.

"And as we read 'Hoopla,' can you find any of the mind games we played before recess?" The energetic, yet comfortable, way in which the children settled into their reading told me that we were swiftly and eagerly returning to our former train of thought. I could tell we were about to have a good time together.

First I read the poem aloud, and then we all read it together. Next I asked, "Did you find any of our games...or any new ones?"

"The first thing *I* saw was that it's got hoops right in it to match the painting!" exclaimed Jesse. "That's not like any of our mind games!"

"Yeah, every single word has hoops in it," Lindsey added.

"It really sounds like someone is rolling a hoop like in the picture because you can hear it going around: 'hoop, hoop, hoop,'" said Jackie, her arm describing a circle. "And you can tell the hoop keeps falling down because of 'oops' and 'whoops.' Hey, that's neat!"

"See, it falls down twice and then it finally really gets going." Allison sounded amazed.

"I wonder how you can tell that the hoop really gets going, Allison," I pondered, pursuing Allison's idea.

Allison shrugged, puzzled. "I'm not sure."

"Why don't we read it once more together," I suggested, "to see if there is a rhythm that helps the hoop pick up speed."

When we had finished, Jason noted, "The 'hoopety' word is the one that makes it sound like it's getting faster and faster!"

"I think the 'hoopety' word makes it sound like the hoop is bouncing along.

It could even be hitting bumps!" added Joanie.

"It's amazing to me," I said, "how the poet used only thirteen words and yet managed to create a whole story in our minds. Maybe this writer's mind game was to see how few words could be used to tell a story."

Then we turned the page:

Jacks

Jacks look like stars,
and the ball you throw to catch them
like a small red moon.
While the moon's bouncing back
your hand must be quick
to collect star after star.
The rules say
If you touch too much
or let the moon roll away
you lose the game.

                    KATHLEEN FRASER

Matt whistled. "Ooh, just look at all those—what do you call them?"

"Similes!" exclaimed Lisa, proudly.

"That's just the way it is when you're playing *one* game, but in your imagination you're pretending something *else*!" said Colleen, the excitement of discovery in her voice.

"Yes!" I responded. "Maybe the person who is catching stars and throwing the moon is pretending to be a...a..."

"A giant!" came back the chorus.

"You'd have to be an awfully giant giant to throw the moon and catch stars!" said Amy, grinning.

We turned to the next poem:

Stilts

Stand tall
Walk tall
See all.
Stilts.

Long fall
Hard fall
Smash all
Stilts.

Stay small
Walk small
That's all.
No stilts.

                    TONIA LAPHAM

I stomped stiff-legged to the rhythm of the poem and spoke in a slow, deliberate voice. Everyone laughed.

"What's so funny?" I grinned.

"You read it like you were walking on stilts."

"You try it," I responded. "You can walk on stilts too!"

So everyone read it, walking stiff-legged, books in hand, as they mimicked the action with their voices.

Several more trips through the poem brought out the stilt pattern of the double *l*s, the patterns in the poem, and its use of rhyme and repeated words.

Then we turned to "Headstand," the last poem:

Headstand

Bend knees,
    Lean on face,
Throw your feet to outer space.
Wiggle woggle twist around
    to keep your head
    flat on the ground.
Spread arms wide
        like elephant ears.
Laugh away your falling fears.
    For now,
because a hand's a foot
and foot is now a head,
a face is at the bottom, and it's
        turning cherry red.

MATTHEW BROCK

I read it aloud in an almost breathless fashion. There was a ripple of delighted laughter.

"Wiggle woggle!" snorted Gabreal.

"I like 'throw your feet to outer space'!"

"I like 'a hand's a foot and foot is now a head'!"

"How many different mind games can you find in this poem?" I asked.

The answers were becoming more sophisticated:

"I see rhyming—like *face* and *space, around* and *ground*."

"I see a...is that thing called a *simile* in 'Spread arms wide like elephant ears'?" Kori put an emphasis on *like* with her voice as she thumped the word on the page. I could tell she was pleased with herself for finding it.

"You're right!" I nodded. "A simile. What about the words 'wiggle woggle'? It looks to me like the poet *invented* these words in order to get the right sound."

Heads nodded.

"That's *another* mind game!" declared Ruth. She had been very quiet this whole time, but I knew her well enough to know she had really been thinking. Now it all came tumbling out. "I like the way the poem goes so fast. It makes you feel exactly like when you throw your legs over your head and your arms are quivering and everything's happening at once."

She paused thoughtfully and then added: "I think this poem has neat words. Like 'elephant ears' and 'falling fears.' I think I like it best."

We'd been sitting a long time and needed to get up and move around; abruptly I changed the challenge. "Let's have a contest. Who wants to be in the Headstand Contest? The winner is the person who can throw your feet to outer space and keep them there the longest without falling. And the winner gets to turn over the next big poster."

Phase Three: Experimenting with Gathering Words

After the headstand break, we sat down in a large circle on the floor to see what the winner would unveil. There it was: a poster of a new painting crowded with simple, archlike shapes in vivid, warm colors—Paul Klee's *Revolution of the Viaducts* (Figure 7–2, A and B).

"With this painting, I want to show you another way of getting your ideas together. I call it 'mind mapping.' Mind mapping is a way of finding out your thoughts. It's like going exploring in your mind and making a map of where you've been." I had thought of the term "mind mapping" as a new phrase for "clustering" because I felt it would carry more meaning for young children.

Figure 7–2   *Revolution of the Viaducts* by Paul Klee (Hamburger Kunsthalle, West Germany). A: The painting. B: Getting into the picture.

A

B

Louise looked puzzled. "I don't get it. How do you know what to put on your map?"

"You just write down whatever comes to mind. As you put something down, you see how it fits with your other words. If it goes with something else, you put it there. If it's something new, you start a new place. If it goes with more than one thing, you might decide to draw lines to connect the two. Or you might put it down in more than one place."

"But that means that everybody's mind map will look different from everybody else's," Louise responded.

"Yes, they will, because each of us thinks differently. And that's just fine."

Luke beamed. "I get it now."

"Okay! Then let's use this picture to try out mind mapping. Let's keep our own made-up name for the painting until we're through mind mapping. Then I'll tell you its real name and about the painter."

The children studied the simple, massive shapes and bright colors.

"*Arches!*" "*Legs!*" "*Marching!*" "*Arches Marching!*"

I interjected: "Why don't we just go with the first one—*Arches?* Okay?"

The children nodded their approval in hasty anticipation.

I laid a piece of poster paper beside the painting in front of me and wrote "Arches" in the center. The children called out words and phrases while I copied them onto the map (Figure 7–3). As I worked, I pointed out that I was making my own connections with their words and that if one of them had been doing the mapping it would look entirely different.

Suddenly the group's thinking began to take a different turn. I began to hear longer phrases, coming so fast that I couldn't transcribe them all. Realizing that the mind map wasn't working any more, I grabbed a piece of acetate from the overhead and began taking down their flood of words in long lines to match their longer phrases. Now I was able to keep up better. I realized that I was putting down a kind of stream-of-consciousness writing. The whole group was locked into what was happening; the ideas that were coming were very powerful and interrelated.

When the flow of phrases slowed, we seemed to sit back a little, as if we were coming out of a trance and were just now becoming aware of what had been happening. "This is beautiful," I thought out loud. "Couldn't we make our own poem out of it?"

"Yes, yes," came the response.

"What if I cut these lines apart and we put them on the overhead and arranged them and changed them around until they suit us? Would you like to try that?"

"Oh yes!" came back the response.

I reached for scissors and began slicing off lines of thought. Then we marked each line with the author's initials and began trying them in different order, numbering the lines when we liked the order, smudging out and changing words

Figure 7–3   Notes on *Arches*

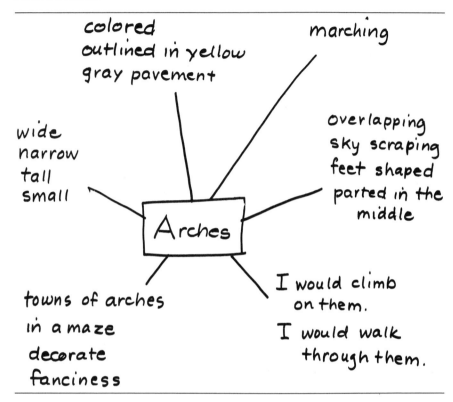

here and there with the author's permission in order to refine and connect
thoughts. Five or ten minutes later we could all agree the poem felt finished:

Arches Marching	(S.F.)
Arches that look back in time	(K.S.)
Arches tumbling back in time	(G.V.)
Arches lingering from the past	(R.G.)
Arches that crumble and fall	(L.F.)
Arches new, arches old	(L.F.)
Giant arches march through centuries	(B.F., M.B.)
Giant arches march through our century	(L.I.)
Arches still marching today	(K.S.)
Arches lead into the future	(C.W., M.G.)
Arches show the way	(A.P.)
Arches from the future	(L.I.)
Arches into the future	(L.B.)
The wonder of the arches	(B.F.)
I wonder about the arches	(K.S.)

Eyes on the clock: we were almost late for lunch. How did we get so forgetful? Everyone was scrambling for lunch boxes, meal tickets, and places in line. Voices were staccato. I promised to type the poem over lunch so that we could have a copy to take home today.

There was that feeling of power again. Kori voiced what we were all feeling: "It gets just so exciting in here sometimes!" She twisted her arms around each other, locking her fingers together in front of her to release the pent-up tension of creative energy. How great we were together, I thought. Then I said it aloud: "How great we are together!"

 ## Phase Four: Time to Reflect and Integrate

That afternoon was library time. We searched the shelves for biographical material about painters. Back in the room, during our silent reading time, many were leafing through art books. I helped a few who were collecting and deciding upon some information to give the others about Paul Klee, the artist who painted *Revolution of the Viaducts*, or *Arches*, as we had called it. I had already brought material on ancient Roman viaducts from the library, anticipating the need to define this term.

After silent reading, we regrouped and enjoyed these spontaneous reports. As we learned about Klee, we needed to return to the maps, the globe, and the time line; we also decided to set aside part of our "Seeds of Greatness" work area for these new materials we were accumulating. Several children volunteered to search at home for more books on artists; some wanted to be in charge of fixing up the display area.

We spent the last part of the day in our math adventure clubs, cooperative learning groups of three, making paper time lines of the lives of Brueghel and Klee with rulers and adding-machine tape. I usually like to have math earlier, but the more urgent need for putting together our new understanding about our artists had preempted the earlier time slot. So, as the day was ending, we were right in the middle of experimenting with the time lines as number lines, making up problems that used estimating, rounding, and comparing these life spans with the others we'd studied. Each small group was engrossed in thinking up ideas of things for the other groups to use for estimating, rounding, and comparing dates. As I looked around the room, I could see the collaborative groups discovering their own purposes for math skills as well as for the new historical data. Problem solving of this kind offered content learning as well as process learning: mathematics, history, and oral language all in one. It could make a good ending for tomorrow also, I thought; it would add variety to what would probably be an intense day of writing poetry.

The groups did not want to be interrupted. We were deep in the event now.

Phase Five: Choosing Our Own Paintings, Choosing Our Own Words

We like to begin each day with journal-writing time, usually followed by journal-sharing time, one of the favorite and most productive parts of the day. The next morning our opening journal-writing time was naturally given over to individual experiments with mind games. I could hardly wait for the sharing time in order to discover what was happening on paper, to see what was actually carrying over from yesterday's experiences. Children really like using journal time for experimenting with writing as long as they have the chance to talk over these experiments, to try them out on a real audience right away. As they watch the response of other writers to their pieces they are at once both affirmed and challenged; as they discuss other pieces, they discover many new possibilities for their own. Because I believe writing response groups are one of the most stimulating means of inspiring more and better writing, I was counting on the morning's journal-sharing time to serve as a significant part of the mind games event.

I was not disappointed! Several hands shot up when I asked if anyone would like to share something written in response to yesterday's experience. As we talked about the different journal entries, we could feel the momentum building again. There was a natural urgency to focus less on what *others* had created—the paintings, the poems—and more on what *we* were about to create. Now was the time to focus on our own needs for expression. The children had also noticed a beckoning pile of upside-down art prints on the table that seemed to be suggesting a way.

I was fascinated by all the kinds of learning represented by the different journal entries. There was a factual biographical account of the artists' lives, a page of experiments with similes, a list of all the games the writer could find in the Brueghel painting, a mind map of a teddy bear picture on the calendar, a diary account in which the writer picked out a few of yesterday's activities to describe, and a poem by Gavin about playing jacks (Figure 7–4).

Gavin's poem led us forward. "This poem is exciting to me, Gavin," I said. "You wove in ideas you got from yesterday and yet wrote your own poem. And it really worked. I can see some of yesterday's mind games right in your poem. Read it again for us, Gavin, and let's see what other people find in your piece, okay?"

Gavin was clearly pleased to be the writer whose work was going to be used today for others' instruction. He read it again in a clear, expressive voice.

"It has rhyme," said Adam. "And you can really hear the rhythm too!"

"There's no question—is there?—about what part of the painting he is picturing again in his poem," I smiled. "His poem uses words instead of paint to give me the picture in my mind of playing jacks."

I reached for the upside-down pile of art prints. "Are you ready to follow Gavin's lead? How about choosing a painting all your own to play mind games with?"

Figure 7—4   **"Jacks" by Gavin**

Jacks

Playing Jacks
All the while
Picking them up
Right by the pile
When having fun
Touch one you're done
When throwing the ball
Don't touch all.

An unhesitating "Yes!" came back to me.

"Great! Let's take just a moment, then, and make a quick list of all the mind games we can think of to try out. I'll make the list on a transparency as you call them out to me."

In just a few moments, we had the following list:

Ways to Play Mind Games with Words

1. Choose words by their sound.
2. Make patterns with words.
3. Make patterns with lines of words.
4. Let words rhyme.
5. Choose yummy words.
6. Look for rhythm in words.
7. Let words surprise you!
8. Put words to music.

I knew there were more things that could have gone on the list; however, its main purpose was to remind us how much we knew as a way of building our sense of readiness and urgency to create. Since everyone wanted to get their hands on the paintings, I didn't want to take long with the list and, in so doing, dull the excitement of the moment for initiating writing.

Making the list did, however, give us the chance to mention briefly some of the problems with getting overly concerned with rhyming as the main, or even a necessary, ingredient of a poem. Also during the list making, Luke added a new mind game — putting words to music — which prompted the insight that music lyrics are one important use for poetry. When we had finished, I promised to make a poster of the list so that we could refer to it any time and keep adding to it whenever more mind games came to us.

It was just about time for music class. "If you are singing songs in music class today, watch for poems as the lyrics!" I suggested. Making connections. New ways to be in charge of learning. New power.

As we came back into the room after music class, there was a sense in which everything was ready. The painting, the poems, the talk, the experiments with mind mapping and group poem writing, the reflections and experiments in our journals, Gavin's first step, our list of the mind games we knew. Everything seemed to have led us to this point. We expected the writing experience to be just as good as all that had come before.

I turned over the first picture. There was one instant of silence as minds engaged with the art. Then the quiet moment melted away swiftly into the excitement of hands reaching, voices claiming posters, paintings being passed eagerly from hand to hand. Pairs and trios of students moving about the room, finding floor space to spread out with paper and pencils to share the same painting. Heads together thinking, fingers pointing, voices excited. Hands waving at me, questions to be answered, reassurance to be given: "It's *your* mind game now. You hop right into the picture. Let it happen to *you*. Write down what happens. . . ." (Figure 7–5).

Figure 7–5   **Hopping into the picture**

I moved around the room from painting to painting, kneeling beside the writers, noticing each first step, looking for ways to acknowledge each writer's unique risks that were now coming in black and white. My instinct was to be everywhere at once. I wanted to be in touch with every writer, to let each one feel my presence as soon as possible during the writing process, to respond to every writer according to individual needs, to help "unstick" anyone who was still not quite ready to get going on paper. I wanted to validate, to encourage, to be stimulated by incredible nine-year-old minds. Maybe this was my favorite moment of teaching: when kids were urgently needing to express their learning through their own creative energy.

I looked around the room. Every spot was occupied by a writer or small group of writers. A few seemed to need absolute isolation in order to incubate their thoughts. Others needed the company of a like-minded writer or two to share the nervous excitement, the tentative words, the frustration of trying to get words to obey needs (Figure 7–6).

I settled down with Chagall's *I and the Village*, a painting I had always wanted to understand better. I let words come to me, putting them down into my own mind map, trying out the effect they seemed to have on one another. I didn't want to be disturbed either; it was hard to pull myself back to Ruth, who was

Figure 7–6   Writers at work

standing behind me trying to wait patiently for me to notice her.

"How're you doing, Ruth?"

"Well, I want to know if it's okay to go on to another painting when you're done with one."

"Oh, yes, sure! Do you like what you have?"

"Yeah, I *really* like it, but I want to do more."

Raising my voice to the whole class, I said, "Ruth wants to go to another painting. If any of the rest of you want to, fine. Just quietly move around the room to a new one you want to try...or go through the pile of posters till you find the one you want to work on next. I'm going to come around to everyone again and see how you're doing. Be sure to let me know if you have more than one piece of writing to show me. I'll try not to interrupt you unless you have something you want to talk to me about."

This tour of the room let me know that people were ready for an immediate audience. My voice stimulated more voices; there was more talking in the room now as writers were reading their poems and pointing out things from the poems in the painting and going back to their papers to make quick revisions as new ideas came. I announced recess time. A half dozen popped up right away. Nobody else seemed to want to budge.

"Please find a good stopping place as quickly as possible. I really want you to go outside and run or do something. Your mind has been playing all the games; your body needs to play some too."

Finally, the words began to take. One by one they pulled themselves away from their thoughts and began to line up. I noticed that some were telling others what they were doing while a few stood passively, perhaps still caught up in their own private world of composing, not really ready to be interrupted. Several of them had drafts in their hands, bringing them up to me or to their friends or carrying them to the playground to share.

As the line was forming, I took the opportunity to skim several poems and give quick affirmations. Now I knew how we would pick up the thread after recess.

"Adam, Julia, Louise: may we share your poems after recess? Okay? The rest of the class needs to hear what you're doing."

 ## Phase Six: Responding and Revising

With recess over, an hour was left before lunch. How to regroup and get the most out of the remaining time without anyone burning out? How to make sure all the writers could feel their writing had been received and reworked to a point where they could comfortably leave it for the day?

"Those of us who wish to have our drafts read or want to listen to other beginning poems, please gather for a response group meeting at the green rocker."

We used the big old platform rocker placed in a carpeted area as a focal point for sharing writing. One or two people could sit in it, read, and lead the discussion while others could listen and respond comfortably, cross-legged on the rug. Most of the children rushed for their drafts and hurried to get prime positions in front of the green rocker. Some, clearly needing to write a little more before they would be ready to come to the response group, were quickly crouching again over their paintings and lines of writing.

During the next hour, almost all the children came and went from the rocker. Each read. Sometimes I read their writing back to them. Together with whoever happened to be in the circle at the time, we discussed and experimented with the words, admiring their strengths, acknowledging when they were not clear or precise, rearranging and brainstorming, and pointing out ideas and techniques we all could learn from. The scene was one of laughter and clapping, differences of opinion and surprising insights. New energy began to explode, sending writers returning to their pieces before ideas became misty and lost. New, unpredicted possibilities emerged from working together. I could tell that writers were feeling an increased sense of control, of being in charge, and of contributing to the whole.

There was purposeful movement: in and out of the circle as writing was revised and tried out again; into other, smaller circles around specific paintings; around the table with the pile of prints as people searched for new paintings to connect with words.

More poems were being created. More groups were forming. Important questions were surfacing out of immediate need. For a moment I was a spectator, observing the process unfold at the hands of twenty-five creative eight- and nine-year-olds.

At my suggestion, Chad had hurried to the office to ask the secretary to make a transparency of his writing to use at the overhead projector so that the whole class could see it. He and I had agreed that the morning would end with a quick demonstration between the two of us on how to think through choosing the words for each line of poetry. Now he was back, positioning the overhead projector and finding colored projector pens to use.

Speaking to the whole class, I said, "Writers, I need to interrupt you because I see several people ready for some important information. Because you are writing poetry today, everyone is going to need to know the difference between writing stories, where you are used to filling up every line automatically, and writing poems, where you use lines in a different way—as what we call 'poetic lines.' The poet chooses very carefully the words for each line in order to help the reader know how the words are supposed to sound.

"Chad and I want to demonstrate for you how a writer might plan, either by himself or with another writer, the way he wants to divide up words or groups of words into poetic lines. He and I are going to work at the overhead projector so that you can watch us try his words several different ways until they begin to sound the way he wants them to. While we're experimenting, we'll make diagonal slash marks [/] with colored pens to show where we are thinking about ending a line. We'll use a new sheet of acetate each time we try different groupings of words. When Chad gets the one he likes, he'll be ready to recopy it as the final draft."

By the time Chad and I had finished working together at the overhead, he had incorporated suggestions from several classmates, and I had fielded lots of suggestions clarifying how much variety and individuality there can be in poem formats. The children were beginning to see that each poem is a unique set of sound patterns that requires careful thought as to how the poet can best transfer the poem's message to the reader. I had also taken the opportunity to demonstrate how they could begin each new line with a capital when making a final draft.

I drew the demonstration to a close by saying, "This afternoon I want you to try planning your own poetic lines. When you come in, experiment with the words that you want to go together and then mark them with the slashes. Then, during independent reading time this afternoon or journal writing time tomorrow morning, I will have a writing conference with each of you. We can work on poetic lines together then, if you like, and give your poem a last polish."

Independent reading time that afternoon was a mixture of mulling over the pile of poetry books I had checked out of the library and rereading, revising, and formatting poems. Then we returned to our math adventure club activities of the day before. Throughout the afternoon, some new questions were beginning to emerge: What shall we do with our poems? What about making our own pictures to go with our poems? Why don't we make a book of poems?

 Phase Seven: Planning for Publishing

The third morning, we continued writing conferences and revision on the poems as a part of journal time. Then we gathered at the green rocker to make sure everyone had had a chance to share at least one poem with the whole group. The response to these poems reflected the growing concern: what shall we decide to do with our poems? From the beginning it seemed clear that publishing a class book of poems satisfied the wishes of all.

Already some of the children had been making large poster art to go with their poems, and so we also decided to make a simple hall display outside our door of these pieces of art, their handwritten drafts, and the appropriate reproductions, choosing the title "Masterpieces of Art and Poetry" to go with it. Making hall displays like this was one of our quick, favorite ways of providing an immediate audience for our projects. Planning the class book, however, required more thought.

After much discussion, we had in mind black pen-and-ink drawings for each poem, with one poem on a page. We would bind with plastic rings and leave the cover page plain so that each poet could make an individual cover design. We would make enough books so that every poet could have two copies to keep or give away. Knowing that a class book was probably in the works, I had stopped this morning to ask Mrs. Hart, one of the two school secretaries, if she would be willing to type poems as children finished them and brought them to the office.

Figure 7—7   Samples of children's work

Blue horses
Green hair
Eating away,
Eating away.
Turning and
Twisting and
Bellowing for more.

                    -Jenny Palmer

It is night out
The stars are glowing
The wind is blowing
And the mountains are like waves
The moon is peachy orange
And the bushes look like cherry red
   with sky blue pussy willows
The sky is black
With little ashes falling down
And one big mountain looks like smoke
While the people are asleep.

                         -Doug Zuuring

He kills his fish
   In one blow of his harpoon
Right through the heart and
   He has a fish
            fish
            fish
            fish
            fish.
            -Pat Malone

Now I told the children how I felt we were lucky to have Mrs. Hart, who really enjoyed helping us out when she had the time.

Planning the publishing of our poems seemed to serve as the needed stimulus to launch all twenty-five writers back into their individual sets of final tasks. The discussion of publishing had brought with it a feeling of genuine accomplishment. Something very important was in the final stages of birth, and it belonged to us all.

Later would come lessons on using pen and ink for line drawing (Figure 7−7) and on lettering and lay-out for the book cover. Then we'd do the final proofreading before sending the pages off to be printed.

Last would come the time when we could read our own book: a time to savor the power of our own words, to believe in creativity, to know we had helped each other figure out the process, to recognize the poet in us all—to name our personal seeds of greatness.

I was beginning to sense that the questions were coming again. Where do we need to go from here?

Personal Reflection

What did we learn through our mind games? This particular event gave us opportunities to use the language of poetry to express our experiences with great art. Basically we were trading word pictures for visual pictures, and in the process we were discovering how poets and artists play very similar, parallel mind games, though they are using different media—or languages—to express themselves. We also were discovering from the inside out how the impact of these visual images create an enormous need for expressive language. It was as though our visual discoveries stirred art forms within us, granting us powers to express ourselves that we didn't know we had.

There were other layers of learning also. We were discovering how language helps us interpret content: in this case, the content of great art. We used language to make connections between art and history, art and mathematics, art and biography, as well as art and poetry. Through these many connections, we experienced the unity of learning and the unifying effect of language.

A third layer of learning: we saw once again how important and necessary language skills became as each writer urgently needed them for very real, very demanding purposes created by each piece of writing. Every writer prized these skills learned in the context of authentic writing. The new skills will not be forgotten, for they have grown out of the students' insight that a writer needs them and not out of the teacher's insight alone. Direct instruction has had a critical place: at the point of the writers' need. We have learned about language through language use. Skill instruction has not been abstracted and isolated from a genuine, practical need for the skills. We have implicitly understood that to learn the language arts we must speak our language, listen to our language, read our language, and write our language. As we *use* language, we acquire the skills and abilities to understand and express content, but do so while engaged in a process that is a unified whole.

Perhaps the key layer of learning: language is an action, in fact a specialized action, an *interaction*. Language understood as interaction is always real and genuine because it is something that inevitably makes connections between people. Because language is a shared experience, the only way we truly learn it is in the process of doing it. We learn it as participants. Just as language is an interaction, so are we the actors, the ones who interact. The interactions we make with each other are of first-rate importance, then, if language is important at all. And if our interactions are of first-rate importance, so are we — we, this company of language users, these people united through language, this classroom of friends. Our classroom is a special place. We have learned this also.

As the teacher, what am I learning? With each language event, I am learning more about the need for balance among the different layers of learning. For instance, as I guide the direction of the language event, I watch for opportunities to give specific instruction in language processes and skills that come to life through the event. At the same time I watch for ways to draw out the initiative of my students as shapers of the event also.

I am learning that children need me to be an active and assertive part of the learning process, just as I expect them to be. They need me to offer, through clear, sequential demonstrations, the benefits of my own knowledge, experience, skills, and vision. At the same time I must also facilitate the expression of all their many talents, insights, and interactions so that they can provide demonstrations for one another.

I am learning that when children enter into the shaping of their event, they increase their sense of ownership of the experience, their acceptance of responsibility for their own learning, and their feelings of pride in their decisions. They learn to see themselves as responsible partners in the learning process. Because the event belongs to us all, it grows and changes in ways I have not anticipated. These changes do not detract at all from the learning; in fact, they enhance it.

Each language event helps me learn new ways of showing children how they can use language to clarify and express their thinking. Because each of their experiments with language naturally centers around a specific cluster of thinking skills, their language development automatically demands the refinement of their thought processes. Here, then, is the real payoff of language learning: the development of the child's array of critical and creative thinking skills. I want my students to become aware that their language is an expression of their thinking, for this awareness connects them to the real source of their language power. By making these intuitive connections, children can sense how language skill is a primary pathway for personal growth. I am convinced that young children already know when they feel this power of language in their lives. I am equally convinced that, in the discovery of this kind of language power, students are acquiring a lifetime gift. They are actually changing their whole understanding of the possibilities for using language.

I think I will always be enlarging my understanding of how much has been entrusted to me in teaching children how to use language. Every day I too am discovering more about the richness and capacity of language—and therefore about the enormity of my task. For this reason, I want my students using language as frequently, actively, and naturally as possible. I want them reading, writing, looking, listening, talking with purpose and precision in every learning context. This is language power.

If I should retreat from this trust and choose to simplify how language is used in my classroom, I choose to narrow the meaning of language. If I should impose a simplified formula for learning language (containing such ingredients as certain allotted minutes for reading and language arts, certain allotted workbooks and worksheets for filling in, and certain allotted spelling words only), I cripple the capacities of language itself. Furthermore and most dangerous of all, I teach children that's all there is.

I see whole language as the alternative to this constricted, passive, simplified use of language. I see, too, that it demands more from me as well as from the children. Far from being "unstructured," as some assume, whole language demands complex, intricate structures in the classroom—because language itself is complex and intricate.

Each day, then, as I create language events in my classroom, I know I must

- □ plan freshly and actively by focusing on these classic and complex whole language issues and by allowing the creative anxiety that goes along with addressing them;
- □ be willing to set an idea loose as a framework for learning and then discover the possibilities of it along with the children;
- □ have a clear grasp of the scope of language lessons for which my students are developmentally ready;
- □ capture every opportunity to weave these language lessons into the whole;
- □ learn every day also.

If my own learning is among the important learning events in my classroom, then I believe I can guarantee each event will be authentic, our experiences will be purposeful, learning will be genuine, and language will be experienced as whole.

References

Rowland, Pleasant T. 1982. *The Dictopedia*. Menlo Park, CA: Addison-Wesley.

8

Making Learning Real for Intermediate Kids

ERIC STONE

At the intermediate level in the typical elementary school, the day tends to be segmented into specific content areas. "Get out your language book and open to page———" and "It's time for reading, get out your reading book" are common directions given by teachers across the country. My fifth-grade classroom, in a school in rural Owen County, Indiana, relies upon integrating the curriculum as much as possible. My attempts at crossing the curricular barriers have led both myself and my students on a most adventurous and stimulating journey—one that makes learning real for us all.

I only recently became aware of whole language philosophy. As an under-graduate, I minored in special education, in which my courses tended to be more "remedial" in nature than traditional methods classes. I am still exploring the relationship of whole language philosophy to my beliefs about kids and learning. I do know that I am a firm believer in allowing students to bring their personal ideas and experiences into the classroom. Together, as teacher and students, we become a community of learners. I am a learner first, a teacher second.

I have tried to create a classroom climate that reflects equality. All of the children in the room believe their contributions are meaningful and will be accepted by the entire class. This aspect of a whole language classroom may frighten some teachers who are not willing to give up the power they feel is their right to possess. In more traditional classrooms, the teacher plans the curriculum, makes the assignments, grades the papers—in other words, "calls all the shots." In a whole language classroom, students often choose what they want to learn and, in many cases, how they will learn and share their understandings with others. Although their ideas and abilities are different, these students have one thing in common: they are trusted to take responsibility for their learning. My job is to support them and help them form guidelines to assist them in their study. This element of whole language teaching makes my profession interesting and rewarding.

The social nature of learning is evident in our classroom. Students are grouped heterogeneously into learning teams; they are encouraged to collaborate on their assignments and to work in pairs and small groups. It is quite common to see kids lying on the floor, sitting under tables, or cozily curled up on a recliner reading and writing. The focus of the team is cooperation, not competition. The desks (I wish we had tables) of each team are grouped together and members select a name for their team.

There is an emphasis on self-discipline in our room. Because I believe that involving students in setting expectations helps to empower them, I encourage them to be responsible for their own behavior. The students are much more conscientious about their work when they know they are collaborating as a community of learners. They all feel a duty to themselves as well as to the team to ask questions, make contributions to the class, and complete the assignments.

Cross-age learning activities also play a significant part in the classroom curriculum. We visit other classrooms so that older and younger students read and write together; they often develop research projects on individual topics related to class themes.

The Day Begins

The morning bell sounds at 8:15 A.M. As I hear the familiar sound, I look forward to another productive day with the students. Our classroom is located up in the gym (second level) of our school building along with five other classes. While I anxiously wait for renovations and new building plans, at present I must be content to reside in a converted girls' locker room.

Rick, Sarah, and Jason dash up the back stairway in the gym and throw open the door. "Morning, Mr. Stone!" Before I have a chance to return the greeting, Jerry, Jamie, Kari, and Stacy make their way up one of the front stairways and enter from the other classroom door.

"Hi, Mr. Stone. Did you see the IU game last night? We smeared 'em!"

"We sure did! Good morning, gang," I respond from the center of the room, as the rest of the children in the class enter from either side. "Don't forget to check in!" Children take their own attendance and lunch count and then begin selecting learning activities for the day.

"Kari, do you want hot lunch or did you bring your lunch?" asks Kristi, the attendance officer for the week.

"I brought my lunch. Sorry, I forgot to check in," Kari smiles innocently, as she turns over her card.

Kristi continues to fill out the attendance and lunch count slips, which she will post on the wall outside the door for an office helper to collect.

Meanwhile Shamus, Bob, Leslie, and Stacy are signing up for an author's circle, while Jason, Sarah, and Tammy sign up to read in Mrs. Brush's third-grade class. I have invited a group of students reading *The Witch of Blackbird Pond* (Speare 1958) to meet in a literature circle. The remainder of the class can choose from writing at the Poet Tree, free reading, working at the geometry area, or carrying out independent/small-group research.

Class Meeting

"All right, guys, let's meet in circle to make sure we're all clear on who's doing what. Bring your folder and a pencil, please." During a typical day, students participate in several experiences that engage them in language use and development. Each morning, we begin our class meeting by sharing poetry or a chapter or two from a book the class is reading together. Sometimes the kids read, sometimes I do. This is an important way to begin each morning for it signifies to the students that reading and sharing written work are truly valued.

Since there are no schedule conflicts to disrupt our morning, Joey shares his research on Captain Cook. "Did you know that penguins are only found on the continent of Antarctica?...Even though we keep them in zoos sometimes, they really only live there. And no one would even know about them if it hadn't been for Captain James Cook," he tells us. I'm pleased to see that Joey's interest in *Mr. Popper's Penguins* (Atwater and Atwater 1938), which I read to them three weeks ago, has become the impetus for this report on Captain Cook.

"Thanks, Joey. Nice going. Does anyone have any questions or comments?"

Almost immediately, Tammy asks, "Can I do a report on penguins?"

Such spontaneous topic selection frequently determines the direction that our curriculum takes. Children build on each other's ideas, and I support their pursuits by highlighting connections and generating further questions.

While it is my responsibility to cover the curriculum guide, I am not required to follow the textbook. Instead we rely on books as resources for the topics we wish to research. I recommend books Tammy might want to begin reading and suggest that she consult with Joey as well.

After sharing, the children proceed to work on their individual tasks. Patty, Angela, Rick, and Joseph begin to read independently, while others continue working on their research projects. Shamus, Stacy, Leslie, and Bob take their

Figure 8–1   Author's circle. A: The Poet Tree. B: Bob, Stacey, and Leslie listen to Shamus as he reads his rough draft.

A

B

notebooks and pencils and meet for an author's circle (Harste and Short with Burke 1988) under the Poet Tree (Figure 8−1, A and B). We display all writings that go through an author's circle on the Poet Tree wall.

Shamus and the others choose author's circle today because they feel they are ready to receive feedback on their working drafts. The author's circles are low risk by nature; they provide students with a purpose for writing, promote a sense of ownership, and help them to begin to write for themselves and authentic, interested audiences (Figure 8−2). Initially, the children valued author's circle simply as a place to share a finished work. In time, however, they have come to appreciate it as a vehicle through which they can share an unfinished piece and receive input from a reader. Although children offer insights about their colleagues' work, it is understood that an author retains ownership of the writing. (For more information on author's circles, see Gloria Kauffman and Kathy Short's "Teachers and Students as Decision Makers: Creating a Classroom for Authors" in this volume.)

Figure 8−2   The authoring cycle (as adapted and used by Eric Stone and Joy Hellman)

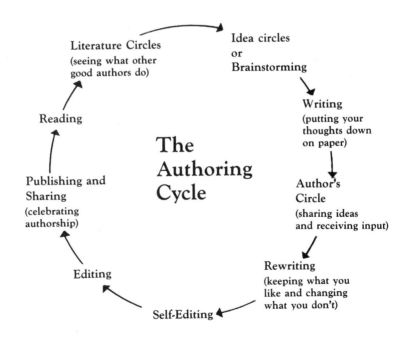

Monitoring Engagements During Work Time

Everyone is responsible not only for choosing learning activities, but for accounting for time spent at those activities. I provide a structure within which students exercise independence and ideas for monitoring individual progress. In each of the areas of the room, I have placed journals in which students log their activities and write comments about how they spent their time. These provide useful information regarding who participates in what activities. The logs also document the students' insights and indicate new areas for exploration. Individual writing folders are kept at the Poet Tree, where children's stories, poems, and sketches are stored. I use the folders when meeting with students to discuss their progress and areas of concern. A literature folder is also used to record individual assignments for the books students are reading.

We spend time reading every day. The children read independently first and then meet in literature circles (Harste and Short with Burke 1988), where they share thoughts and raise questions about their selected texts. Today, while others are engaged in various activities, I conduct a literature circle with a group of students who are reading *The Witch of Blackbird Pond* (Figure 8–3).

"I can't believe people thought Hannah was a witch," says Shamus. "She was just an old lady who lived by herself by the pond."

Figure 8–3   Sharing ideas in literature circle

"Yeah, but she was weird. She acted differently than anybody else," responds Sarah.

"But that doesn't make her a witch, does it?" defends Kari. "They treated her awful."

"Do you think this could happen today?" I interject.

"No way—nobody's afraid of witches any more!" everyone agrees.

"I think this happens all the time, every day, probably even here at school," I tell them.

"Oh, sure, Mr. Stone. What do you mean?"

"Have any of you ever been afraid of somebody you didn't really know?" I ask them, encouraging them to reflect on their own personal experiences. As they share their stories, they begin to see connections.

"This is kind of like discrimination, isn't it?" Shamus observes.

"Yeah, they've been treating Hannah like a witch and they don't really even know her," Jason adds.

The students spend the next fifteen minutes discussing discrimination and stereotyping while drawing analogies from *The Witch of Blackbird Pond*. Allowing time for reflection about the story is crucial to the students' understanding. It takes time to digest what you read, and having the opportunity to discuss ideas with others in literature circles helps clarify those understandings.

At the literature table, Eric and Dana are reading *The Wonderful Story of Henry Sugar and Six More* (Dahl 1977). The book is divided into seven short stories, each having really interesting characters and plots. They have decided to read each story independently and meet every other day or so to discuss the stories. I meet with them when they want to share a particular story. They are very enthusiastic about the book and plan to do a special project afterwards.

Eric has chosen to write a sequel to the book, focusing upon the story entitled "The Hitchhiker." He has adopted Dahl's writing style and is experimenting as he reads with a traditional English accent (Figure 8–4).

Dana is creating a diary that features characters from different stories, each of whom is writing an entry. She talks and acts like each of the characters as she writes. I watch with joy as she works on the diary and shares it with others. Dana has captured the unique personalities of characters in her writing (Figure 8–5).

As the children work, I find that I can best assist them by conducting individual and small-group conferences. I ask questions like "How do you think you can best get your ideas across to your audience?" or "What strikes you as the most important idea in the book?" We spend a lot of time talking about different ways to share newly acquired knowledge before deciding which project or activity would work best.

I remember earlier in the year when the class and I first discussed possible ways of sharing books with each other. We brainstormed on the blackboard a list of previous sharing experiences from other classrooms as well as new ideas of our own. I also looked through many different reading activity books and then compiled a list of various activities and projects from which students could choose.

Figure 8—4   Eric's introduction to his story

March 28th, 7956

By: Roald Dahl

After my first encounter with the pickpock .... forgive me finger-smith in 1945, I have never forgot him. He had a "rat" face, grey teeth, and shabby clothing, he also had matted hair. Ah, remanecing that sly knaves face, teeth, clothing, hair, and of course occupation is enough, save when I remember our 'semi-adventure in my old BMW (it's old now it just sets in my shade-of-a-garage, it's usefulness obsolete) I feel just like a schoolboy. Then I have to remember the pauchie copper (policeman), gleeing inside with sheer pleasure about writing us a speeding ticket. (I was going pretty darn fast if I do say so myself. And then I certianly ...., well I surely didn't pick up pen and paper 11 years later to retell a tale I've already told. So without any futher ado I will begin with the present story awaiting to be told.

Figure 8-5   Dana's diary entries

Dear, Diary,   12-20-78
I'm going to be the
second character to tell you
how I liked being a character in his book!
        I was in the second
story called "The Hitchiker."
And I must say that
I did not like being in
his book. So many people
and reporters have asked
me why and I simply
reply, because he made me
a bad guy. He made me
just exactly like a pick-
pocket. I'm sure all of the
little girls and boys who
read this story thought right
away that I was a pick-
pocket. Or maybe some of them
knew I was a finger-smith
was the same thing as a
pickpocket. And it's not
at all! A finger-smith is
a proffesional job. I'm more
of a Robin Hood, I steel
only for the rich. I don't
actually give it to the poor,
but I only take things that
I know they won't miss. I'm
nothing but a proffesional.
        There were a few
parts in the story where
he made me look o.k. like

Continued

Figure 8–5   Continued

when I gave everything back to the driver, but for the most part I was an evil villan. But there was nothing I could do about it. He was my creator.

ungratefully yours,
The small,
ratty man with
grey teeth

1-11-79

Dear Diary. Good afternoon. I'm suppose I'm supposed to write in this filthy thing. Oh, very well. I really didn't like or dislike being in the book. It was just another one of those boring tasks that you have to do in life.

I liked everything— me getting the treasure and Gordon Butcher being to stupid to know he should have gotten it. And I loved everything up until that awful man came in and saw the spoons on the mantel and I had to give up my precious treasure.

Figure 8—5 **Continued**

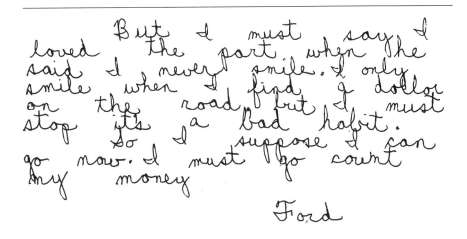

loved But I must say, I said I never smile. I only smile when I find a dollar on the road but I must stop its a bad habit. So I suppose I can go now. I must go count my money

Ford

Examples of literature projects are presented and displayed so others may get ideas from their peers' work or adapt projects to their own individual needs. The following are some of the more common projects chosen by students in my class:

1. Pretend you are your favorite reporter on radio or television and report on a book in such a way that your listeners will want to read the book.
2. Write about a section in your book that you enjoyed. For example, the most humorous part, the most interesting part...
3. Pretend you are the author and tell about your book.
4. Before you begin reading your book, write the story the title makes you think of.
5. Write a conversation between the character in the book and the author.
6. Write a conversation between you and the author.
7. Write a letter to a friend or classmate, recommending your book.
8. Identify a minimum of five conflicts in your book and how the author chose to resolve them.
9. Make a character web.
10. Draw a series (5—7) of original illustrations for a story. Use good judgment in the selection of the incidents you choose and include captions.
11. Keep a diary as if you were the main character in your book.
12. Compare and contrast books or stories that are similar in content.
13. Compare and contrast books written by the same author.
14. Describe how the main character would fit into our classroom. Think about possible friends, activities, and problems he or she might have.

15. Write a dialogue between yourself and the main character.
16. Discuss people, events, and lessons you and the main character have learned from the story.
17. Compare and contrast the setting to our community.
18. Make a time line of events in the story from the beginning to where you are currently reading (or to the end).
19. Use poetry to share about your book. For example, write a diamonte, haiku, or character poem.
20. Tell about the *best* book you have ever read and explain why you think it's the best.

Across the room, Wendy is spending time at the Poet Tree illustrating a poem she composed after a class experience at the school outdoor education area. Yesterday she met with Stephanie, Melissa, and Sarah in an author's circle. Wendy has edited her poem and is now working on her final copy. As I observe her I remember the comments she made that day while we were outside making our way up a small hill. "My hair and coat get stuck if I don't push the branches out of my way!" As I begin to read her text I notice that she has integrated this experience into her piece.

> Walking in woods on a hot spring day
> Pushing the branches out of my way
> Hereing the birds cheaping and frogs leap
> and turtles walking slow, while wind blows
> It just makes me glad there's know more snow.

Cross-Age Sharing

"Mr. Stone, we're going to read in Mrs. Brush's room now," Jason announces, as they begin to exit the room.

"Have fun! What are you reading?"

Sarah responds, "*It Didn't Frighten Me, Where the Wild Things Are,* and *Alexander and the Terrible, Horrible, No Good, Very Bad Day.*"

"Sounds good. Oh, Tammy, be sure to leave your notes on penguins on top of your desk so I can see how it's going."

Suddenly, I realize that the morning is passing quickly. I decide to check the geometry area where Glen, Russ, and James are using protractors and compasses to make hexagons. Building from our study of the Colonial days in social studies, they are using protractors to make Pennsylvania Dutch signs. Integrating content areas is an important aspect of our classroom.

As I glance up at the clock on the wall, I'm reminded that it's about time for lunch.

"Okay gang, let's pack it in. Take everything back to your seats and clean up your work area. I really like the way you've used your time this morning—there was a lot going on and a lot was accomplished." Students from all over the classroom begin to make their way back to their desks. Eric and Dana joke about "The Hitchhiker." Wendy, Melissa, and Sarah straighten up the papers and chalk at the Poet Tree. It has been a good morning.

Afternoon

It's 1:00 and the students enter through the back stairway after recess. "Hoosiers, your group may get drinks first," I announce, while the rest of the class begins to read independently or write in their journals.

"Who has the walking journal?" Jerry asks.

"I do—you can have it next!" replies Melissa.

Students keep their own personal journals and write in two "walking journals" when they wish. The idea of the walking journal came from my work with IU doctoral student Dave Heine, as we researched collaboration in our school. Originally, the walking journal was devised as a way for teachers to share their thoughts and frustrations. One notebook was circulated among them, offering opportunities for them to reflect on each other's perspectives on teaching and learning. In our classroom, we have adapted the walking journal to suit our needs. Here is how the initial invitation was extended:

> This is a walking journal. It is a place to write about what is on your mind. You may reflect on what someone else has written here, or introduce a topic of your own. Your writing in this journal will not be graded. Please do not keep this journal for more than one day. Pass it on to the next person, so that everyone has a chance to write in it.

Figure 8–6 (A , B, and C) shows some samples of walking journal entries.

The real beauty of the walking journal is that it offers everyone the opportunity, through written language, to share important information. There is a certain degree of risk taking involved depending upon what the individual writes. Entries vary from discussions about the weather to more social and personal topics.

About a month after the walking journal began, Sarah asked, "What if we want to write something that's real personal and we only want you to read it?"

The solution to the problem came from the kids. A second journal, entitled "Dear Mr. Stone," is located on my desk top, face up when it's available to be written in, face down when someone has written an entry that needs a response. I read the journal daily and respond within twenty-four hours (typically much sooner). Sometimes the journal serves as an ice-breaker that leads to face-to-face dialogues; other times, personal information is shared and no further communication is necessary. "Dear Mr. Stone" serves as an outlet to channel some of the real concerns that face today's kids—things like peer pressure, drugs, divorce, and sibling rivalry.

Figure 8—6   Samples of walking journal entries. A: Kristi. B: Jamie. C: Russ.

I think the journal is a good idea to share thoughts but I was wondering if the journal is going to be passed around for the hole school year. Rod W.

I can't wait till Friday because I'm going to spend the night with Dana! We will have a geait time but I also have to get a allergy shot and I hate it because it hurts. And my arm always starts swelling up. Oh I forgot I don't have to git it because last time I had a bad reaction to it! Ya! Kristi P.

A

10-14-87

I think the new paper that tells what we are sopose to do is really neat. Today was so fun at recese we got to play kickboll it was so fun. I hope we can play it agian with Mr. Stone Well Bye!!

Jamie

B

Figure 8—6   Continued

I HAVE A COW NAMED LUCKY. HE IS A STRONG, CUTE STEER. HE HAS ALWAYS BEEN NICE TO PEOPLE AS LONG AS YOU ARE NICE TO HIM. IF YOU EVER STICK YOUR FACE UP TO HIM, HE WILL LICK YOUR NOSE.

LUCKY IS REDDISH-BROWN WITH WHITE ON HIS FACE AND BACK.

WHENEVER I PUT HAY IN HIS PEN HE CHASES ME, AONCE HE EVEN MADE ME FLIP BUT HE NEVER RUNS OVER ME.

LUCKY IS MY FAVORITE COW. TONIGHT, AFTER HAVING HIM FOR 1½ YEARS, WE ARE TAKING HIM TO GET BUTCHERED.   Russ

C

Cross-Age Social Learning

"Let's put away our journals and books for now. This afternoon we're going to Mrs. Schrougham's class to share our research projects," I announce. Students need to be given opportunities to explore language and share with others outside their classroom. Working with younger students plays a crucial role in our classroom. Cross-Age Social Learning (CASL) is much more far reaching and powerful than tutoring or simply reading to younger students. During CASL, individuals bring their personal experiences to a situation and, while working together, a metamorphosis occurs. The learning event always becomes far richer when the children collaborate than when each child performs independently. More simply stated: The sum is much greater than its parts.

Figure 8-7   Written conversation. A: Dorian and Joey. B: Susie and Leslie.

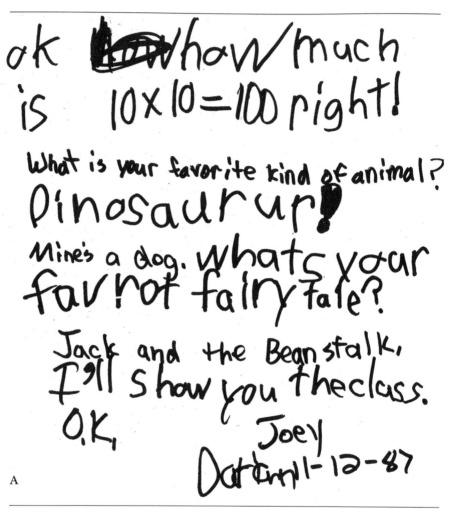

ok how much is 10 × 10 = 100 right!

What is your favorite kind of animal?

Dinosaur up!

Mine's a dog. Whats your favrot fairy tale?

Jack and the Beanstalk, I'll show you the class. O.K,

Joey

Dorian 11-12-87

A

I am pleased that my fifth graders are so eager to work with the younger students. One of the first activities we engaged in when we began CASL time was written conversation (Harste, Woodward, and Burke 1984) (Figure 8-7, A and B). The students discovered they could communicate with one another without speaking aloud. The younger students' confidence in their writing increased (after all, they were writing with the "big kids"!). My students tried hard to communicate their ideas clearly in a way that the younger ones could relate to.

Figure 8–7   Continued

Hi! How do you spell your name? Leslie
How do you spell yours? I spell
it Susie. How old are you? 10 what
about you? 7½ Nov. 13 I will be 8.
when is your birthday? Oct. 8 19\7?. So
you just tened 10? Yes OK! Do you
like this turned class? yes Good!!! If
you were me do you think you would like
my class? ~~they~~ ya! do you
YES!!!   I relly think that
...   as I get to know
OK! You start be- you more I like
couse I didnt   you better let's
know how to.   talk about your
   O K!   class & friends?
~~★~~ Who Are sorry your friends
OK
It's to long of a list. — Kelly, Malinda,
Amber R.. And you! Thanks is my
sister your friend? Yes
I didint want to take to long to write. Who
are your friends? You, Mr. Stone
all teachers, Joey, Dana, Kari,
Jamie, Kirsty, Eric, Rich, and
more

B

Figure 8–8   Sharing projects created during CASL time

"Let's sit by our research partners in a big circle," I suggest, as we enter Peggy Schrougham's room. Today is a culmination of the past two weeks' work. Students are presenting projects that range from posters, reports, and board games to group stories, plays, and songs (Figure 8–8).

"I'm very proud of everyone today. Your presentations showed all of us the hard work you've done together. Let's all give ourselves a round of applause."

After the cheers subside, CASL time is over and we're off to recess and later, off to go home. Again, the day has been filled with accomplishments of which we all can feel proud.

Personal Reflection

One of the joys of learning in a whole language classroom is that it allows both the teacher and the students to rely upon each other and use multiple sources in planning the classroom curriculum. It is a place where learning is viewed as an ongoing process, an environment that values cooperation and trust. Children are treated as decision makers and given the opportunity to learn not only from their successes but from their mistakes as well.

When given choices in the classroom, students become excited about their learning and assume the responsibility of being an integral part of the classroom. Because of this acceptance, everyone feels encouraged to take·risks in author's circles and literature circles, as well as in the walking journal. Students see a purpose for their writing and view themselves as authors. They learn to accept and respect both the teacher's opinions and ideas and those of their peers.

Students develop an appreciation of literature as they are allowed to read and explore novels and many other kinds of works. Not only do they love to read, but they also love to share what they've read—something we've done every day since the beginning of the year. They realize that our classroom is different from the others, especially in regard to reading, and they seem to appreciate the way literature is the foundation upon which the whole classroom curriculum rests.

I've been teaching for nine years and I'm constantly evaluating my curriculum and teaching strategies as my philosophy of learning evolves. I believe there is no "bag of tricks" that can *make* students want to read...to write...to learn.

A teacher can *allow* students to learn by providing opportunities that are truly meaningful. Getting kids "turned on" to learning means "tuning in" to their interests, needs, and abilities. Planning the curriculum with students ensures their interest and commitment while giving them the responsibility of making decisions about their learning. Our classroom is a social place, a community of learners, where our abilities are nurtured, our actions trusted, and our ideas respected. To me, that's what it's all about.

References

Atwater, R., and F. Atwater. 1938. *Mr. Popper's Penguins*. Boston: Little, Brown.

Dahl, R. 1977. *The Wonderful Story of Henry Sugar and Six More*. New York: Alfred Knopf.

Goss, J. L., and J. C. Harste. 1981. *It Didn't Frighten Me*. Mississauga, Ontario: School Book Fairs.

Harste, J. C., and K. G. Short, with C. Burke. 1988. *Creating Classrooms for Authors: The Reading—Writing Connection*. Portsmouth, N.H.: Heinemann.

Harste, J. C.; V. A. Woodward; and C. L. Burke. 1984. *Language Stories & Literacy Lessons*. Portsmouth, N.H.: Heinemann.

Sendak, M. 1963. *Where The Wild Things Are*. New York: Harper & Row.

Speare, E. G. 1958. *The Witch of Blackbird Pond*. New York: Dell.

Viorst, J. 1972. *Alexander and the Terrible, Horrible, No Good, Very Bad Day*. New York: Macmillan.

9

Units of Study in an Intermediate-Grade Classroom

THOM WENDT

U nits of study are a means for organizing the curriculum at Highland Park Elementary in the South-Western City School District, Grove City, Ohio. Highland Park maintains a literature-based reading program with an integrated approach to the curriculum. Units of study help students and teachers explore connections across the disciplines.

The program at Highland Park provides children with a wide variety of experiences that foster a love of reading, writing, sharing, and exploring. The building has an open structure with a central library surrounded by ten classroom areas. Six additional classrooms contain walls. But teachers in those rooms share the same philosophy as those in the open area. Carpeting, easy chairs, sofas, throw pillows, work tables, display boards, shelves, and other furniture items fill the areas where children and teachers work. Classrooms contain areas for class meetings, math, reading, language arts, science, social studies, health, art, and general work. The work areas are stocked with materials to meet children's needs. The environment is set up as an informal community of learners who all share in the responsibility of maintaining a working atmosphere. The walls are covered with displays of childrens' work; this reflects how we value the children and what they do.

Classes at Highland Park are grouped into split-grade combinations of K−1, 2−3, and 4−5, allowing children to have the same teacher for two years in each of the combinations. Ideally, a child would start kindergarten and have only three teachers before leaving to attend the middle school. Mobility, shifts in student enrollment, and the personalities of teachers and students will sometimes interrupt this sequence.

This chapter will focus on a fourth- and fifth-grade classroom of thirty students. Although I will be discussing one classroom, our story is typical of what one would find walking through any of the classrooms at Highland Park.

Many of the fourth and fifth graders in this grouping have worked through units of study before. With the students' background experiences in mind, I talk with the children using much of the Highland Park terminology common to units of study (terms such as *web*, *thought rambling*, *brainstorming*, and *sharing*). Textbooks are seldom the focus of a unit; instead, they are used more as a resource. Students and teachers rely more heavily on trade books from the classroom, school library, and public libraries.

Some units of study are initiated by teachers, while others arise from student interests. A unit of study may result from a previous unit or from an area of interest unique to a particular group of students. The unit of study that I will discuss grew out of my own interest, the childrens' interest in science and plants, and the state and district curricula, which specify that Ohio history concepts must be taught to fourth graders.

Getting Started

On the first day of our study the children came excitedly into the morning meeting area to take lunch count, and they began talking about the Ohio canal unit. I had taught this unit for two years, but each time it had gone in its own direction. These children had heard a great deal about the unit and the interesting activities that would be a part of it. The reading area shelves were loaded with a new display of books related in some way to the unit of study. During the morning lunch count, taken by students, classmates browsed through the display of books that I had collected from several libraries. I listened to the conversations that emerged as the children discovered new information or came across photographs that captured their interest. Some children talked to friends, others talked to me, and still others were off reading by themselves. The atmosphere was relaxed and informal as books were passed from reader to reader.

"Look at these pictures of old locomotives!" Jason exclaimed to Glen. "My dad works for the railroad. That must be a canal boat there by the tracks. Look at that horse. . .or is that a donkey pulling the boat? Here is another old locomotive.

These pictures are great!" With my clipboard in hand, I jotted down on a class list that Jason had an interest in trains and then made a mental note to talk with him about his interest and its relation to the Ohio canals.

With the lunch count and attendance completed, we focused our attention on the large piece of chart paper that was stapled to a bulletin board. In the center of the paper were the words "Ohio Canals." The chart paper would help the students focus their energies over the next few weeks. The children and I talked about what they already knew about canals and what other information they had received from browsing through the books. As ideas came to the children we wrote them on the chart paper. At Highland Park, this is called a "web" of possibilities (Figure 9–1). During the course of the unit children refer back to the

Figure 9–1   Web on the Ohio canals

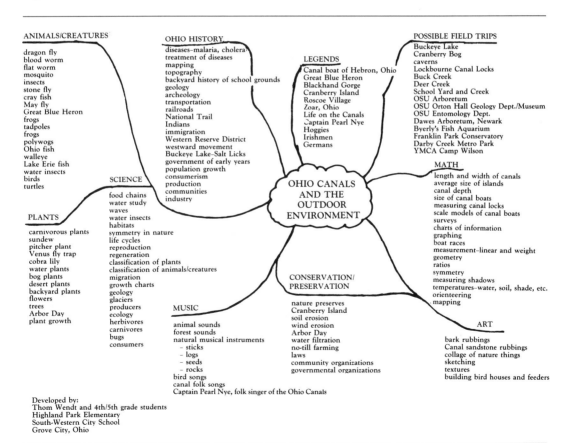

ANIMALS/CREATURES

dragon fly
blood worm
flat worm
mosquito
insects
stone fly
cray fish
May fly
Great Blue Heron
frogs
tadpoles
frogs
polywogs
Ohio fish
walleye
Lake Erie fish
water insects
birds
turtles

OHIO HISTORY

diseases–malaria, cholera
treatment of diseases
mapping
topography
backyard history of school grounds
geology
archeology
transportation
railroads
National Trail
Indians
immigration
Western Reserve District
westward movement
Buckeye Lake–Salt Licks
government of early years
population growth
consumerism
production
communities
industry

LEGENDS

Canal boat of Hebron, Ohio
Great Blue Heron
Blackhand Gorge
Cranberry Island
Roscoe Village
Zoar, Ohio
Life on the Canals
Captain Pearl Nye
Hoggies
Irishmen
Germans

POSSIBLE FIELD TRIPS

Buckeye Lake
Cranberry Bog
caverns
Lockbourne Canal Locks
Buck Creek
Deer Creek
School Yard and Creek
OSU Arboretum
OSU Orton Hall Geology Dept./Museum
OSU Entomology Dept.
Dawes Arboretum, Newark
Byerly's Fish Aquarium
Franklin Park Conservatory
Darby Creek Metro Park
YMCA Camp Wilson

SCIENCE

food chains
water study
waves
water insects
habitats
symmetry in nature
life cycles
reproduction
regeneration
classification of plants
classification of animals/creatures
migration
growth charts
geology
glaciers
producers
ecology
herbivores
carnivores
bugs
consumers

PLANTS

carnivorous plants
sundew
pitcher plant
Venus fly trap
cobra lily
water plants
bog plants
desert plants
backyard plants
flowers
trees
Arbor Day
plant growth

OHIO CANALS AND THE OUTDOOR ENVIRONMENT

MATH

length and width of canals
average size of islands
canal depth
size of canal boats
measuring canal locks
scale models of canal boats
surveys
charts of information
graphing
boat races
measurement–linear and weight
geometry
ratios
symmetry
measuring shadows
temperatures–water, soil, shade, etc.
orienteering
mapping

CONSERVATION/ PRESERVATION

nature preserves
Cranberry Island
soil erosion
wind erosion
Arbor Day
water filtration
no-till farming
laws
community organizations
governmental organizations

MUSIC

animal sounds
forest sounds
natural musical instruments
– sticks
– logs
– seeds
– rocks
bird songs
canal folk songs
Captain Pearl Nye, folk singer of the Ohio Canals

ART

bark rubbings
Canal sandstone rubbings
collage of nature things
sketching
textures
building bird houses and feeders

Developed by:
Thom Wendt and 4th/5th grade students
Highland Park Elementary
South-Western City School
Grove City, Ohio

web for reminders of areas to be studied. The web also offers words that children may use in their writings. Children often take their personal spelling word books to the web to copy down a word for a piece of writing (Figure 9–2).

Another common activity in the beginning of a new unit is the reading aloud of related books. I may introduce a book to the whole group during a quiet time in the meeting/reading area. The book is then read and discussed. Children ask questions and share information from their own readings and understandings about the unit.

Figure 9–2   Heather's word book (excerpt)

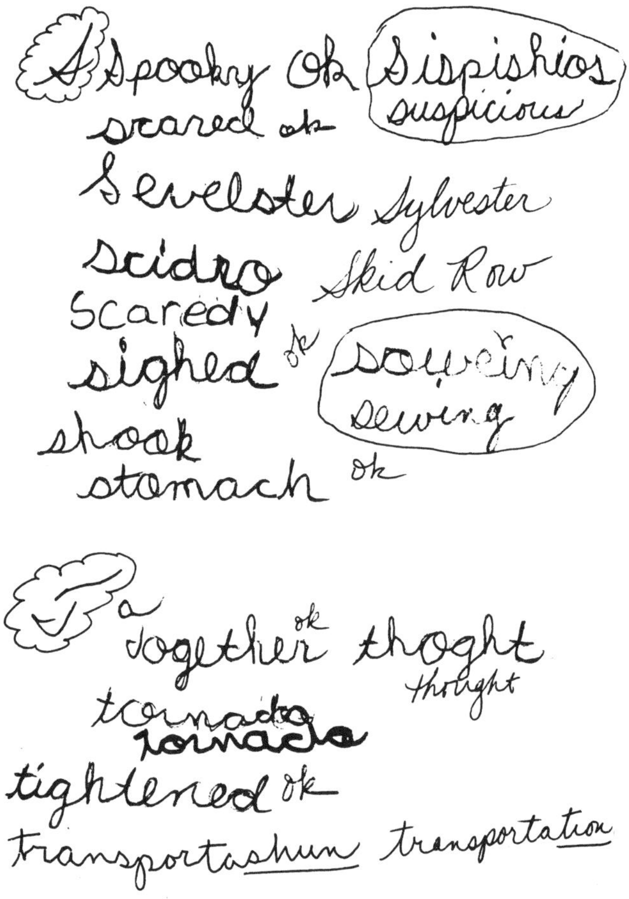

After my reading aloud of a book about carnivorous plants, Todd and Steve became very excited and wanted to share their information about a wasp that lays its eggs in the pitcher plant. The boys scrambled to the carnivorous plant display with live specimens and found the book with photographs that illustrated the layering of food between clusters of eggs for newly hatched wasps. They carefully explained the process the parent wasp goes through in preparing the egg nests. The boys talked a little and then read sections that they felt were important for us to hear. Bobby raised his hand to ask, "Don't the pitcher plants eat the wasps and eggs inside the plant?"

"That's a real good question," Todd remarked with a look of puzzlement in Steve's direction.

"Didn't it say someplace that they only lay their eggs in last year's pitchers?" Steve asked. Both boys looked through the pages as we waited in anticipation. "Yes, they only build a nest in the dead parts from last season."

"Well, that makes sense," Bobby said to himself. "That way the plant wouldn't be able to eat the baby wasps."

"Isn't it amazing how a plant that kills some insects could be a home for other insects to have their babies in?" Rachael added.

As the teacher, I found out something new about the reproductive habits of some wasps. The sophisticated dialogue between the children indicated to me that they were trying to process the information that they were receiving about the mysterious plants that eat insects. Bobby was trying to make sense of what he knew about pitcher plants, and Steve and Todd responded to his quest for knowledge.

Such discussions help me to gain a better understanding of the student's interests and comprehension of the subject matter. Much of the actual teaching of the unit takes place during such informal talks among class members. Students learn from each other by listening to the information others have already acquired. Personal insights and information are valued and welcomed through the spoken word. In this way, children talk their way into understanding. These discussions also indicate to me who really understands the subject matter and who still needs some clarification. I can choose to address those students as a group or individually, depending on their personalities as learners.

Quiet reading times are also provided each day so that students have time to read books of their choice. Some days I sit with the students on the sofa or floor with a favorite book. On other occasions I may hold a book discussion with one or more students. I am always writing and recording the information I learn through the discussions with children. The written records help me track a student's history with books and also provide information about how to help extend the student's understandings of a particular concept.

The students keep a written record of what they are reading, which they show to their parents each week to keep them informed of the literature experiences at school. I use student reading logs (Figure 9–3) to gain a better understanding of the books each child likes to read. The reading logs also help me

Figure 9–3   Heather's reading log

READING LOG

Name _Heather Ann Smock_

Monday I read: _Manhattan Is Missing_

I read from page _19_ to page _47_   Date _4-4-88_

My comments about what I read:

Peter, Adam, Benjie, Mrs. Clarke & Mr. Clarke are in America. They live in London but are in New York now. Peter is taking Manhattan the cat for a walk.

Tuesday I read: _Manhattan Is Missing_

I read from page _48_ to Page _85_   Date _4-5-88_

My comments about what I read:

Peter & Benjie took Manhattan to the park. She got away. They met a boy. He is really smart. Manhattan is Missing now!

Wednesday I read: _Manhattan Is Missing_

I read from page _85_ to Page _137_   Date _4-6-88_

My comments about what I read:

Manhattan is still missing. They are still looking for her. They found a ransom note. If they didn't bring $200 Manhattan will be killed.

Thursday I read: _Manhattan Is Missing_

I read from page _137_ to page _170_   Date _4-7-88_

My comments about what I read:

Manhattan is STIll missing. Benjie had to give $200. dollars to a kid. (He didn't) Now they think they know where Manhattan is.

Friday I read: _The Cat Sister Mystery_

I read from page _1_ to page _19_   Date _4-8-88_

My comments about what I read:

Beth just moved into a new home. The house next door is strange. Weird things happen. Mrs. Goodall lives in that house. She has 5 cats.

Have parents read and sign this form. Return form on Monday.

_✓_ Yes, I have proofread my reading log. _Heather S_
                                          Student Signature

_✓_ Yes, my child has shared his/her reading log with me. _Jew Smock_
                                          Parent Signature

determine whether or not students need guidance in making selections. If children are having difficulty finding books that interest them, the reading log will reflect new books started each day but never finished. I sometimes find that a child chooses to read only one type of literature. With this awareness, I can suggest books that will expose the student to a wider variety of readings as well as books appropriate to their reading level.

Read Aloud with Chapter Books

Selecting chapter books to read aloud to the class can be difficult. Today's market is flooded with many wonderful books for intermediate-age children. I am aware of the books children naturally choose and usually leave those books for individual independent readings. I choose books for reading aloud that tie in with the current unit of study and stretch the imagination of children. By having children talk about their current readings, classmates begin swapping books and making lists of books to read during the year. Some classes have a box in which children can keep a three-by-five card that lists books read on one side, books to be read on the other side, and the student's name on the top. Children often refer to a classmate's card for good book recommendations (Figure 9–4, A and B).

Zoar Blue, by Ohio author Janet Hickman (1978), was the read-aloud book during our canal unit. The story begins in a village located on the Ohio-Erie Canal and is about the communal Separatists that lived in Zoar during the Civil War and canal days. Reading this book gave me an opportunity to call attention to the language used in historical fiction. We discussed the ways in which the author describes the feelings of the orphan girl, Barbara, and the layout of the village of Zoar, which children can visit. We talked about how the descriptive language allows our imaginations to take us places we have never been before. With no illustrations, the descriptive language "paints pictures" in the minds of children, allowing them to create images of Barbara, the other characters, and the village of Zoar. When I read aloud I often say, "Listen to that again," and I reread a portion that is exceptionally descriptive. When I started Zoar Blue, Tiffany said, "Oh, Mr. Wendt, read that again! I like that part about the roosters having their say and the jobs that must be done around Zoar."

I read the first paragraph again and Keleigh added, "I can't wait to use that idea in one of my stories." This attention to "book language" is later reflected in the students' work when they try to describe something through writing.

The children found the characters of Tante Bertha and Rosina to be their favorites. They loved hearing about Rosina playing with apple dolls and felt sorry for Tante Bertha, who often became frightened and confused. They found out later that Tante Bertha was a special character for the author, too.

Figure 9—4   Michelle's cards. A: Books read. B: Books to read.

Michelle

Books Read

The Cay   Theodore Taylor
What do You do When Your Mouth Won't Open
Rat Teeth   Patricia Giff
The Indian in the Cupboard   Lynne Banks
Witch's Sister   Phyllis Naylor
Blubber   Judy Blume
Freckle Juice   Judy Blume
Are You There God? It's Me Margaret
Sky Full of Poems   Eve Merriam
The Stranger   Van Allsburg
The Polar Express   Van Allsburg
Jumanji   Van Allsburg

A

Michelle

Books to Read

Round Trip   Ann Jonas
Reflections   Ann Jonas
Black Beauty   Susan Jeffers
Cinderella   Susan Jeffers
Hansel and Gretel   Susan Jeffers
Over Sea, Under Stone   Susan Cooper
Be a Perfect Person in Just Three Days   Stephen Manes
A Circle of Seasons   Myra Cohn Livingston

B

After hearing the ending to *Zoar Blue*, Steve decided to write his own ending to the story (Figure 9–5). He referred to John Keffer, who was a German Separatist from Zoar and returned to the village after fighting at Gettysburg. He had been sent back to Zoar because of illness.

After reading *Zoar Blue*, the class had the unique opportunity to talk to Janet Hickman. During the author's visit she listened to several children share their writings and extension projects from the canal unit. She talked with the class about researching information for historical fiction, and about her feelings about writing. The most moving element of her visit was her reading of a portion of one chapter that described Tante Bertha and Barbara's role in the Keffer family. When she finished she told us about a special family member who was much like Tante Bertha and also told us that she could remember the exact spot where she had written that portion of the story.

The children fired questions at her about how the characters developed throughout the story. They also wanted to know about her visits to Zoar and Gettysburg. She shared stories about the people who had helped her gather information for the books.

Zoar Blue took on a whole new meaning for this group of fourth and fifth graders as we interacted with the author. The author's visit was much more than an enjoyable experience. It allowed this community of learners to learn more about the content of Hickman's text. It also enabled us to uncover the strategies that professional authors use when researching and writing. The children's writing experiences and exposure to quality literature were evident as they carried out a sophisticated discussion that had meaning and depth.

Extensions

Theme extensions are projects such as dioramas, writings, poems, wallpaper books (blank pages of paper with wallpaper coverings for children to make their own books), roller movies, plays, music, murals, and other similar activities that serve as a means for children to express their knowledge about a given topic and then share that knowledge with others. In our classroom, children are expected to extend their learning and are offered a wide variety of options from which to choose. Some children make good choices easily and naturally, while others require teacher direction and input.

The web is used for generating a focus or idea for an extension. The children research their topics and convey what they've learned through the extension. They then share these extensions with classmates, who provide positive comments and suggestions. Sharing may take place informally in small groups, in whole-group meeting areas, individually with teachers, with other classes, or with the school principal, secretary, custodian, visitors, and anyone else who acts as an audience.

Figure 9–5   Steve's version of *Zoar Blue*

Steve Brann
Writing
May 9, 1988

<u>Zoar</u> <u>Blue</u>

    John woke up in a tiresome sleepiness.
"Get up soldier," demanded the Union sergeant.
"The south is coming to raid the train house
ahead!"
    John looked up and the sun was
flickering over the heads of the men in front
of him. The train suddenly stopped and John
turned around to pick up his backpack and
jump off the train. He heard a gunshot
and flew to the ground.
    "Men, come on quick!" shouted the sergeant.
"Get to the train house! The south are running
away! Come on John Keffer! Get to it!"
    John ran trampling over gray coats of men
shot on the railroad bed. "Keffer, get your
group together. We've got to chase them back
to—" John felt a sting in his stomach,
fell to the ground in pain, thought about Zoar
and his mouth was open, paralyzed in
death. Short life for Keffer.
    "Keffer, Keffer!"

The End

Theme extensions are highly valued within the classroom and throughout the school. These attractive displays create a visually stimulating environment in which children, teachers, parents, and visitors come to respect the knowledge of others within and across grade levels.

Field Trips and Field Trip Booklets

Field trips provide an opportunity for students to acquire information outside of the classroom setting. Field trips tie in with the current units of study and normally include a field trip booklet that the teacher designs as a focus for the children.

During the canal unit, our class participated in three field trips related to the canals and their impact on Ohio's environmental and industrial development. On one trip, children explored the maps and drainage patterns of one Ohio stream. Wading into the creek with fish nets and seine in hand, we caught and identified many water creatures. Books were on hand for identification, as well as hand lenses for closer observation.

The second trip took us to an old abandoned canal bed where we had the opportunity to measure the old canal locks and lock stones that were cut and put into place with mules during the 1800s. Many of the topics that had been discussed in the classroom began to make sense as the children explored the historical landmark. The conversations among children and parent chaperones indicated a great deal of excitement:

"Look at these old stones! They are huge!" Rachael exclaimed as she ran a respectful hand across the bumpy surface of a canal lock stone.

"I didn't think the locks were so big," Keleigh remarked to no one in particular.

"Wouldn't you like to go back in time and walk along this canal while it was still working, Mr. Wendt?" Michelle asked. "I would love to ride one of those old boats. We could sing the canal songs and dance like we did in Music."

Greg pulled a yardstick out of the trunk of the car and raced to the canal lock for some measurements (Figure 9−6). He quickly jotted down some numbers and shouted, "Mr. Wendt, I have a great idea. We can measure these locks and take sizes back to class for our aqueduct extension. I can tell people in my writing how big a lock was." Greg opened his trip booklet and made more notations. "I wonder if people driving by on the road know that these are locks from the old canal. They look like basements without houses on top of them. If you stand up on the top of the lock you can see how the other three locks are lower, just like in the books. The locks are like steps for the boats to go down."

Greg returned to the classroom to construct with his friends the rest of his aqueduct extension and a model canal boat built to scale. The boys carried on many conversations about how to create an aqueduct model that looked authentic

Figure 9–6   Greg measuring stones in the canal lock

(Figure 9–7, A and B). Together they wrote a piece that included some of Greg's measurements on the field trip.

The culminating field trip for the canal unit was a trip to Cranberry Bog State Nature Preserve on Buckeye Lake, a man-made feeder lake to the canals during the 1800s. Cranberry Bog was created when canal builders flooded the swamp once inhabited by buffalo, deer, and Ohio Indians. The bog is composed of a Canadian glacial peat moss deposit that absorbed water and rose to the surface level of the lake. Carnivorous plants from the glacial period continue to grow, along with cranberry bushes and a population of great blue herons on the nineteen-acre island. The children rode pontoons to the island and experienced firsthand many of the topics discussed in books and class meetings throughout the course of the unit. Seeking out the delicate sundew plant and pitcher plant and watching the great blue heron's majestic flight and stately capture of fish were some of the many highlights of this experience.

The bog is now in danger of extinction because of the changes in climate and public use of the state lake. Measures for preservation have resulted in the realization that the bog may last for years to come, or may disappear as suddenly as it appeared in the canal days.

Figure 9–7   The aqueduct model. A: Greg puts the finishing touches on his canal barge. B: Steve
looks over the canal barge that will be placed on display with the canal aqueduct.

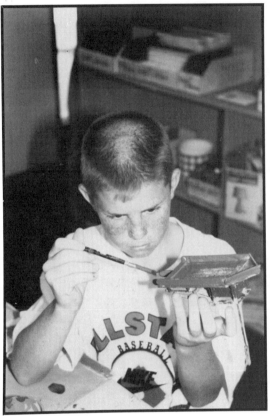

A   B

The children and I left the field trip with a better understanding of the environment and natural history. We could sense a deeper appreciation for the preservation of the environment as we made the forty-five mile trip back to the school. As Layla was browsing through her trip booklet (see Figure 9–8), she would occasionally stop to sketch in an additional feather on her heron or add grass to the base of an alder tree. She glanced up at her mother, who had accompanied us, and said, "This was the best field trip. Mr. Wendt was right. Cranberry Bog is a special place. I hope it stays around for a long time. I would like to go back."

Figure 9—8   A sample page from a child's trip booklet. Trip booklets help students record their findings to take back to the classroom.

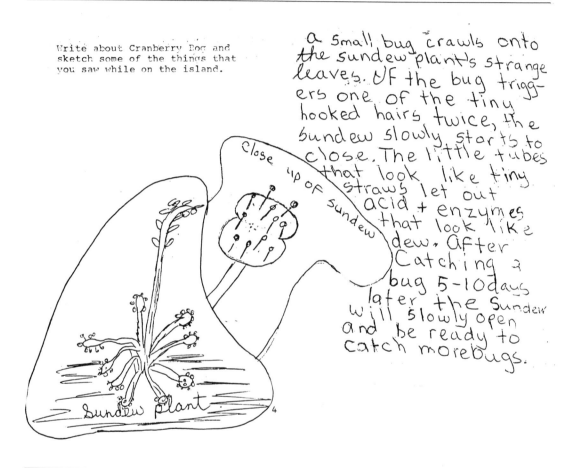

Write about Cranberry Bog and sketch some of the things that you saw while on the island.

a small bug crawls onto the sundew plant's strange leaves. If the bug triggers one of the tiny hooked hairs twice, the sundew slowly starts to close. The little tubes that look like tiny straws let out acid + enzymes that look like dew. After catching a bug 5-10 days later the sundew will slowly open and be ready to catch more bugs.

Close up of sundew

Sundew Plant

Keleigh leaned over toward Layla and added, "It's too bad that they can't do anything to save the bog. I hope that people will take care of it. It is such a neat place to visit." I silently thanked Keleigh and Layla with my own glance of appreciation. "I know Mr. Wendt loves that bog and wants to take more kids there some day," Keleigh said to Layla as she watched me smile at her from across the seat.

Personal Reflection

Working at Highland Park has allowed me to grow and explore along with the children. I find that each new group of students adds to my understanding of children and the world around us. Having the freedom to make use of the wealth of resources available throughout the community as well as within the school allows me, as a teacher, to find better ways to work with children. I have worked through the canal unit three times during the course of my nine-year career and I continue to be amazed by the new information that the children and I discover together. They know that I enjoy hearing about their discoveries, and I always ask them to teach me what they know. Such sharing of knowledge makes for a very relaxed relationship based on trust and understanding. I trust that they have something valuable to share, and they know that I am interested in them as students and people.

In planning all of our units I follow a basic strategy for creating student experiences. The following list helps me to develop a solid foundation upon which to work:

1. We choose a topic based on student interest, personal interest, and/or curriculum mandates. Sometimes the topic will evolve from a current unit of study or read-aloud book. Getting to know the individual interests of the students helps. I often notice that they are really interested in things that I show an interest in.

2. I research the unit by finding out what is available in the way of resources (speakers, literature, field trips, parents, and so on).

3. I develop a web of possibilities from a teacher's point of view. In what direction do I think the unit should go? What areas must be covered?

4. I collect books from libraries and display them attractively in the classroom. I hold a discussion about the books and draw attention to topics that interest my students.

5. Students browse through the books. I listen to what they are saying to each other. I make notes to myself about my findings, which are often useful during parent-teacher conferences. The parents love to hear stories about their child's discoveries.

6. I develop a web with the children by stimulating the conversation to include areas the children may not have thought of as possibilities. Sometimes we may need to return to the web several times in the early days of the unit.

7. I make arrangements for special activities and events (field trips, speakers, films) to occur throughout the unit. Posting a calendar of unit events helps children maintain a constant focus.

8. I choose a book that relates to the unit of study to read aloud to the

children. I read to the children every day. The book should stretch their imaginations. Looking for the book is often difficult but, along the way, I discover other books that can be used in a variety of ways.

9. I provide time for children to read, write, and work on extensions or projects related to the unit.

10. I include whole group, small group, and individual sharing as part of my daily plans, and I display childrens' work so that others can share in the discoveries made by my students.

These simple steps make teaching enjoyable for me. I find that I do not become bored with teaching units more than once. Each time I experience a unit there are new avenues and directions that are determined by the class groupings. I also find that students remember a favorite unit after they have moved on to other schools and return for a visit with me. My former students tell me that learning didn't seem like work when they were able to read good books, take exciting field trips, and write about new discoveries. That kind of feedback makes me feel good. I know then that Highland Park and my teaching has made an impact on someone's life. My hope is that through their discoveries at Highland Park they have developed a desire to be lifelong learners who ask questions and seek answers.

References

Hickman, Janet. 1978. *Zoar Blue*. New York: Macmillan.

10

Learning Together in the Resource Room

PATRICIA TEFFT COUSIN   ALANE LANCASTER

S prunica Elementary School sits at the top of a steep knoll in a wooded and hilly section of southern Indiana. This rural school serves about three hundred children in kindergarten through grade six. The special education resource room, (officially called the Learning Resource Center and referred to in this chapter as the resource room) serves several functions: it provides an alternative curriculum in language and mathematics for those students who haven't been successful in the regular classroom program; it offers additional support, particularly in social studies and science, for some students working in the regular classroom; and the learning resource teacher acts as a consulting teacher for regular classroom teachers, providing suggestions and materials for the successful mainstreaming of special needs students and others having difficulty in the regular classroom. All of the students served in the resource room qualify for special education services according to state and federal guidelines. Because of retentions they are typically one to two years older than their peers in the same grade.

As in other schools, our resource room schedule is determined by the regular classroom schedule; the students travel from the regular classroom to the resource room. As a result, some of the students are in the resource room only for a short period of time before they must return to an activity in the regular classroom. And like other similar programs, the students come to receive additional support in the academic areas. But here the similarities between this program and traditional resource programs end.

Figure 10−1   Classroom schedule

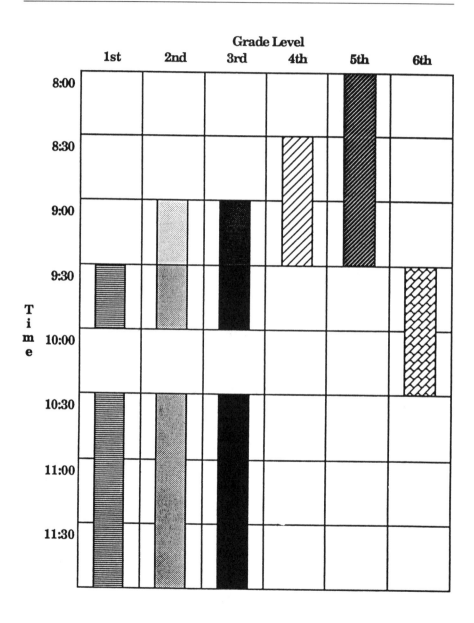

We, the teachers in this resource room, are in the midst of shifting to a curriculum based on reading "real" books, writing for a purpose, learning strategies for understanding content area materials, and learning to use mathematical skills to solve real problems. We also support students in assuming more responsibility for their learning and help students to change their self-image, an image often shaped by previous failure. In addition, because we recognize the social nature of learning, we organize the classroom so that students and teachers work and learn together. Finally, we want to improve the coordination of regular and special programs so that these students and the regular classroom teacher are supported as they work together.

This chapter describes a typical morning in early spring. The change in the curriculum from an individualized, skill-based program to one based on whole language principles began in September. As the curriculum changes were planned and implemented, we have identified several characteristics—interest, choice, reflection, and participation—that contribute to successful learning experiences in this room. We believe that:

- Student interest should be an entry point for curriculum planning.
- All aspects of the curriculum should involve *choice*.
- Students and teachers need opportunities to reflect upon and evaluate their language use.
- Teachers should participate in language activities and encourage students to control their own learning.

These components are critical in encouraging students to develop more sophisticated reading and writing behaviors. In our story of one morning in the resource room these characteristics are highlighted. But let's first take a look at the typical classroom schedule in the resource room. It shows the intermingling of grade-level groups throughout the morning work period (Figure 10–1).

The Day Begins

It's an early spring day, still chilly enough to wear winter clothes. On this particular morning, we (Alane Lancaster, the teacher, and Pat Tefft Cousin, the teacher-researcher) are in the classroom. We are later joined by Lynn, a field experience student from a nearby university. It's the second day back after spring break, and some of the students are still sleepy as they readjust to their early morning schedule. Some of the fifth graders—B. J., Charlie, Michelle, Ida, and Bradley—stroll into the room around 8:00. "Look at my new Garfield folder," B. J. tells Charlie, pulling out his new purchase from the school store.

"I made four baskets last night at practice," Michelle says to Alane.

Steve, a sixth grader, and Angie and Shawn, fourth graders, come in. They sit at desks clustered together in the middle of the room, chatting about the upcoming field trip and about the bus ride to school.

Alane welcomes the group and asks them to get out their spelling books, designed for students with spelling difficulties. They work quietly in their spelling books for a short time, completing the exercises on one page of the week's unit, and sometimes asking questions of Alane and each other. Alane moves from desk to desk, checking their answers and responding to their questions. We still maintain a traditional approach with spelling instruction. The spelling curriculum is one of the last areas to be dealt with in changing the focus of classroom instruction. Just as we, as teachers, believe that we need to provide time for students to grow and develop, we also recognize our need for time to develop the curriculum area by area. Our spelling program remains intact while we spend our energies on changing other areas of the reading and writing curriculum.

Author Study

The group has been here about twenty minutes when Alane asks them to put the books away. Gayla and David, two fourth graders, and Jeremy, a fifth grader, come in and join the group. She tells the class that she is going to read another book by the author the class is studying this week, Chris Van Allsburg. The name of the book is *The Wreck of the Zephyr* (1983).

Author study demonstrates different styles of writing, such as use of description, humor, and so on. We support the students in developing their individual voices and hope that by reading and discussing several works by the same author, they will become aware of how that author has developed a distinctive voice. Once the students begin to recognize their own strengths in one aspect of their writing they are less inclined to dwell on the areas in which they are having difficulty. Author study also helps students become more aware of terminology related to writing, such as author, illustrator, and publisher.

The room is very quiet as Alane reads the story of a sailboat that sailed in the sky. She stops to ask, "Have any of you been on a sailboat?" Shawn waves his hand.

Alane continues, "You're going to hear some sailing terms."

As she reads the story, she occasionally makes a comment or asks a question. "Have any of you ever eaten oyster stew?"

Bradley scrunches up his face as he answers, "No-o-o."

Near the end of the story she asks, "Anyone want to predict what happens?" Some students make predictions and she continues. The book ends rather ambiguously. The reader is led to assume that the narrator of the story is really telling about himself as a young boy.

Alane finishes the book and waits. Michelle is the first one to comment. She says, "That was the boy!"

Alane answers, "How do you know?"

"He says he broke his leg and he would know the waves could carry him," says B. J.

Michelle adds, "The boy would be the only one who would know every little detail."

Alane asks how the book is similar to *Jumanji* (1981), the Van Allsburg book that was read the day before.

Aaron answers, "The pictures."

"There's something you know is going to happen," offers Michelle. "First the animals," she says, referring to *Jumanji*, "and then the boat" in the *Zephyr*.

The discussion continues, not according to preconceived questions written by the teacher or gleaned from some book discussion guide, but with the teacher letting the students take the lead by building upon their comments and questions.

Aaron finishes the discussion by asking, "What does the author look like?"

Alane refers to the book jacket and finds some descriptive information about Van Allsburg. "I think his picture is in one of the other books," she says, pointing to the shelf where a group of Van Allsburg's books are displayed for students to read while they are in the resource room. "You know, when I'm reading, I also do that," she tells them. "I wonder what the author looks like." Alerting the students to strategies used by proficient readers encourages their use of similar strategies. Previous instructional experiences had often convinced these students to abandon these very strategies, leaving them with the impression that there was some type of trick to learning to read and write.

Since we also want students to value their strategies, we create opportunities for them to respond to, reflect upon, and evaluate classroom experiences. We call this particular activity "informal evaluation." Informal evaluation encourages them to reflect on what they are doing and why; it also helps them make connections between their own learning and what is going on in the classroom.

Today Alane involves the students in an informal evaluation experience. She passes out small pieces of paper and asks the students to write in response to the questions "Why are we doing author study in the classroom? What have you learned from it?" Michelle, a fifth grader, writes:

> I like the books we read—mostly the Steven Kellogg books. They are really good books. And they are funny to read. I enjoy the books. They are interesting to me. Are they to you? I also enjoy the pictures. In the Dr. Seuss books—the pictures are O.K., I guess. But they don't really show very much detail in them like the Steven Kellogg books. I have learnt a lot from the books we have read so far. I understand more about writing a story and how to express what I want to write or what I feel while I'm writing. I mostly write what I feel. If I'm sad, my story is sad. If I'm happy, my story is happy. If I'm bored, my story is boring, but not to me. I really don't know. Sometimes I can't think of anything to write about.

This type of informal evaluation provides useful information on what the students are thinking about. It is most helpful when we find out that the students envision a different purpose for what we are doing than what we had in mind. We can then begin to understand how they are interpreting our demonstrations.

The informal evaluations are used along with two other types of evaluation experiences to help students reflect on their classroom experiences. The first, which we call evaluative conversations, incorporates reflection into class discussions. In our conversations about written texts we ask the students to discuss their strategy use. For example, the previous week Pat noticed that Bradley strongly relied on pictures to figure out unknown words. She asked him how the pictures helped him to decode. As Bradley discussed this, she pointed out that this was a useful strategy and then asked him, "What other strategies could you use?" This discussion supported Bradley's use of one productive strategy and introduced him to several others.

The other type of self-evaluation experience we call formal evaluation. The students complete a form that poses questions such as "What do you like about the way you read?" or "What do you want to change about your writing?" Then we discuss the answers in small-group interviews. Often other students comment on what one of their friends is doing well. Using these forms in a supportive social context keeps the students and us aware of the changing focus of a particular student's work.

These experiences provide a variety of opportunities, in different contexts, for reflection to occur. Reflection has become a key element of the change process in this classroom.

The informal evaluations are placed in the student's folder with the other literacy products collected over the school year, including the formal evaluations. We share these folders with the student, parents, and other teachers when we discuss the student's progress and growth.

Research Groups

Having completed the informal evaluation, Alane now discusses the status of the seven research groups that were organized based on student interests and friendships. The research groups mark one of the first times that the third, fourth, and fifth graders are working together on formal reading projects. In addition to promoting intermingling of the diverse age groups in our resource room, the research groups are also a method to coordinate better our work on reading and writing. The structure of the resource room and the constant coming and going of students pose certain time constraints when considering a diverse set of reading and writing invitations.

Pat sits with a group of students on one side of the class, while Alane sits with another across the room. Each group is gathered around a large table. Bradley, Gayla, and Pat are studying horses. Shawn and David have decided to study castles, and Aaron is working on tigers. One of his partners, Matt, is absent and the other, Richard, hasn't entered the room yet. Alane is working on unicorns with Michelle. Ida and Angie are studying teaching as a career, and B. J. and Charlie are researching motorbikes and four wheelers. Jeremy has decided to study the planets, an interest he has held for several years.

The children in each research group have a stack of books and magazines on their topic in front of them. The printed material ranges from easy to difficult, reflecting our belief that students can read and gain information from a variety of materials. As far as the teachers' roles are concerned, we do not simply act as directors of the interaction, but also participate as members of the research teams. If the students are reading, we read. If the students are writing, we write too.

Earlier in the year, most of these students did "research" by copying the encyclopedia and then were not able to tell much about the topic. However, we found that when students begin research by asking their own questions, rather than those of the teacher or text, they are involved and motivated; they are pursuing interests that are important to them. And in the process of researching relevant topics, they naturally become the expert on their topics. Some of the students also demonstrate their expertise in their regular classrooms. For example, Jeremy completed one of the more sophisticated projects when his science class studied space.

Today Pat asks the groups working near her to write down some research questions in their reading notebooks. Shawn, David, Bradley, Gayla, Aaron, and Pat start to work.

"How do you spell tiger?" asks Aaron.

"What's it like to live in a castle?" Shawn wants to know.

Aaron draws a little tiger in his notebook as he makes growling noises: "R-r-r-r." As he pages through several of the books on tigers he wonders aloud, "How would tigers growl?"

Shawn ignores Aaron's noises and records another question: "What's it like to be king, to be a queen?"

Aaron is having some difficulty getting started. He tells Pat he doesn't understand what to do. Aaron, like many students who have been identified as special needs learners, does not have confidence in his ability to read and write. In addition, the strategies he uses when he does read and write are very limited. He often attempts to arrange the situation so that someone else does the work or "fools around" in order to draw attention to his behavior rather than to his reading and writing. Pat, aware of this, hopes to set up a situation of demonstration and support, so that Aaron engages in the experience.

"Maybe you can brainstorm with Shawn," Pat suggests to Aaron, knowing that he seems to attend better to demonstrations from other students than from teachers. "Shawn's good at thinking of questions. Talk to him about tigers."

"Think of some questions. Tell me everything you know," Aaron says as he asks Shawn to give him some ideas.

Shawn tells Aaron, "How big are they?"

Aaron writes the question down and asks, "Any more questions?"

Shawn responds, "What color are they?"

Aaron answers, "Orange and black."

"There are albinos," counters Shawn.

Aaron stays with his agenda of eliciting questions from Shawn, asking, "What else?"

Shawn is wondering aloud about his own topic, castles. He says, "Ohhh," and ignores Aaron's probing.

As Shawn thinks, Aaron begins to develop some of his own questions. He says to Shawn, "How fast they can run? How they got their name?"

"Yeah! That's a good one," Shawn tells him. Then Aaron begins to work without Shawn's help. Aaron has gained confidence in his own ability to generate questions through the seemingly one-sided collaboration with Shawn. Yet Shawn's support gave him the needed push to recognize that he could accomplish the task.

One experience like this does not change the stance of students like Aaron. However, such successful reading and writing experiences help these students to view themselves as readers and writers rather than failures. They begin to change their self-image and engage themselves in reading and writing rather than in avoidance behaviors.

As he finishes Aaron exclaims, "All my questions, here they are!" and then shares them with Shawn. In the process of reading them, he comes up with another: "Can they camouflage easily?"

It's 9:00 and Richard comes into the class and joins the group. He sits next to Aaron and begins to write his questions about tigers in his notebook.

As the groups are recording their questions, David and Shawn are discussing the correct spelling of the word *for*. David says, "For...f-o-r."

Pat asks about the use of the word and confirms David's correct choice. We discuss the different forms of the word: the number *four*; the preposition *for*; and the golf term *fore*. Aaron then says, "There's four *fors*," and adds, "Fo-o-o-r out"—his southern Indiana pronunciation of "Fa-a-ar out." The group laughs as we discuss Aaron's new form of the word.

Discussions like these occur naturally as students write and discuss their writing. They learn the conventional use of specific words in the context in which they are appropriately used. The students then demonstrate their understanding by incorporating this conventional use in their writing. The students better understand the form of a particular syntactic structure when they directly experience the function of that structure while writing.

Pat asks each group at the table to share the questions they have developed. "Finish up, then we'll share the questions and see if the group can suggest any more for your list." Aaron volunteers to share first and reads his list (Figure 10–2).

Figure 10—2   Aaron's list of questions

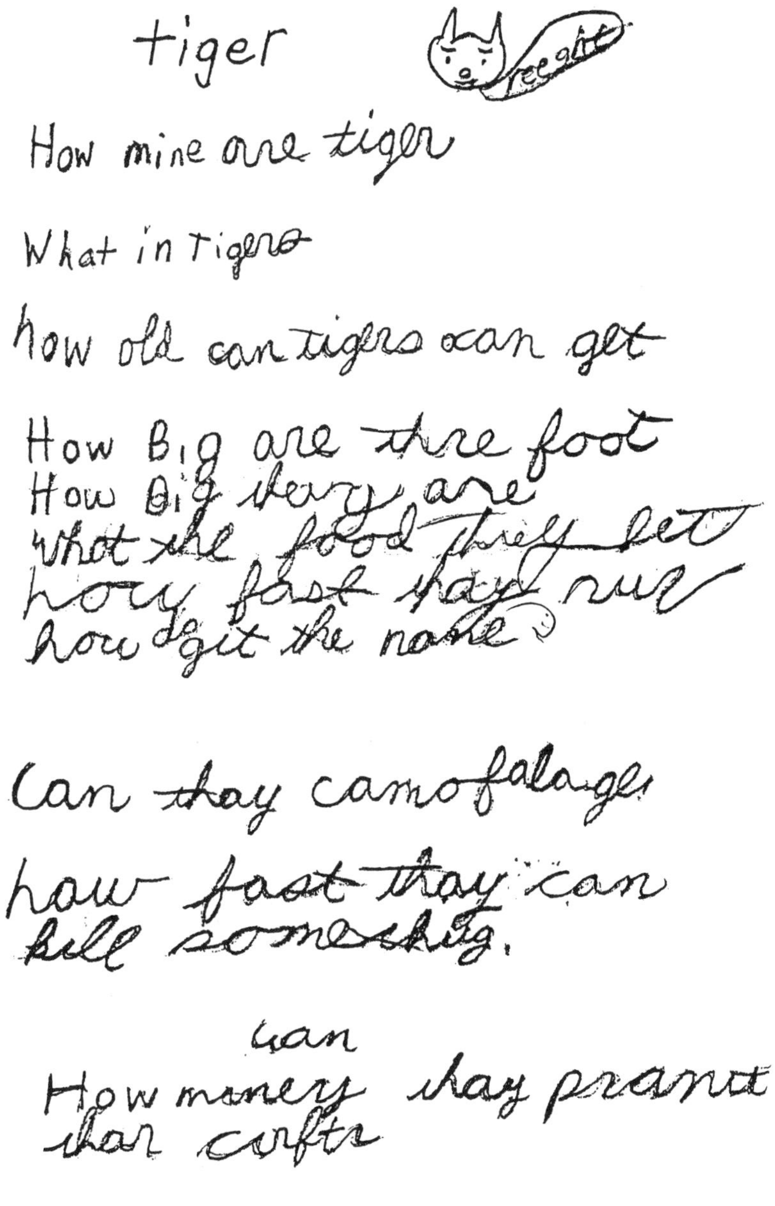

tiger

How mine are tiger

What in tigers

how old can tigers can get

How Big are thre foot
How Big they are
what the food they let
how fast thay run
how git the name

Can thay camofalage

how fast thay can
kill something.

                    can
How money thay prant
that cufts

Figure 10−3   Shawn and David's list of questions

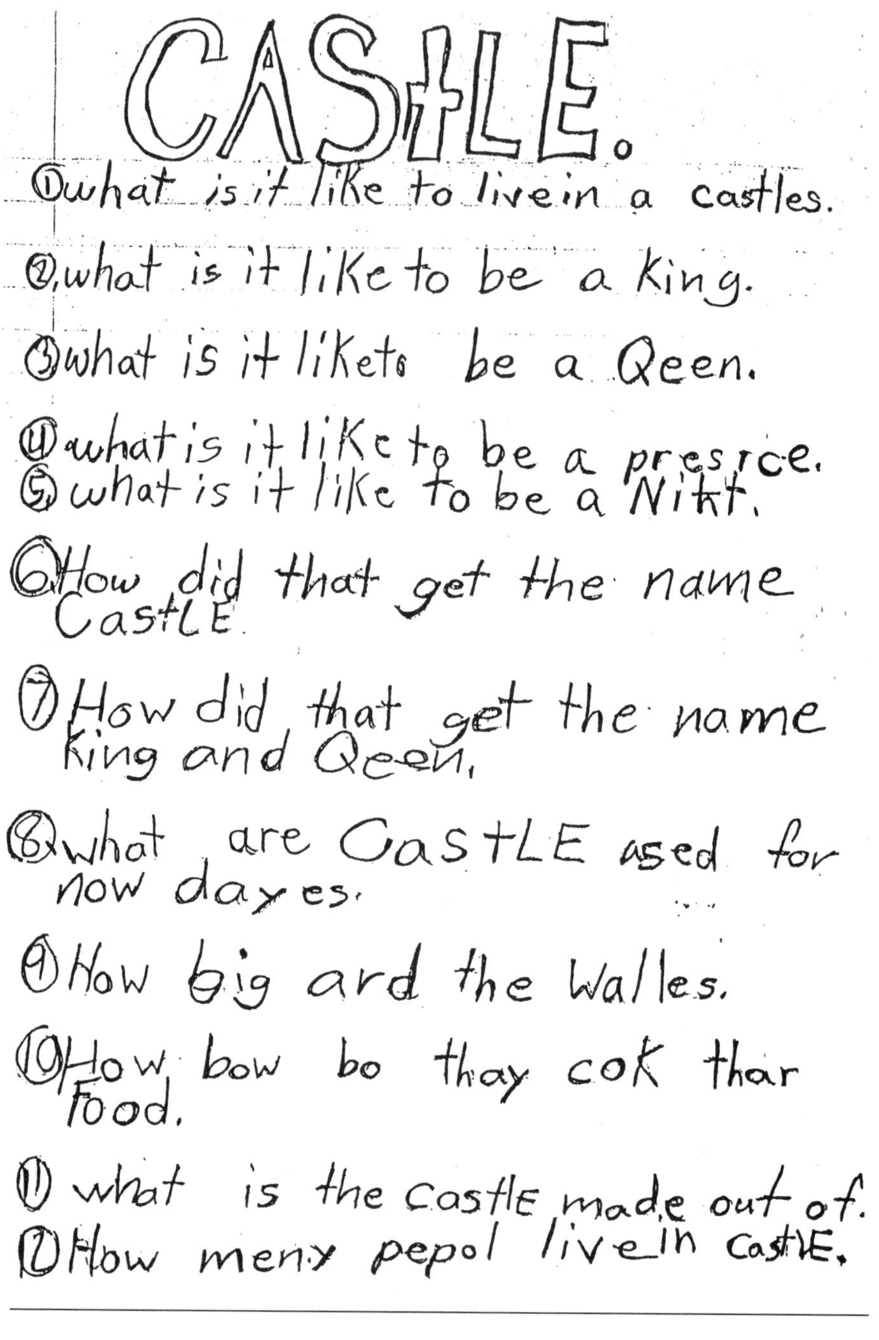

CAStLE.

① what is it like to live in a castles.

②, what is it like to be a King.

③ what is it liketo be a Qeen.

④ what is it like to be a presrce.
⑤ what is it like to be a Nikt.

⑥ How did that get the name
Castle.

⑦ How did that get the name
king and Qeen.

⑧ what are CastLE ased for
now dayes.

⑨ How big ard the Walles.

⑩ How bow bo thay cok thar
Food.

⑪ what is the castle made out of.
⑫ How meny pepol live in castE.

After Aaron finishes sharing his own list of "tiger questions," Pat asks, "Any suggestions?" Some of the others volunteer questions about tigers.

"How do they protect themselves?" asks David. "And how many babies can they have?"

Gayla asks, "What color are their eyes? How do you know how old they are? Where do they live?"

Aaron decides to record one of the questions.

Shawn and David then share their list (Figure 10–3).

The group sharing continues with each member choosing to write down some of the new questions. The group also discusses each person's topic. Sometimes a member of the group adds information about a particular area. David, for instance, knows quite a lot about horses. When Bradley reads his question about how fast horses can run, David says, "I read this book and it says horses can run up to fifty miles an hour." A few minutes later, when Gayla reads a question about the number of babies a horse can have, David adds, "My grandpa had a horse and he had it for years and he said it had six or seven litters—I mean babies." Bradley and Gayla have found a resource on horses right in the classroom.

Next Pat passes out notecards and asks the students to record their questions on them. She explains that this will help them keep track of what they want to find out and give them an easy way to record the information when they find it.

After several days of reading about and researching their topic, each group decides on a method to share their information with others in the class. Aaron, Matt, and Richard decide to write a story and make flannel board figures to accompany it. David and Shawn write a report relating facts about castles and also create a three-dimensional castle that even has a fire-breathing dragon!

The groups on the other side of the room have been conducting research as well. It's 9:20 and the fifth graders put their cards in their notebooks, return the notebooks to the bookshelf, and leave to return to their regular classroom. Shawn and David, having a few minutes before they return to their class, begin to look at some of the books on castles that Alane and Pat have gathered from the school and public libraries. Shawn is intrigued by the latrine pictured in the book *Castle*, by David Macaulay (1977). After some discussion about this with Pat, they leave for their homeroom.

Reading Together

The first, second, and sixth graders arrive at 9:30. Pat invites the sixth graders to join the younger children for a reading of another book by Van Allsburg. "Do you want to hear the story *Jumanji*?" she asks. Their other options include writing, working on their research projects, or reading a novel currently being studied in their literature group. Two of the three sixth graders decide to listen to the story. "Have you ever heard this story?" Pat asks the group.

"Uh-uh," mumbles Chris.

While they are waiting for Greg, a first grader, to arrive, Pat reads the information on the book jacket. She mentions that Van Allsburg won the Caldecott Medal for the book they are about to read. "Who did he dedicate the book to?" Steve wonders, prompting Pat to read the dedication.

Dedications have become an important part of the books written by the students and, as a result, many of them are interested in the dedications of the books shared in class. Through observing children's reactions to books, we have recognized that hearing stories read aloud is important for all age groups, older and younger children alike. And we can see, too, another benefit of mixing age groups as well: they provide demonstrations for each other. Steve's comment about the dedication brought this feature of books to the attention of the younger students. However, the older students are not the only ones who provide demonstrations to learners. The situation is often reversed. For instance, the younger students frequently demonstrate that it's all right to take a risk with reading and writing. They show the older students that our first attempts as learners do not have to be perfect.

The students are now deeply engrossed in the story, and as Pat reads the conclusion, they react. "Uh-oh!" Chris sighs, aware that the ending suggests there might be trouble ahead for two of the characters.

They discuss Van Allsburg's unique drawings. "I like the lion," says Chris.

"The piano," adds Greg.

"His pictures look like photographs, don't they," says Pat.

The book discussion draws to a close, and the students move to different areas of the classroom. The sixth graders go off to work on research projects that they started the day before. Kevin is researching kangaroos, and Pat is reading books about the Seminoles with Betty S. and Steve. They are discussing aspects of the books along with recording some of the information. They propose several strategies for organizing their reports, such as using an outline, a schema map, or a chart. These research strategies help the older students link what is happening in the resource room to the regular class. Alane has also been sharing some of these strategies with the regular class teachers to ensure continuity between programs.

Several days later, these students share their reports with those in the class. Again, everyone uses informal evaluations to record what they learned from the report. "It was really organized," Steve writes about Kevin's report. "I like his drawing."

Sharing Books

As the sixth graders are working on the reports, Alane tells the two second graders, Betty J. and Chris, "We're going to share a book."

She then passes out multiple copies of a book that includes short riddles. As they read together, Alane supports the two students in using all the cueing systems. Chris, in particular, mainly uses the letters and sounds, rather than trying to make sense as he's reading. Alane encourages him to focus on comprehension by asking questions like "What makes sense?" and "Does this sound right?"

At the same time, Greg decides to share a book he has been reading, *I Love You, Mouse* (Graham 1978), with the field experience student, Lynn. As they move to the far side of the room in search of a quiet corner, Greg says, "I've been practicing with my Momma."

As it nears 10:00 A.M., Alane, Chris, and Betty are just finishing their book. Alane extends an invitation to the two that builds on this riddle experience. "Do you think we could write some riddles?"

"Yeah," Betty answers.

Chris adds, "Sur-r-re." Alane suggests that they do that after recess, and she dismisses the first and second graders. The sixth graders work on their research projects for the next half hour as Alane prepares for the younger students to return. Steve has decided to write an ABC book on Native Americans, and he consults with Pat about the topics he should include. She shows him the index of a book on Native Americans and points out how he can use it to get ideas. Discussions of the uses of reference materials, just like the discussion of word forms, take place in the natural context in which they occur rather than with a worksheet on the topic.

Pen Pal Letters

At 10:30 the first, second, and third graders come back into the room. Greg works on his pen pal letter to Barb, an undergraduate student in elementary education at a nearby university, as Lynn observes his composing process. "Dear Barb," he begins, writing slowly and carefully (Figure 10–4). He repeats the name to himself and then begins to write, saying each letter, "B...R...B." "Barb," he repeats and then continues with the letter. He rereads each sentence several times as he is writing, gaining additional experience in reading what for him are the most predictable of texts—those that he himself has authored. He places his pencil under each word as he rereads:

Dear Barb,

I'm going to John Cougar's house for my birthday. What do you like? Is it John Cougar? Do you like his concert? I'm going to give you a picture of him. I bet he wants to meet you.

Greg finishes his pen pal letter, rereads it to Lynn, and folds it up. The pen pal letters provide another meaningful opportunity to write for an audience. For some of the students, this experience constituted their first attempt at communicating a message of personal importance. Sharing letters with other teachers, classmates, and parents has made this exchange one of the most exciting experiences of this year.

Figure 10−4   Greg's pen pal letter

C DerBrB Greg
I MGento Jokaogrs
has FoorMI B+ha
W4t Do you IIk is It
Joncoqr Do you
I his kost
I Gento Gev youa
Pihrqvhm
D
I Bithe WStoM+You

Publishing Books

Pat then suggests that Greg might finish putting together his book about birds, since Lynn is there to help. She gives him the typed version of a fictional story that he has written; each page has been typed on a separate strip of paper. The strips have gotten out of order and Greg has to reread the strips and put the story in proper sequence. He begins to paste the strips onto blank pieces of paper, which will eventually be the bound pages of his book.

The formal publishing of written material has also become an important aspect of the class. With each published volume, we celebrate the student's writing. This experience not only increases their confidence in themselves as writers, but it provides a natural context to work on revision and conventions as part of the "formal" publication process.

In both the pen pal letter and the book, Greg's best efforts are accepted and praised. Greg, although still a beginning reader, has multiple opportunities to read and write in the resource room and the regular classroom. Greg is beginning to believe that he *is* a reader and a writer, a belief he did not have in September.

Writing Riddles

Meanwhile, Betty J., Jeff, and Alane are writing their own mystery riddles. Chris and Richard have been invited to join the group, but both have decided to continue to work on their books about foxes, a research project begun several weeks ago.

"Think of something in your mind," Alane says to Betty and Jeff. "Then you can think of the words to describe it."

Betty says, "Okay, I got one," as she decides to write a riddle about a mouse.

"What does a mouse look like?" asks Alane.

Betty describes a mouse—"fuzzy, a long tail"—and she begins to create her riddle.

The students create their riddles by folding a piece of paper in half; the question goes on the outside and the answer on the inside. Betty and Jeff are also drawing pictures to accompany their texts. Since they tend to write very unconventionally, the use of art also helps those reading their texts to understand better what they are trying to communicate.

In contrast to book publishing, which is a formal writing opportunity, these riddles are examples of more informal writing invitations, the kind that get displayed immediately after being composed. These types of texts are usually not revised and published. The use of different types of writing in the class helps the students understand that writing is used for multiple purposes and takes multiple forms. It also helps them to understand the reasons to focus on conventions when we want a more formal, published text.

Wrapping up the Morning

As the clock inches toward 11:00, Betty and Jeff come to share their riddles with Greg, Chris, Richard, Lynn, and Pat. Betty giggles as she hands one to Chris: "What is this? Guess it!"

Chris begins to read the riddle: "What has round ears?" But then he sneaks a peek inside the folded paper.

"You aren't supposed to look!" Betty exclaims, clearly annoyed with his peeking.

There is much laughing and talking as they tape their riddles onto the bulletin board for the other students to read. Alane reminds Chris and Richard to put their books in their writing folders. They hurry across the room to find their folders in a basket near the reading area.

Chris then checks out a book from the classroom library. He records the title of the book and his name. This simple activity provides not only another natural context for writing, but also a record of each student's "outside" reading. The teachers say good-bye as everyone returns to their homeroom classes for recess and lunch.

As Lynn gathers her things to return to the university, Alane and Pat begin to discuss the morning. They focus on the research groups, discussing how things went in each area.

"I think Richard is going to enjoy working with the older students," Pat tells Alane.

"I noticed that he seemed happy in that group," adds Alane. As they walk through the halls to join others in the teachers' lounge, they discuss Aaron's work that morning, laughing together about his new definition of the word *for*.

Summary

Our class deals with transitions—transitions in the roles of teachers and students, the roles of reading and writing in the curriculum, the relationship to regular class programs, and our ideas about students who have learning problems. We are working together to set up a classroom community that focuses on student success rather than failure. The changes we have made in the resource room curriculum support the students in improving their self-concept, redefining themselves as learners, and developing more effective reading and writing behaviors. Some of the students are also changing in their regular classrooms, becoming successful in those contexts.

But this story is not just about how students learn; it is about how teachers learn. As teachers espousing holistic principles, we are always dealing with change. As we observe and interact with students on a daily basis, we continually develop our ideas about learning and curriculum. The same processes that support the students in reevaluating their stance toward learning and uses of literacy also support us in reevaluating our roles as teachers. We have seen many demonstrations of what is gained when we, as the teachers, give up "directing the show." As we work together and take opportunities to reflect and evaluate our roles, we are able to redirect our actions in the class. These processes also help us in recognizing that curriculum change is a continual process. We no longer feel guilty when everything is not yet how we envision it should be.

Perhaps Jeremy, a fifth grader, said it best when he described his work in the resource room. "I go to the regular class except for reading, but I am working on it," he says, expressing his goal to do all his classwork in the regular classroom.

Like Jeremy, we are "working on it," learning together and searching for better alternatives in supporting students who have difficulty in reading and writing.

Personal Reflection

Time has passed since our year of working together. Yet our collaboration changed both of us as teachers and learners. We better understand the relationship between negative self-image and learning difficulties. We know we can begin to support a change in self-image through a curriculum that centers on student interest, choice, opportunities for reflection and evaluation, and participation.

We recognize the paradox of being identified as special educators. On one hand, we are able to support students successfully and help them reposition themselves as learners, readers, and writers. Yet the act of pulling the students away from the regular classroom perpetuates their view of themselves as failures. We are still confronted with a system that must identify the student as a failure in order to provide any type of special support.

Finally, we have a better understanding of the difficulty of change for both students and teachers. We observed why it is so difficult to support the students in changing their stance. They have to give up behaviors that allowed them to survive in the regular classroom, the same behaviors that have for so long helped them avoid reading and writing. They have to develop a trusting relationship with the teacher before they will consider trying to read and write, but learning to trust takes a great deal of time.

Change is difficult for us, too. Our year together formed the basis for our continued work with high-risk students, work that continually confronts us with new questions and concerns. But our collaboration helped both of us to be comfortable with that situation. As learners, rather than experts, we can now enjoy the uncertainty and let it fuel our continued work in this area.

References

Graham, J. 1978. *I Love You, Mouse*. Orlando, Fla.: Harcourt Brace Jovanovich.

Macaulay, D. 1977. *Castle*. Boston: Houghton Mifflin.

Van Allsburg, C. 1981. *Jumanji*. Boston: Houghton Mifflin.

———. 1983. *The Wreck of the Zephyr*. Boston: Houghton Mifflin.

11

Whole Language in the ESL Classroom

LIA RIDLEY

Ponderosa Elementary, one of three Cherry Creek schools in a suburb of Denver, Colorado, has an elementary ESL (English as a Second Language) program for foreign students. ESL students from five nearby elementary schools are bused to Ponderosa every day for the entire year to participate in the ESL program and to attend mainstream classes with American students. On average twenty-two students take part in the Ponderosa ESL program each year, with the length of stay ranging from one to three years. They attend class from one to two hours daily, depending on language needs, age, and scheduling availability. The classroom teacher, the parents, and I work together to determine when a particular student is capable of functioning well in a regular classroom on a full-time basis.

Program Goals and Learning Environment

Language learning through meaningful communication is the focus of our ESL program. Students are provided with a safe, secure setting in which making mistakes, taking risks, or simply not knowing are accepted as natural aspects of learning. Our physical environment is filled with stimulating artifacts from the students' native countries, books, magazines, and newspapers. Our classroom contains a science corner; a corner with writing materials; a corner for designing and creating puppets, dolls, and other craft projects; and more. Our walls are decorated with students' written and illustrated compositions, and the shelves are lined with craft projects that the students have created around the themes they explore in literature, social studies, and science.

As an ESL teacher in this whole language classroom I enjoy assuming the roles of (1) facilitator — a caring coordinator, encouraging and stimulating, conferring with students and drawing out their potential; (2) participant — an equal contributor with students, voicing my own experiences and perceptions; and (3) teacher — monitoring, questioning, and providing information. As facilitator and teacher I circulate throughout the classroom to spark interest, ask questions, direct and redirect a student's focus, and assist with problems. As a participant I enjoy interacting and motivating my students to do the same, thereby building a sense of trust in a safe learning environment.

Daily meetings are not rigidly structured to cover a predetermined topic. Instead, I try to adopt a "listening attitude," so that I can shape a curriculum that addresses the immediate needs and current interests of my students, as well as my own goals (see Appendix). In essence, the individual needs of the students dictate the rhythm of the class. Through talking together, students learn to negotiate and to compromise their needs with one another and with me. As you will see, language born out of the students' interests and needs forms the core of our curriculum.

Regardless of their level of English proficiency, I encourage students to interact with each other and take risks in order to convey meaning. This means I must provide them with diverse opportunities to practice speaking, listening, reading, and writing. While exchanging information, students learn from each other, gain an appreciation of each other's cultures, and in the process ultimately come to appreciate themselves. Spontaneous, casual sharing, playfulness, and humor are important elements in the daily interactions. Sometimes, though, students confront painful subjects. On occasion they are deeply touched by reading selections that enable them to draw parallels between their personal experiences and those of the books' characters. This important intellectual and emotional connection challenges their reasoning abilities while touching their hearts.

A Typical Morning

 ### First Period: 9:00 A.M. — 10:00 A.M.

In my first-period class are four monolinguals (students who speak and comprehend only their native language) and three intermediate-level students (students who are able to express and comprehend basic ideas with a mild degree of sophistication) from five countries: Korea, Paraguay, Iran, Japan, and the Philippines. All four monolingual students have been actively involved in making and sharing meaning through drawing and pantomime. They also keep language-experience stories in a small notebook, which they like to reread to themselves and to each other. In addition, they enjoy listening to taped stories while reading along with a variety of books.

Learning to read and write takes place through purposeful activities, offered without threat or pressure. The beginning ESL students are free to choose any book, to read or to have it read to them, and to write on any topic of their choosing, using a variety of materials from the writing center. Bill Martin's *Instant Readers* (1972), which consists of familiar stories and enticing language rhythms, challenges the children by requiring them to make meaningful predictions as they read.

Kyoung Sok. Kyoung Sok, a second grader from Korea, likes to make "little books" by stapling combinations of five-by-five lined and unlined paper together and adding laminated construction paper covers. He particularly enjoys making books based on the Mr. Men series by Roger Hargreaves (1978). After Kyoung discovered the books, he asked me to read them to him. Even though he didn't understand many of the details of the stories, their illustrations and my dramatization of the actions enabled him to follow the main story line. Today he is working on a new little book, which he entitled *Mr. Snow.* Sheh Mai, another Korean student in the class who is more familiar with English, helps translate for Kyoung Sok. Kyoung relays a sentence in Korean to this friend, who then translates to me: "Mr. Snow is a fat man who likes to live in cold weather."

"Sheh Mai, tell Kyoung that we're going to write what he said," I say, keeping him involved in the process.

Sheh Mai then translates for Kyoung as I point to his illustration and dramatize his ideas for him.

"Mr. Snow is a fat man," I repeat, spreading my arms wide, "who likes to live in cold weather." I continue demonstrating being cold with chattering teeth.

Kyoung Sok continues to embellish his story by adding illustrations while Sheh Mai provides key words verbally for each picture. By relying on my demonstrations, Kyoung Sok is able to continue the process of illustrating while Sheh Mai supplies a few words. Kyoung Sok is beginning to repeat some of the vocabulary and reads his first sentence without prompting with Sheh Mai's help.

"Mr. Snow is a fat man who likes to live in cold weather."

He listens to the second sentence and follows along as I draw a line under it with my finger. Regardless of the age or English capability of the students, their message should be rendered in complete thoughts rather than only doled out in short, choppy phrases. While many would predict that short phrases would be easier to remember, I have found that complete, lengthier sentences are best because they more closely reflect the students' original intention.

Amin and Abbas. Two of the four monolingual ESL students, Amin and Abbas, brothers from Iran, are attempting to read their completed pieces to each other. Amin, the older, is showing off to Abbas: "Abbas, Abbas, look what I read! 'This is my house in Iran. There is an ocean in front of my house, flowers, trees, and grass.'"

Amin takes a long breath and silently counts the number of words he just read.

"Nineteen words, Abbas," he says as he lifts his head proudly.

Abbas quickly reads his story to himself. He seems to do this to count the number of words he has written.

"Sixteen words, sixteen words!" he exclaims. Suddenly, though, he realizes that his brother has beaten him and begins to speak to Amin in Farsi, their native language, in an argumentative tone.

Amin responds, half smiling and half teasing, in Farsi.

I walk over to them to refocus their attention on the enjoyment of reading rather than brotherly competition, and I suggest that they take turns reading their stories to each other and to me.

Amin, the third grader, goes to the bookshelf where he seems to be looking for something specific; he quickly returns with *Nana Upstairs, Nana Downstairs* by Tomie de Paola (1973). He leafs through the book, which he has already heard during literature-sharing time. He points to the picture of the oldest grandmother and says, "Grandma," and mimes her death, by making a moaning sound and closing his eyes.

"Dead," I respond, offering a word that seems to fit his actions.

"Yes, grandmother dead," he says. "Me grandmother dead."

"I'm sorry," I tell him, while gesturing toward my heart. "Are you...," I ask as I mime tears falling down my cheeks. He nods, turns to the page in de Paola's book containing an illustration of Tommy, the little boy in the book, crying over his grandmother's death. "Me grandmother dead," Amin says again as he continues to point to de Paola's book. He pauses. "Picture."

I now understand that he wants to make a picture of his grandmother, and I repeat his thought in expanded form. "Are you going to draw a picture of your grandmother who died?"

"Yes," he answers. "Tears," he continues, remembering the word from a previous conversation. In sharing something important from his life, this student is acquiring new vocabulary in a natural, meaningful way.

Meanwhile, Abbas holds up *The Gingerbread Man* (Schmidt 1967), one of his favorite books, and in a half-questioning, half-pleading voice asks, "Story?" I know that he wants me to reread this book (for at least the eighth time!). He already knows all the repetitive lines by heart and remembers everything about the book, from what the author is going to say to the language she uses. Listening to and repeating his favorite memorized lines is one of his preferred strategies in learning to read, and it also provides ideas for his writing. He enjoys the repetitive and cumulative patterns and rhythm of the language, and he always reminds me that he first heard this story in Iran. *The Gingerbread Man* also offers a good match between text and illustrations, which this monolingual second grader uses when retelling the story to the other students.

Now Abbas decides to use this and other predictable books that he has enjoyed listening to and reading as a starting point in composing his own predictable book. He takes all the predictable books from the shelf, looks at the titles, reads them, laughs at some, smiles at others, and begins to read *Q Is for Duck* by Mary Elting and Michael Folsom (1980). He reads the first page: "A is for Zoo. Why? Because...animals live in the zoo."

He then piles them together and begins speculating on a page of his own. "B is for dog. Why? Because a dog is big." Pleased with his rendition of the pattern, he runs to the shelf where the teacher-made blank books are kept, selects the smallest size (three by five inches), and starts drawing a picture of a big dog on the plain side of the paper. On the lined paper he writes, "B is" then stops to look up the spelling of *for* in *Q is for Duck*. I am pleased to see that he has discovered that he can use many resources for the words as he writes. Abbas has never before tried to spell anything by himself, so he turns to me to ask how to spell *dog*. Recognizing that he has developed some knowledge of sound/letter relationships, I encourage him to write by himself.

"Dog," I repeat for him, orally "stretching" the word to enable him to hear the sounds. He quickly writes *d a g* and shows me what he has written. He feels proud of his first attempt to write by himself and chuckles as he turns the page and begins thinking of another word to describe an animal.

Fukami.   Meanwhile, Fukami, a third grader from Japan, is playing with puppets she has created to represent herself, her sister, and her mother. She is enacting a story she has written in the form of a movie. Her "movie" is actually a four-inch adding-machine tape, which she divided into small sections that fit into the screen of a box that she had built and decorated at home. All the ESL students have created similar movie boxes and presented them to invited guests. Several children chose to create puppets of important family members. Like Fukami's, they represent many aspects of their native cultures.

"My ESL class, I am ready for you to come here, sit down, and look at a show," Fukami announces.

All the students gather on the floor to watch. At one point in her story when she reads that she had slipped in the shower, she bursts out laughing, and everyone joins in her contagious, joyous laughter. Amin and Abbas look at each other and repeat in unison, "Fall down in the shower." Fukami laughs and laughs.

Like the others, in the process of conveying her imaginary family story, Fukami is learning a great deal of new vocabulary, which is becoming part of her everyday language. After her perfomance she decides to write another sequel for the family adventure, starting out, as usual, with illustrations. With scotch tape, she splices more four-inch tape onto her existing movie. "Yuka, my sister, and my mother is going for vacation to ocean!" Fukami exclaims with much enthusiasm. "When at the ocean Yuka. . ." she laughs as she imagines some mishaps Yuka will encounter.

For Fukami, learning to speak, read, and write has been an easy and natural process. She started the school year by speaking in two-word phrases about herself, her interests, and her needs. Now she likes to read to anyone willing to listen: her ESL peers, guests, her regular classroom teacher and students, our principal, our secretary, and me. She has enthusiastically written a variety of works. She seeks out opportunities for writing, and joins in with her regular class-mates in all types of reading and writing activities. She has exhibited a delightful sense of humor from the beginning of her involvement with the ESL program. Her regular classroom teacher agrees that Fukami is a pleasure to work with and has told her that her contributions are an asset to her fellow students.

David.   David, a second grader from China, via Paraguay, arrived three months ago. He likes to emulate his American peers and occasionally asks if he can bring an American friend to the class. I encourage this since I know that when a friend comes they will write together, taking turns illustrating and assisting each other with mechanics. David is a natural writer, and spelling is easy for him. He utilizes his limited knowledge of English to extend an invitation to his friend: "You, I read." He motions to his friend and himself several times.

His friend asks, "Do you want me to read with you?"

"Yes!" David exclaims. "You read, I read." He motions again to himself and his friend. David already recognizes the value of reading together, and he enjoys working with a more capable language user.

The friends also spend time talking about the objects in the science corner and looking through books about shells, sea creatures, the ocean, and mountains. In the process of enjoying each other's company, David hears conventional English being used by a peer. The relationship is informative for his friend as well, who enjoys being shown all the resources in the room, particularly materials from other countries.

Today David arrives very excited and quickly finds the picture he drew yesterday. Because he was planning to go swimming, he had drawn a picture of boys swimming and diving into a pool. He has learned the words *swimming* and *diving* and has been provided with simple sentences corresponding to the action depicted in his illustrations. David combines his memory of how his message sounds with the actions of his drawings to recall the text. As he points to the word *diving*, he cannot recall how to pronounce it. I simply point to the diver in the illustration and David remembers the word he has heard earlier when we discussed his picture. He then shows the other students how he dives by going through the motions and landing on the floor.

Chi Hwan and Chu Ho.   Chi Hwan, a sixth grader, and Chu Ho, a third grader, are reading multiple copies of *The Amazing Bone* by William Steig (1977) in a corner of the classroom. They are discussing the illustrations and asking each other questions. Chi Hwan rereads the first paragraph. "What was Pearl doing?" he asks Chu Ho.

"Pearl was watching the people in the street," Chu Ho responds. Now it is

Chu Ho's turn to ask a question on the same paragraph of Chi Hwan.

"Why does Pearl like to watch the grownups?"

"That's a good question, Chu Ho," says Chi Hwan, and they proceed to discuss possible responses.

As they continue reading, Chu Ho stands up from time to time to act out the fox and the pig in the story. Chi Hwan looks at him with amusement, taking on the role of the older and wiser student.

Sheh Mai.   Sheh Mai, another sixth grader, is deeply engrossed in reading predictable books and easier literature. She is beginning to integrate more sophisticated language into her writing based on what she can already verbalize.

This is the first year in which Sheh Mai has been introduced to reading and writing. She spent her beginning ESL year in another state, where she was seldom involved with literacy. She has talked of this experience, having to practice speaking, and keeping a list of new words in a dictionary. The majority of her time was spent cutting out pictures, underneath which her teacher wrote labels.

Because Sheh Mai already speaks and understands the language to a considerable degree and has extensive life experiences, she has been encouraged in our room to rely on her predictions to deal with unfamiliar words. She makes use of "nonvisual information" (Smith 1978) to determine meaning and has learned to take risks with oral and written language. She effectively employs self-monitoring strategies by asking "What word would make sense here?" "What words sound like correct language?" "What words start and end this way?"

Evidenced by the themes of the stories she has composed and the books she has selected to read, Sheh Mai's interests center on family relationships. Uprooted from her native country, Korea, and separated from her mother, she is now living with two of her sisters and her father. When reading and writing on the theme of family, she does so with keen interest and sympathetic feelings. One of her favorite compositions is a touching story about a mother and daughter awaiting the return of the father from another country, though in real life it is her mother who still lives in Korea.

As Sheh Mai and the other ESL students demonstrate, students learn to speak, read, and write through active involvement with language. Sheh Mai's speaking, reading, and writing have evolved out of her need to express her own experiences, as well as the desire to read about others' lives and feelings. She uses oral and written language to express herself and discover more about her abilities. Her purposes for reading and writing are personal, and she has become her own audience.

 Second Period: 10:00 A.M—11:30 A.M.

At 10:00 the monolingual group leaves and six other students (two beginners and four intermediates) join the remaining three intermediate students in the classroom.

Two naturally cohesive groups have evolved: a less experienced and a more experienced group. The former is composed of two second graders and two fifth graders. The fifth graders are on the same "level" as the younger students, but have already achieved a degree of independence in selecting their own books, can comprehend what they read to some degree, and are able to initiate related creative activities.

One of the fifth graders, Afsoon, a natural teacher, takes it upon herself to be my assistant. She surveys the class to find out what each of the students, beginning and intermediate, want to do today.

"Chi Hwan, what do you want to do today?" Afsoon asks.

"I want to read a funny book. I like funny books," Chi Hwan replies with a smile on his face.

"And you, Mary Jean?" Afsoon continues.

"I want funny book too," Mary Jean answers, looking mischievously at Chi Hwan.

Afsoon writes something in her notebook and proceeds to find out how the others feel about reading funny books. "Okay!" she announces. "Let's go to our ESL library and find a funny book."

All of the money allocated for materials in the ESL program has gone toward purchasing literature. Today students decide to read together the recently purchased *Chicken Soup with Rice* (Sendak 1962).

Young Sin, a second grader who is thrilled to be part of the reading group with the older students, asserts herself. "Let's put two tables together and take turns in reading."

When no one responds to the contrary, Young Sin continues enthusiastically, "Afsoon, you will read first, then Chi Hwan, then Chu Hyon." She points to the children, one by one, sitting around the two tables. "I will read at the last," she exclaims happily.

Afsoon, who has had enough of following someone else's plans, now decides to offer an alternative suggestion. "Let's look at each of the pictures and talk about the story before we read it."

Chu Hyon, Mary Jean, and Chi Hwan, for whom the reading of this book is easy, go along with Afsoon's suggestion. Chi Hwan has one more idea. "Let's take turns talking about the pictures because it's fun," he suggests.

Inspired by Sendak's book, they begin a general discussion about what kind of chicken soup they like and how they prepare chicken soup in their countries.

"We like chicken soup with rice like in book," says Young Hee.

"We like rice, too," asserts Min Ho, a second grader from Korea.

"My mother puts chicken in, and I like it very hot in the winter," Afsoon adds.

"I look forward to eating my mother's chicken soup with vegetables at her house," I add as one of the participants in this conversation.

Supporting Reading and Writing Projects

Most of my time in this period is spent with the other five highly animated and verbal fourth, fifth, and sixth graders who are working on individual reading and writing projects. Two weeks ago they began talking about their families. After they compared their relationships with brothers and sisters and talked about what they liked to do with each family member, they decided to see what books their library had on the topic of family. After much discussion they chose to read Vera B. Williams' *A Chair for My Mother* (1982), a book about a grandmother, mother, and daughter who, following a fire, accumulate change in a jar to purchase a comfortable chair. They also read Tomie de Paola's *Now One Foot, Now the Other* (1981), the story of a tender, loving relationship between a grandfather and his grandson. Over the next two days they explored these books together and discussed the various ways of reading them. They decided to have me read *A Chair for My Mother* to them and with them; they constructed the story of this book by consulting the illustrations in sequence. They liked this "assisted reading" so well that they wanted to use this strategy to keep the story line going.

Two students decided to read the Tomie de Paola book silently. The others discussed various ways they might, with my assistance, read it together. They considered (1) taking turns; (2) having one student read while the other two listened, asked questions, and participated in a discussion; (3) having one student serve as a narrator while the other two enact the conversation; and (4) engaging in choral reading.

Mary Jean began the negotiation. "I like to read all the many ways, but now I want us to each read a page till we finish the book."

"Okay," Chu Hyon readily agreed. "That's good for first time, but then we read like in reader's theater. Remember we did this before with Mrs. Ridley, she and two children. There were three, like now. We sit looking at that wall [pointing to the south wall], and then one of us read, we face this way [pointing toward the area in front of the room where an audience usually sits]."

"Yes," Mary Jean concluded. "After we take turns we will be better so we can be in the reader's theater."

On the third day of exploring the theme of family through literature, I introduced a book the students hadn't yet seen, *The Hundred Penny Box*, by Sharon Bell Mathis (1975). Prior to reading it, we spent some time discussing painful and joyful family relationships. Next I asked them to predict what they thought would be the difficulty between the family members in *The Hundred Penny Box*. We recorded our predictions on butcher paper, which we left on the wall so that we could refer to them during and after the reading. Each prediction was written on a line extended from the prediction map (Figure 11–1).

Figure 11-1   **Prediction map for** *The Hundred Penny Box*

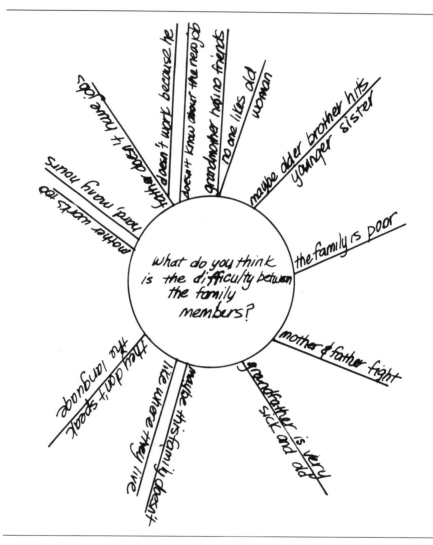

This realistic dramatic story about a black southern family has themes relevant for any culture or country. The students were visibly touched by the simple but profound story. To help them expand on the author's ideas and at the same time discover their own, I invited the students to respond to the story in writing. Since they were accustomed to sharing their ideas orally, I provided a few sentence openers to choose from if they felt they needed them.

- ☐ I began to think of . . .
- ☐ I love the way . . .
- ☐ I wonder why . . .
- ☐ I was surprised . . .
- ☐ I can't believe . . .
- ☐ The best part . . .

We then shared our thoughts on the story.

"I miss my father so much," Afsoon confessed. "He doesn't know I'm learning English fast."

"My grandmother loves me and my sister like Aunt Dew loves Michael, and I miss her now," Chi Hwan added.

"I'm sorry for Michael's mother because she is jealous that Michael, her boy, doesn't love her anymore," Mary Jean claimed.

"We have a very love care family," Young Hee sadly explained. "We all live very happy in Korea. Now it's hard. My mother and father are not only happy." She smiled as she looked at us, yet her eyes revealed her true feelings.

"I never had the opportunity to meet any of my grandparents on either my mother's or father's side. This still makes me very sad." I added my own thoughts to this conversation. Several students were curious about why I never met my grandparents and I explained that they all died during World War II.

This family theme became the topic of the special books they created with the librarian. Figure 11–2 shows an excerpt from ten-year-old Mary Jean, who chose to write a touching story about her life in the Philippines. Kyoung, a sixth-grade boy, wrote and illustrated a book entitled *My Cousin and Me* (Figure 11–3). In the conclusion of his book he wrote, "If he was here I would be his best friend and I'd live with him forever."

Instead of pursuing the personal family theme, Chu Hyon asked if he could write about families from other countries. He began gathering information about the U.S.A., Mexico, Canada, Korea, Japan, China, the Soviet Union, Greece, and India. He selected facts from books obtained in our school library and wrote them on notecards before transferring them into book form. He expanded his use of media by drawing the flags of the countries he researched on a blank filmstrip, then he made an audio recording of his story to accompany the individual drawings of the flags. Aware of his audience, Chu Hyon was careful to speak slowly and clearly to make this a practical learning tool for beginning ESL students. Finally, he chose a musical recording to accompany his "production," which added an extra dimension of involvement for his classmates. Figure 11–4 presents samples from the "family" book that Chu Hyon prepared for beginning ESL students.

Chu Hyon's filmstrip and audiotape inspired other students to explore alternative ways of making and sharing meaning. He and others created puppets representing favorite members of their families, including pets. They also built sets to represent rooms in their houses and yards and planned to put on a puppet show for all of the ESL students.

Figure 11–2   Excerpt from a ten-year-old Philippine child's family story

The most beautiful place in world is the plaza in the Philippines. This plaza has Bushes, Flowers, water, trees, two stages, a slide, boxes of trees, a royal statue, green grass, road, tennis and basketball courts, Stone chairs and a watching house.

My brother, sister and I were always going to the plaza. We played a lot of games. We looked at all the flowers in the plaza. We went actors and actresses. My friend Georgina and I were walking at the plaza. Next, at the royal statue we played tug with each other.

Every morning I always went to work because we had to finish our work. We worked taking weed from the ground. Everytime I got tired. I never picked of weeds well and I always broke the bottom of the weed. My real mom always came to my place to start again to help me out. Sometime my moms got mad at me because she saw me walking if I didn't finish what I did. Sometime we took a break from working too hard. We went to the house of my cousin or my friend of my cousin's. We ate a little bit. Sometime I played with my brother and sister.

Figure 11–3   Excerpt from a sixth grader's book *My Cousin and Me*

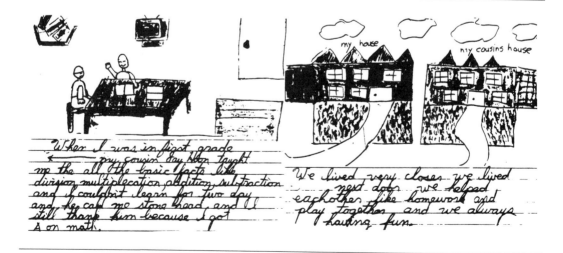

"When I was in first grade my cousin Jay Jun taught me the all the basic facts like division multiplecation addition, subtraction and I couldn't learn for two day and he call me stone head, and I still thank him because I got A on math.

We lived very closes we lived next dor we helped eachother like homework and play together and we always having fun.

Figure 11—4   Samples from Chu Hyon's family book

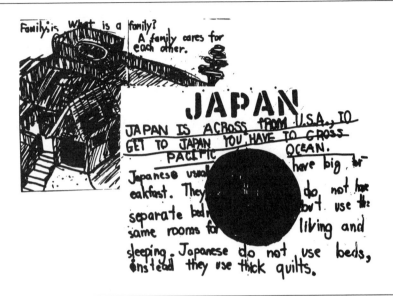

Turning Classroom Interactions into a Language-Rich Environment

Today during second period, the fourth, fifth, and sixth graders enter the classroom ready to begin discussion. Their excitement is immediately apparent. Each hopes to be the first to speak during the conversational sharing period. Every day we begin with ten to fifteen minutes of conversation. Any student can initiate this verbal sharing time and speak about any topic. We can begin to see here how casual interaction can lead naturally to language-rich experiences.

Chi Hwan, speaks first. He is excited and appears slightly anxious, talking faster and louder than usual.

"I didn't do my homework this Saturday and Sunday."

"Why not?" I asked.

"I had so much fun, I had no time to do it!" Chi Hwan exclaims.

"Tell me about your fun," I respond. I am quite curious about what could have generated such enthusiasm.

"My father, me, and my sister went to my uncle and played games with all the children. Then my father and me went shopping and then I went to play pool in a place with my friends. I had so much fun!" He says all this quite seriously, as though he has not considered that his excuse might be regarded as invalid or humorous.

As he concludes his lengthy and elated discourse, there is no question that in sharing his adventures, Chi Hwan has made as much use of language as he might have in his written assignment.

Summary

Providing opportunities for meaningful communication was the purpose of our language-rich, print-rich, and visually rich classroom environment. Students used features of this environment as springboards for exercising their current knowledge of the language. They learned to express themselves in oral and written language with increasing confidence and clarity.

Personal Reflection

In my eight years of working with ESL students, I have learned that language enhances personal growth and ultimately empowers these second-language users. By experiencing the language in a natural, holistic manner, in a peaceful environment of acceptance, students feel comfortable being themselves and demonstrate an appreciation of their differences. Allowing spontaneity and fresh ideas to circulate freely has enabled me to continue learning. In doing so, I have refined my interaction with the students and have found new ways to support their growth.

Appendix

 ### Lesson Plan

There are general long-term goals for all students as well as daily objectives for individual ESL students. The overall goals are to provide a language-rich, print-rich, and visually rich environment to stimulate students to participate in the four language skills: speaking, listening, reading, and writing.

Specific objectives for monolinguals and intermediate-level students:

Monolingual

1. Experiencing language: illustrating, listening, speaking (repeating), reading and writing, rereading (in this order).

2. Reading predictable books: listening, "assisted reading," reading, and repeated reading.

3. Sharing literature: language acquisition and enjoyment of various topics.

4. Writing: the beginnings of using invented spelling (sound-symbol association), selecting topics on their own, and writing predictable books using published, predictable books for ideas.

5. Using creative expressive arts for language acquisition, self-expression, appreciation of each other's cultures.

Intermediate Level

1. Reading process: prereading, reading, and postreading strategies.

2. Selecting topics on their own for writing and for reading, emphasizing verbal exchanges of likes, dislikes, perceptions, feelings, etc. among the students, and between the students and the teacher.

3. Exploring various reading styles so that students begin to experiment with their individual styles.

4. Exploring themes in literature through speaking, listening, reading, and writing. Extending these into expressive arts: creative dramatics, arts and crafts, reader's theater, musical accompaniment, jazz chants, creative movement, dance, puppetry, movie making using filmstrip and TV boxes with written scripts.

5. Writing process: prewriting; revisions; conferring with peers, teachers, and guests. Writing in a variety of formats for various audiences and a variety of purposes.

6. Reading like a writer: identifying themselves with authors, as authors.

7. Engaging in deep/light, sad/ humorous discussions, which become a springboard for more reading and writing activities.

References

de Paola, Tomie. 1973. *Nana Upstairs, Nana Downstairs*. New York: Penguin Books.
———. 1981. *Now One Foot, Now the Other*. New York: Putnam's.

Elting, Mary, and Michael Folsom. 1980. *Q Is for Duck*. New York: Ticknor and Fields.

Hargreaves, Roger. 1978. The Mr. Men Series. London: Thurman.

Martin, Bill. 1972. *Instant Readers*. New York: Holt, Rinehart, and Winston.

Mathis, Sharon Bell. 1975. *The Hundred Penny Box*. New York: Penguin Books.

Schmidt, Karen. 1967. *The Gingerbread Man*. New York: Scholastic.

Sendak, Maurice. 1962. *Chicken Soup with Rice*. New York: Harper & Row.

Smith, Frank. 1978. *Understanding Reading*. New York: Holt, Rinehart, and Winston.

Steig, William. 1977. *The Amazing Bone*. New York: Penguin Books.

Williams, Vera B. 1982. *A Chair for My Mother*. New York: Scholastic.

12

Language Learning Through Family History

PHYLLIS E. WHITIN

I rmo Middle School, Columbia, South Carolina, serves approximately one thousand seventh, eighth, and ninth graders. The student body is largely composed of children of professionals. The day is structured in the traditional seven-period format, with all seventh graders taking two periods of language arts a day. The eighth graders described in this chapter are above-average students who take one period of advanced language arts daily. Despite the restrictions of a fragmented day, the family-history project described here encourages students to cross subject lines, involve the home, explore writing and the purpose of language, and add a little piece to that age-old puzzle, Who am I?

The family-history project reflects several key beliefs of the teacher:

☐ Language in the middle school must be meaningful to the learners. The family-history project builds on the need of young adolescents to understand and accept their unique identity.

☐ Choice must be provided to middle school learners. Variations on the family-history theme are welcome.

☐ Trust is a key element in the language arts classroom. It is essential that we work together to create an environment in which students can share drafts without criticism. Only when students feel free to take risks will they learn. The teacher must also trust that students are capable of making appropriate decisions.

- It is important to capitalize on the naturally social nature of middle school learners. This requires encouraging students to share their information, artifacts, and drafts. Students learn from hearing the strengths of others as well as from being coached and supported by peers.
- Opportunities to express meanings through alternative communication systems are important. In this project students collect artifacts, use the telephone, write letters, and tape-record and videotape those interviewed. Many students present their final products in an artistic form.
- Language learning in the middle school should encourage reflection. Students reflect on the nature of writing as they encourage those that they interview to be specific and to give details. Also, through this process they begin to sense connections to past generations and to respect the value of the spoken and written word as a vehicle for preserving personal history.

The Day's Lesson Begins

Scott, thirteen, glances nervously around him. Encouraged by the smiles and interested looks of his peers, he picks up his paper and reads the following:

Barn Sliding

After their chores were done, my grandfather, who was seven, his brother Jay, who was ten, and their sister Ferd, who was the oldest at thirteen, were sitting in the barn trying to think of something exciting to do before lunch. Jay suddenly thought of something. He said, "I've got a great idea! We can have a contest to see who is the bravest of all of us here."

"Well, what is it?"

"All right, this is the object of the game. We all get on top of the barn and we slide down head first and see who can stop before falling off the barn."

"Jay," my grandfather said, "that's a great idea!" So they all went and got on top of the barn.

"Well, here we all are. Now who's going to be first?"

Jay said, "Let's go from oldest to youngest." Since Ferd was the oldest, she went first. She was a little scared about going first, well, I guess about sliding at all. So down she went. She slid about two feet away from the edge. By this time my grandfather was ready to go. He could not wait to slide, but since he was the youngest, he had to wait one more turn. It was Jay's turn. Boy, by this time Jay was so cocky that he was the bravest. He was already sure he had won the contest. But my grandfather had another winner in mind, and that was himself. Jay was ready, and down he went. They thought he was going right off, but he stopped thirty inches away from the edge. That was a good slide that was going to be tough to beat, but my grandfather thought he could do it. His turn was now. He knew he could slide. He prepared himself and down he went and kept on going. He didn't stop and off the edge he went, using his head for a landing pad. He hit the ground hard, and dust flew up everywhere.

Ferd and Jay climbed down the barn as fast as they could. By the time they got there, the dust had cleared. There was my grandfather lying on the ground, crying. Ferd and Jay picked him up and carried him off into the woods until he quit crying. Ten minutes later everything was fine: no bumps, cuts, lumps, or bruises, just a headache. That was the last of barn sliding for my grandfather.

As Scott puts down his paper, he is met with broad smiles and exclamations of praise. No teacher recognition could ever match that spontaneous show of approval by peers. Hands shoot up.

"Scott, you may call on your friends for comments," I say. Scott surveys the room and calls on several classmates.

"I like the way you used dialogue to tell the story. That made it so realistic."

"I like the way you kept us in suspense by telling how the oldest kids went first. I began to suspect that your grandfather was going to have the hardest time because he was youngest."

"I like the way you get into the story. I was interested right away when you said that they were looking for something exciting to do."

Although these observations support Scott as a writer, this sharing time has been no easy task for him. Early in the year he had met me after school at his request. He admitted to his weak skills in writing and spelling, as well as to a deep fear of reading in front of classmates. "I start to mess up, and then I get embarrassed and I mess up more." Scott's early behavior in the class was tentative, and his written work was full of run-on sentences and improperly used possessives. Beneath the veneer of errors, however, lay a keen wit and observing eye and ear. By building on his strengths, Scott was able to overcome his fears. When he read his "Barn Sliding" story to the class that day, he was a model of confidence. Because he saw the assignment as a keepsake of family memories and not just another task unconnected to his life, he was willing to invest extra energy into polishing and was able to deal with guidance about mechanics with less frustration. Scott has learned to trust.

After his classmates have commented on the story, I pose a question to the class. "This is Scott's grandfather. How about brothers and sisters today? Does anyone have a story to share about when you covered up a mishap with a younger sister or brother so that you wouldn't get in trouble?"

Now there are more hands waving in the air. Jason says, "When I've been mean to my sister and I think she's going to call my parents, I bribe her with candy." Other students add similar incidents.

"Scott, how did you feel when your grandfather told you this story in your interview?" I ask next.

"I was really surprised. I had no idea that kids were like they are today way back then. I guess we really are pretty much the same."

The depth of Scott's insight surpassed my preconceived notions. I had trusted that during our family-history project students would learn more about writing. I had expected them to gather, sort, delete, and order information. I had wanted them to develop interviewing techniques. I had also hoped that the students would realize that they were a part of a larger wheel of time and generations, and that their worries, troubles, pranks, and fears matched those of their forefathers. I could not put this idea into a lecture, but Scott taught it to the class that day.

A Family-History Project

My own family's interest in gathering, telling, and writing down family history stories served as the impetus for this class project. Susan Gundlach's "Teaching Writing with Family Stories" (1986) and Norma Livo's "The Golden Spoon: "Preserving Family History" (1984) provided additional resources.

My seventh- and eighth-grade students were used to writing a journal piece two or three times a week. Although I would write a suggested topic on the board, they were allowed to write on a topic of their own choice. I would also write, and we would spend a few minutes sharing and commenting on one another's journals after writing. In the weeks that preceded the project, I suggested such topics as a childhood school memory, a tooth lost, a first bike, or a lesson learned as a child. In this way the students began considering personal history as significant for written stories. By hearing and discussing each other's stories, they generated more ideas. When it came time to initiate the project, many students interviewed parents and grandparents about topics similar to those about which they had written.

I introduced the actual project two weeks before Thanksgiving, since many students would be seeing extended family over the holiday. Because a schoolwide open house fell at this time, I urged parents to visit on the day of our first brainstorming activity. In one class a mother wrote her own journal entry on a childhood memory. She met with a small group, listening to the pieces and sharing her own. Her contributions provided an important demonstration of the home-school connection.

Early in the year I had surveyed parents to find the ways in which they used writing for pleasure or business. One mother, a Dutch native, replied that she kept journals, letters, and even notes from phone calls. She was so afraid that her children would lose touch with their rich Dutch heritage that she felt compelled to record as much as possible. She visited one class and related dozens of stories and descriptions of life on a European farm in the 1940s. As an adult other than a teacher, the theme of her talk carried great weight: if one does not write down family history, it is often lost forever. All of us must research, listen, write, and preserve. The students listened with wide eyes.

Each class brainstormed both possible topics and ways to interview. Several students related amusing, touching, and informative anecdotes. As always, when one student spoke, a half dozen new hands would signal that the first story had generated similar incidents in the minds of others. I shared a piece that my father had written for me about his Model T. I told the class that in my twenty-one years of living in the same household with my father, I had never heard that story. I would never have known it if I had not taken the time to interview him and to have him write it down. Quoting Norma Livo, I warned, "Families are diminished and deprived when we permit important family lives to go mute to their graves" (1984, 9). Gathering a family-history story would be more than a writing assignment; it would also preserve a family's identity in a busy age. As a teacher, I knew that middle school students struggle with their own identity. I felt strongly that this activity would enable them to broaden their understanding of their own identity by allowing them to discover and preserve the uniqueness of their own family heritage.

Each student was to choose a person to interview personally, over the telephone or by letter. Diaries, letters, photos, and artifacts (such as jewelry, a tool, or a game) could be additional resources. Students could tape-record or videotape their interviews if they wished. They were to guide those that they interviewed to be specific and to give details. The student would then compile the information into a story that would reveal the personalities of the characters. As a culmination, the art teacher offered to help interested students make a Christmas gift by helping them create an old-looking "manuscript" with an illuminated first letter (Figure 12–1).

Figure 12–1   Kathy working on her final manuscript

Individual Responses to the Family-History Theme

The drafts were as varied as the students themselves. The most common topics were how parents or grandparents met, how they misbehaved as children, or how they responded to particular events in history. Other themes included immigration, holiday traditions, first cars, and school experiences.

Mandy had recently approached me about a specialized project. She had unearthed a photo of her parents on their engagement night as part of her early research. She wanted to collect photos that traced their early marriage, parenthood, and other events that led into the present. As a Christmas gift, she planned to create a photo album with anecdotes. I had agreed, and Mandy had arranged and mounted the photos during class.

Today Mandy has hit a stumbling block. "I want an introductory essay to my album," she explains. "I want to begin with my parents' meeting and falling in love. I just don't know how to start." I suggest that we bring Mandy's problem to the class.

"What interests you about your parents as a couple?" I ask Mandy in front of the class.

"Well, they're so different! I never imagined that they would have been attracted to each other. My mom is outgoing and talkative, and my dad is quiet and so straight! I want to emphasize their differences, and how funny it seems that they fell in love. I just don't know if I should begin with my opinion of them now, or how they each felt on their first date, or what."

Suggestions from classmates begin to flow. "You could just say, 'My parents are so different,'" one offers.

"You could start with your mom's reaction to your dad, and his reaction to her."

"You could start with their wedding, and flash back."

The last idea appeals to Mandy, and she begins to toy around with ways that she could use the marriage ceremony. Again students raise hands to suggest going up the aisle, each parent contemplating the wedding day or the wedding vow, "Till death do us part." Suddenly Mandy's face lights up. "Yes, that's it. I'll start with, 'Till death do us part,' and then describe each of my parents. Then it will be obvious that even though they are different, they loved each other and got married."

Mandy's need for help had been genuine. She risked sharing her problem because she trusted her fellow students. She knows that one idea generates another, and that collaborative thinking is a legitimate way to gain perspective on writing.

The focus of Beth's investigation is quite different. She is intrigued by her Tennessee mountain heritage. She has spent many vacations on the old homestead, and she is fascinated by the dialect, country meals, dress, and regional way of life.

She has delved into family albums, talked with her parents, and called her grand-mother. She knows that mere description would destroy the rich regional character of her story, so she chooses to write in dialect. Like the snapshots that Beth photo-copied for her project, the flavor of the dialect is worth "a thousand words" (Figure 12–2, A and B):

Figure 12–2   Beth's story. A: Beth's caption: "Grandpa Cobb going hunting up the hollow." B: A draft of "Grandparents Are the Greatest" (excerpt).

A

Grandparents are the Greatest.
   Four am. and Grammy Cobb was almost done. She was my great great grandmaw. She had been up at least one hour earlier making breakfast. There was some rich, dark brown chocolate to go on the biscuits. mouth watering sausage and lightly browned fried potatoes. She had fried apples and gravy with grits. The biscuits were on the counter just a waitin to be patted out then baked.
   "Kally why don't you take these here pieces of bacon and put them over younder on that table, Would ya do that for grammy?"
   "Sure," Kally said. She was my grandmaw (I call her mamaw)- her grand-parents called her Kally short for Kathuleene She was only four but according to grand paw and grammy she was ready for the world.
   "All you gotta do is pat 'em out and put 'em on this here plate." Kally was instructed to make the biscuits
   "OK, grammy." She said trying to act brisk

B

Grandparents Are the Greatest

Four A.M. and Granny Cobb was almost done. She was my great, great grandmaw. She had been up at least one hour earlier making breakfast. There was some rich, dark brown chocolate to go on the biscuits. Mouth watering sausage and lightly browned fried potatoes. She had fried apples and gravy with grits. The biscuits were on the counter just a wait'en to be patted out then baked.

"Kally, why don't you take these here pieces of bacon and put them over yonder on that table, would ya do that for Granny?"

"Sure," Kally said. She was my grandmaw (I call her mamaw). Her grandparents called her Kally, short for Kathleen. She was only four, but according to Grandpaw and Granny, she was ready for the world.

"All's ya gatta do is pat 'em out and put 'em on this here plate." Kally was instructed to make the biscuits. "OK, Granny," she said trying to act brisk.

"Well, I'll be. Kally, whatcha doin' up so early," asked the new arrival?

"Makin' breakfast Grandpaw." (My great, great, grandpaw only stood 5 feet but in Kally's eyes he was 10 feet tall, and he was the sherrif around these parts). He walked in the room still buttin'n up his overalls, gettin' ready to plow them fields.

"Boy, Kally, these are the best biscuits you've made yet. Why don't you make biscuits like these Nancy?", Grandpaw asked. "Don't know Bill. Kally really does do a good job. Tell me Kally, how do you do it," Grandmaw asked her? "Well, I guess it just comes natural, watch me next time, you'll catch on".

That wouldn't be to far from then because Kally practically lived there, at Granny's house, and was up there as soon as she could get her clothes on every other time. Now don't get me wrong, she loved her parents, but her grandparents were something special.

After breakfast was over Grandpaw took Kally outside to shoot some. He got out a tobacco can with a picture of Prince Albert on the back. As he finished the last bit of tobacco he set the can on a stump not too far away. Then he strolled slowly accross the dusty dirt road. He found a branch in almost a perfect "Y" shape. The black barrel of the old gun was placed where all three lines met, right in the center. He lined the gun perfect and muttered, "go ahead, pull the trigger". Kally pulled as hard as she could. Eyes squinting — BANG — !!!! She jumped back at least five feet, her heart was beating like a big brass band.

"Oooo-Weee, I can't believe it. You shot the eye plumb out of that old Prince on the first try! Boy your almost as good a Dan'l Boone himself," said Grandpaw.

"Dan'l Boone! Really"? "Sure". Kally was tickled to death.

My great, great, granny and grandpaw were just simple country, mountain folk, who never had a car, T.V., or camera. Their life style was simple and basic. Love of family and kindness to neighbors and friends. They did what they had to, to survive, and never knew any other way to live.

Other students use dialogue for other purposes. Marielle uses it to include herself in her own story as well as to set the stage for the incident she plans to relate: "'Marielle, you better listen to me! I told you to be careful; I told you, didn't I? You never listen to me.' My grandmother paused as if thinking. 'You know what? I did the same thing at my age....'" Her format is much like the organizational scheme used in the Uncle Remus stories (Harris 1977).

Dan also uses dialogue with his grandmother to communicate his anecdote. However, instead of interviewing a family member, he relates a story that occurred spontaneously during a visit. He feels it is important to describe the circumstances that prompted the telling of the story. When Dan ruined his bike brakes, his father punished him. The family visited his grandmother shortly afterwards, and Dan asked about riding a bike that was kept in his grandmother's garage. When Dan's father said no, Dan's grandmother reprimanded her own son for his harsh treatment of Dan. She reminded him about a bicycle incident in his own boyhood. These circumstances provided Dan the opportunity not only to learn a family story, but to gain his father's permission to ride a bike again.

The open-ended nature of the project enabled these students to explore the most meaningful way to communicate their family stories. Beth felt strongly that the use of dialect would best convey the richness of her Appalachian heritage. Mandy thought that a scrapbook was the most appropriate medium for her project. Other students drew upon art, photography, videotape, and dialect to emphasize the important facets of their family histories.

Social Aspects of the Project

The social nature of learning in this project was evident in the students' peer and family relationships. They shared stories and artifacts with each other. One student displays a thirty-year-old checker set; two show videotapes of their interviews; and many others share photographs, news clippings, and yearbooks. As Spencer passes around pictures of his dad as a boy, students exclaim, "He looks just like you!" Spencer beams. He has shared more than a photo; he has shared a part of himself. Spencer's unique identity as a class member is enhanced by his revealing more about his lineage.

Sitome's Ethiopian heritage has afforded her the opportunity to broaden her classmates' understanding of both another culture and another period in history. Her father was five when Italy invaded Ethiopia in 1941. His vivid eyewitness account of the murder of a young man by a group of soldiers impresses Sitome. Her father had watched as the young man stumbled onto a piece of discarded corrugated tin roofing and bled to death. Sitome has written an emotional rough draft, which she shares with the class. The students sense the horror of being trapped as a child in the confusion of gunfire, but her facts are not sequenced clearly. In a peer conference, they pepper her with questions.

"Why was your dad outside? Was it a surprise battle?"

"Why were the soldiers there?"

"If the man was on a piece of roofing, was he on top of a house?"

I help Sitome clarify her writing by asking her to retell the basic background history first. Then I suggest, "It seems that what your father remembers most vividly is the man lying on the corrugated tin with his blood dripping down the grooves." Sitome nods vigorously. The poignancy of the memory is what she is striving to preserve. She becomes more aware that she needs to give more background information before she describes the key image. Sitome has gained insight into what communication is; she has learned that she must enable her audience to picture what she herself can visualize. The questions of her peers and my reflecting her thoughts help her to shift from writer to reader. She bends over the paper, adding notes while they are fresh in her mind. Her final paper has the impact that she desires, and her classmates gain a greater appreciation for Sitome as a person, for her unique heritage, and for the history of another country.

Fostering positive family relationships is the second social aspect of the family-history project. It is the dream of every teacher that learning initiated in the classroom will be carried beyond the school walls. The family-history project fulfills this high expectation. At an age when many students feel out of touch with their parents or grandparents, these middle school students instead feel new bonds.

Sometimes students discover a clue to their own personalities: "Family history shows where you got a trait or habit," remarks Holly.

Many students delight in discovering their parents' or grandparents' misdeeds. "My dad has always been businesslike. He never does anything wrong. If he does, he says it's a first. To learn that my dad was a little rascal cracks me up," laughs Cynthia.

"My dad and his brothers got into trouble even though they were 'preacher boys,'" adds LaChanda.

Anthony notes, "My mom's brothers and sisters were no different from the brothers and sisters of today."

Jay D. smiles, "If [my parents] get mad at me for doing something, then I could tell them they used to do it."

Kerry enjoyed learning about a prank her father played as a boy. Because she has a flair for drama and storytelling, she plans to act out this story for relatives at a family gathering.

Middle school students also enjoy comparing notes about dating with those of older generations. That the parents of a young couple disapproved of a relationship is particularly enlightening to these student researchers. John relates that his grandparents had to hide their marriage so that his grandmother would not be ousted from nursing school. Andi relishes the fact that her grandmother married at age fifteen. Heather displays the scrapbook of mementos and pictures of her parents' early dating days.

Nora's experience is more emotional. She had never heard the story of her grandparents' courtship. Her grandparents are both dead, and Nora's mother rarely talked about their personal lives because of her own grief. When Nora first questioned her, she knew that her mother was upset. In telling the story of her parents' elopement, of being married "Tuesday at two" in the morning, and in showing Nora the newspaper write-ups that followed, Nora's mom experienced a fresh joy. Nora then gained a deeper respect for her own background as well as a stronger bond with her mother.

Figure 12–3   Brent's artwork reflects his father's career decision

Many students admit that they gained respect for their parents and grandparents by researching the project. Jay L. is astounded by the simplicity of his grandmother's Christmas. He learned that a simple orange and apple were cherished gifts. Matthew is surprised to find that his mom's special attachment to pets as a child matches his own feelings for animals. Ashley admires her grandfather for sweeping the college gym floor to earn his tuition. Matt respects his grandfather's coming to the United States from Ireland with so few possessions. Being at an age when decisions about one's future loom large, Brent feels a new understanding for his father, who after high school faced the choice of going to college or joining a major league baseball club. Brent's artwork reflects his father's career decision (Figure 12–3).

By sharing research and drafts, students not only develop their writing ability but also gain an understanding of each other's heritage. They also discover similarities between their own lives and those of their parents and grandparents and in this way form new or renewed familial bonds.

The Value of the Project

The family-history project helped students develop new knowledge about writing, speaking, listening, and reading in a meaningful context. They sharpened their understanding of the concept of audience by working with peers. They struggled with adding and deleting information to make their writing clear. And, most important, by interviewing they gained new insights into the nature of the writing process. When the students interviewed family members, they were forced to reflect upon the story as writers. In class we had worked on good writing technique for months, stressing two main concepts: first, an author must provide a clear main idea and details to support a theme; and second, there is a difference between "showing" and "telling" (Murray 1968). "I was surprised" merely tells, while "My mouth dropped open when I heard the news" shows the reader feelings. When interviewing, students found that their subjects were not practiced storytellers. "I had a hard time getting the storyteller to elaborate," commented Robyn.

Other students needed to explain to their parents the difference between "showing" and "telling." Students were impressed with watching the learning process in their adult subjects. Marty remarked that teaching the adult interviewees "made you be more conscious of your own writing because you taught someone else to ['show,' not 'tell']." This statement is significant. By engaging in an authentic language experience, these students could evaluate and reflect upon the communication potential of their own writing.

In the family-history project students gained a new respect for the power of the written word. They realized with greater depth that without a written record, oral stories could be lost forever. Parents and grandparents reacted similarly. All recipients treasured the finished scrapbooks and decorated manuscripts. Beth's mom typed and photocopied Beth's story for her relatives. Mandy reported, "My parents opened my scrapbook first on Christmas. They said it was the best Christmas present ever!"

Several pupils remarked that once those interviewed started one story, other stories were generated. In fact, the interviewers learned much that had nearly been forgotten. Nora wrote in her evaluation of the project: "[Family history] tells you about yourself and about why you are the kind of person you are. It makes you feel closer to someone who was close to your parents. This person should be important to you even if you never met them." Other students agreed. "Feeling closer" to parents and grandparents was a major effect of participating in the project.

Family history helped "people we love to open up more to us and to others," commented Marty.

"If you know a lot about your family and your history, it brings you closer," added Shannon.

"I got to see my grandfather happy to remember his experiences," smiled Chrystal.

Souraya's insight summarized the most basic of all functions of language: "The real value of doing a family-history project is to feel the feelings of the person."

Summary

In the family-history project, students were valued for their unique heritage and individual response to the given theme. The unit took shape as students and teacher worked together. Students helped parents and grandparents take the risk of revealing themselves and develop a unified story. Class members trusted each other and so were able to share drafts and discuss impasses with their peers. The teacher served as a guide, listener, and fellow learner. Students pursued individual expressions in art and video. In reflecting about the experience individually and as a group, all participants gained new respect for that marvelous human tool, language.

Personal Reflection

Although I knew this project offered great learning potential, in no way could I have anticipated the breadth of the responses, the diversity of projects, and the depth of emotions experienced. I also found that the appreciation for ties between generations came in unexpected ways, such as the lesson that Scott taught the group. Students reflected about themselves as authors and as individuals, and I reflected about their unique personalities. I grew to appreciate each student's rich heritage through the stories they told. Similarly, as I related the short anecdotes I wrote to the class, my own fluttering heart reminded me how vulnerable fledgling authors of all ages feel when they share their writing with others. As I participated in every step of the writing process with my students, I learned from them the same lessons I sought to teach. I could only laugh when my husband read this chapter and commented to me, "You've become a much better writer." I knew whom to thank.

References

Gundlach, Susan. 1986. "Teaching Writing with Family Stories." *National Storytelling Journal* 3, no. 4: 17–20.

Harris, Joel Chandler. 1977. *Uncle Remus: His Songs and Sayings.* New York: Grosset & Dunlap.

Livo, Norma. 1984. "The Golden Spoon: Preserving Family History." *National Storytelling Journal* 1, no. 3: 8–10.

Murray, Donald. 1968. *A Writer Teaches Writing: A Practical Method of Teaching Composition.* Boston: Houghton Mifflin.

13

Learning on the Job: Whole Language in a Middle School Remedial Program

BETTY ANN SLESINGER

Looking for both meaning and well-being in my profession during eighteen years of middle school teaching, I have inched my way from English through reading to writing. I have found a whole language approach, encompassing and connecting all modes of communication, to be most compatible with my goals and practices. As my understanding of language and learning deepen, my classroom changes. And, because whole language expands the definition of "teacher" to include colleague, decision maker, learner, and researcher, I continue to find my own potential stretched. I have accepted these new roles and have come to value change. Becoming a researcher in my own classroom is an important change; exploring my observations through my writing is another. Thinking and writing about what's happened in my room help me to understand my successes, erase the indignities and frustrations of the day, and restore my calm and energy. Learning, as well as classroom success, makes teaching so rewarding.

Last school year, as I tried to understand a new group of students and fine-tune a curriculum to meet their needs and interests, I recognized that my teaching approach and my assignments were continually evolving. Of course my ultimate goal had always been student growth, but it had become increasingly clear that my changes influenced *our* learning. Despite my commitment to adapt, I was not consistently successful at it. Change was difficult and uneven. It is impossible to detail all of the interruptions, emotions, and problems that occurred with my classes; there was plenty of confusion, some wasted time, and even periods of hostility. But I did experience moments of insight and success, and, more important, so did the kids. I believe that positive accomplishments resulted because I learned and changed while on the job.

All of my middle school students had failed state writing tests, and most had very low reading scores as well. Although my classes usually numbered between ten and fifteen, some classes were in the midtwenties. Most of my students were unhappy about being scheduled for extra writing instead of their elected mini-courses. Besides losing electives, they were embarrassed about being singled out for a remedial class—one that was frequently a combination of sixth, seventh, and eighth graders. Often they reverted to unproductive roles that had previously helped them cope with their inadequacies. With little or no experience in the writing process, many children balked, expecting writing to be more penmanship and fill-in-the-blanks worksheets.

It was not just the kids' lack of writing experience that first overwhelmed me, it was their indifference to school learning. Not only had years of school repetition and failures contributed to their indifference, so had their home lives. Many of them were from unstable families, without models of school literacy, school values, or routines.

My children, like some students in all our classrooms, had to contend with a great deal in their lives that is beyond their control. Many had given up caring or trying. Certainly these kids did not need more drills and worksheets in grammar, usage, and rhetoric that had been so ineffective and unrewarding in the past. Overcoming their indifference became a priority. I wanted to do more than simply weather the year. To make any difference, it was essential to get in touch with the language and the experiences my kids enjoyed and felt comfortable with. I needed to build on their pastimes and friendships, to capitalize on their love of "juicy" gossip and their proud stories of dangerous deeds. I wanted to transfer to their drafts the lively language, so full of comparisons and fresh descriptions and real conversations, that I saw and heard in their journals, class discussions, and peer chatter. But what would work for them also had to be manageable for me.

While not all days were like this one, I have chosen to describe a day when my students were involved in different phases of a similar project. I have made this decision in order for the reader to get a sense of continuity for the entire experience.

The Day Begins

 ### First Period: Making the Most of My Prep Period

My schedule is an unusual one, not envied by many. Being assigned to a different school each quarter means lots of moving, reorganizing, and coping with newness. In addition, I work with more than three hundred students in one year. However, each school offers learning experiences that shape my notions of teaching.

It is an early morning in the last quarter, and I have recently arrived at my fourth and final school. I begin the six-period day in this new placement with a planning period. Because the rest of the day will be completely full, I am happy to have this early time to organize my resource cart and do any last-minute preparation. In addition, I sometimes use the ten-minute homeroom period to seek out and spend personal time with those of my kids who seem to be distant in class. Chatting one-to-one with them in the neutral area of an empty hallway is relaxed. They usually drop their "hard" classroom facades; I probably do, too. Often at these times, students will make a commitment to try harder. I make a commitment as well, to work on understanding life and learning from their perspective.

Occasionally during first period I browse in the library for books and articles that will interest the kids or that might work as the basis of a lesson—either one they have demonstrated they need, or one that I believe will help them with a future project. I want the reading and writing experiences to flow naturally together. A list of their interests, accumulated from their free-write entries, gives me ideas. I look for both fiction and nonfiction selections that not only are readable for them but that also illustrate qualities of good writing.

My prep period is also a good time to organize and send out pen pal letters. We had various pen pal projects last year. In the first quarter we wrote to students in my previous, out-of-state school district. Initially this was the most exciting arrangement since it seemed more exotic to the kids, but it proved to be least successful because of the difficulty in motivating and promoting replies from distant, inexperienced correspondents. In the second and third quarters, the students chose pen pals in an unusual way: they made "literary" choices on the basis of student pieces that appeared in the quarterly writing magazine(s) of my former classes at sister schools.

> I picked you out of a writing booklet from North that we had to read. I enjoyed reading your story about the beach. I've tried surfing before and about the 20th time you give up.
>
> I read your story [about your family] and your mother seems nice to me.
>
> I have two animals that are my favorites the shark and the monkey. Your piece about sharks interested me.
>
> I enjoyed reading your paragraph about your friendship with Amanda. I feel that friendship with a close friend is vital to success. I would be pleased if you wrote back.
>
> I liked your paragraph you wrote about hawks. . . . Your paragraph was good. . . . I like the way hawks land when they are looking for food. I saw a lot of [animal] paragraphs in your school's magazine. When are you going to write another one?

How exciting for these published authors to receive personal responses from a peer!

During the fourth quarter, a couple of my classes wrote to fifth graders who would be incoming middle school students in the fall. This arrangement also worked well since there was a timely purpose and my students could assume the role of the older authority. These letters seemed the most successful because students knew there was the genuine prospect they might meet each other. My students had information and advice to give; the fifth graders were eager for both. During the exchange, as personal data were included, friendships were established. Many of my students offered to meet their pen pals on the first day of the new school year and to act as guides or "big brothers" and "big sisters." Others invited their pen pals to write over the summer and included their addresses, phone numbers, and photos. A few enclosed their own drawings or embellished the stationery (Figure 13–1). Clippings of favorite hobbies or products accompanied a couple of letters. Over time, the amount of writing and attention to correctness increased.

Seeing the excitement in the letter exchanges helped me to appreciate the impact of real audiences on writers. My students anticipated the arrival of letters, read and reread them, and shared them with classmates and me. There were no complaints or goofing off during the writing of replies.

Time slips away during prep period. Before I know it I must collect my cart and push out into the hall, into the sudden mayhem of adolescents given three minutes to see friends, get the right books out of lockers, have drinks, make phone calls, and use bathrooms. Of course, friends take precedence.

 ## Second Period: The Interview Assignment— Sharing Student Writing

Just before the second-period class bell rings, I have scuttled down two hallways and arrived at my assigned classroom. While students pick up their color-coded folders from my cart, I usually put the class agenda on the board or on an overhead before the bell, hopeful that this will help provide the focus and organization my students need so badly. It should also alert them to the homework and materials they will need to have ready when the bell rings.

Today I begin second period by sharing booklets of classmate interviews "published" at a sister school. As readiness and motivation for their next project, their first activity is to skim through the pamphlets and write down the names and pages of some pieces that they like. Next, the students are invited to read carefully the three choices they think are best and justify their selection decisions. Excitement and interest are high as students read, perhaps about a cousin, or about someone they know from an old neighborhood, or about an athlete from an opposing team. Since the students from all four middle schools will be in high school together, kids in this class are eager to know what students from other areas are like. They are usually comforted by the similarities they find.

Shy and quiet Janie, who is sometimes on the verge of tears because of classmates' brusqueness and remarks, ventures that she likes the interview about

Figure 13—1   Sample letter to incoming student

May 17, 1988

Dear: Robert

Well, nice to meet you Robert. So you like girls. Do you have a girl friend? Let me give you some advice "when you get my age they start causeing you trouble and money." Do you like any thing else? I like to draw, and I am good arodamics. Arodamics are how things fly. I also design aircraft. I got a idea why don't we be penpals at home also that way we could keep in touch over the summer. I think me and you will get along. I forgot to ask you what type of music do you like? I like country music. Like Hunk Williams J.R. Well got to go. Oh yea there is a drawing to. By. my address is: 1911 Blue Ridge Terr. W.C.S.C. 29169

Your Friend,

Michelle. She whispers, "Well, I know Michelle and she is a little fat. Saying that she likes to eat tells you that, but won't make her feel bad." Ron, who is catching on to looking at the elements of good writing, as we have done with some overhead models, notices that "She used food in her ending because it was in the rest of the interview." Hyper Patrick relates to pieces that share his experiences or interests. Jiggling in his seat, he grins as he adds, "I'd go over to her house for dinner."

> One of my classmates is Michelle. Michelle is in the eighth grade. She has gone on many vacations, but her favorite trip was to Rossford, Georgia because it had many different things. Michelle's fondest hobby is cooking, simply because she likes to eat. I can just imagine her cakes, cookies, pies, and gingerbread boys. Michelle does not like music. She thinks that it is too loud and sounds alike. I have enjoyed interviewing Michelle and I hope she will invite me over to have one of her home cooked meals.

A couple of kids who take karate lessons believe that the interview with Sam shows that he is really good in martial arts, because the interview includes the color of the belts and the term *tae kwon do*. Rocky pauses after drawing a music group's emblem on his folder. As his leather-gloved hands rake his shoulder-length hair, he concedes, "This interview might make you want to get to know Sam."

> My friend Sam is new to the writing class. Sam is a boy that is easy going, tall and slim. He like "Kiss" a rock group. He like loud music and their lead singer. He has a cat name Tony that he had for about three years. Sam likes playing football and karate. He has won three karate bouts and is a blue belt in Tac Kwando. He want to be black belt in his own. I hope to know Sam better this years.

A third choice is Chris's interview of Denise. This assignment productively channeled for a brief period some of the constant social talk that Chris and Denise were always engaged in.

> I would like you to meet Denise (NEE-CEE is her homey name). She is intelligent but has a smart mouth. But that is why a lot of people like her because she speaks her mind. She is in seventh grade and has a boyfriend by the name of Kelly. He is in the 8th grade. She gets along very well with her family. Denise favorite foods are pizza and junk food. We have know each other for a long time and she is a very good friend.

"Ooo-ey," laughs Tawana, and so do a few others in the class who know Denise from an old neighborhood. "Nee-cee's mouth is loud and smart so that's really important about her, but he also tells that she's intelligent and has friends, too. So you know both sides to her."

Finally we look at Dan's interview with Daniel. Several kids point out that the paragraph begins and ends by naming Daniel, who is the subject of the piece.

> A friend of mine is Daniel. He enjoys activities like telling jokes and playing pranks. He doesn't like school but his friends are here. His best friend is Shane. Daniel thinks friends should have loyalty and humor with each other. His switchblade makes him proud and he collects things like all kinds of knives. It was nice finding out more about Daniel.

I am always impressed with the kind and supportive tone of these interviews. Here were the school's "toughest kids" writing and talking positively about classmates, who may not necessarily have been their friends.

Next, we begin to discuss real, professional interviews. What makes them good? Why do people seem to enjoy them so much? All the students are familiar with such TV interviewers as Oprah Winfrey and Phil Donohue. They are eager to share the other sources of interviews that they have read or watched, including those in popular music, sports programs, and publications. Anita, who is often absent or tardy because she has to get her younger siblings off or stay with one who is sick, believes that "everybody watches Oprah to find out about families and their problems and what people are doing about them." Dressed and polished like models, Chrissie and Stacy suddenly seem young when they giggle and nod in agreement that "rock interviews give you pictures of the cute guys and tell you what they do when they're not in a video or concert."

The students' interest in an assortment of characters is important for me. I know that next time I do this activity, I will have copies of interviews with popular celebrities to read and share. When working with actual interview examples in class, these students seem to understand the importance of using follow-up questions to find out what someone is really like or what he or she is thinking or feeling.

Yesterday, in this second-period class, we brainstormed together and made a list of possible interview questions. In addition, we reviewed a handout I made up that emphasizes the kinds of questions an interview should ask.

Today, on the overhead, I show a draft of an interview I did with a former student. Again I am impressed with the attention I get when I use examples of current student writing or, in this case, my own writing. This draft has errors and needs revision. Hands wave. They love correcting the teacher, and although many of them start out with surface features, they do explore language, content, and organizational problems. "Briartown is Briarton"; "You kept saying 'he likes'"; "The part about his job should be separate from the stuff about school"; "You told too much about his family. It's supposed to be about Gerald." We work on these changes together on the overhead.

After reading my sample over, the students make a list of three to five questions that they think I asked to be able to write my interview. Their list includes: "Do you have pets?"; "What is your family like?"; What do you do in your free time?" We discuss these and the kind of follow-up questions I probably asked. I take time to talk about the importance of asking good questions. They come to understand that they will need to ask questions when responding to other students' writing.

At this point in the project most of the students are able to begin to write a list of questions they think would elicit interesting information from a classmate. But even with the brainstorming questions on the board and the questions in the handouts, a few students still have trouble getting started. I have found that for the kids who need extra support, a sheet of actual questions other students have asked provides a sense of security.

As the end-of-the-period bell rings I quickly remind the kids, "Questions, including follow-ups, are due tomorrow so you can begin interviewing!"

 ## Third Period: Student Interaction and Notes for Interviews

My third-period class is supposed to be prepared with questions to begin their interviewing today. Some kids entering the classroom look at my homemade "Western Union telegram" copy on the overhead with curiosity. They think I have forgotten the interview preparations and begin to chastise me. "Miss, you said we'd do our interviews," says Amanda, who is one of the few kids who regularly comes prepared to class. Kim has begun to sulk because she's been counting on sitting with her friend Cindy for interviewing. "What's that, Teach?" questions Joey as he literally slides around the corner of the door while the bell rings. I point to the class agenda, now completed and boxed off on the board. Then I ask them to make a prediction of how we'll use the overhead transparency. "We're going to send a telegram to someone like the president" and "You got this telegram from your kid" are a couple of their assumptions.

Before responding to their inferences we discuss how we will gather the replies our interview partners give. Because of the nature of the interview assignment, students discover the need to jot down their partners' responses. In the course of this engagement, the students develop skill in capturing the essence of a message or conversation. I teach key words for note taking as "telegram words"—specific nouns, strong verbs, sentences that send the "message." Unnecessary words are dropped in telegrams, since the sender pays for length. The overhead telegram sample makes this point nicely. I show them a few standard abbreviations and a couple of my own strategies for speedy note taking. They enjoy designing and sharing some of their own, too.

While students are experimenting with abbreviations, I invite them to put their best three on the board to share with the class and I begin to make a quick check of their interview questions. While circulating, I help them group together related questions. "Couldn't you group basketball, skateboarding, and biking together under the idea of sports or free time?" "What do cleaning up the kitchen and folding laundry have in common?" Putting a letter or star next to related questions provides the organizational support they need and facilitates the production of a cohesive text. When ready for a partner, they draw numbers from a prepared envelope.

Now students with matching numbers get together in assigned locations around the room to talk and write together. Although there is some hesitancy in this imposed intimacy, they love the opportunity for interaction, and with the very specific assigned tasks and the limited audience, most engage successfully.

As I wander among the animated pairs I hear popular questions like "Who's your favorite group?"; "What pets do you have?"; "What do you think about this school/writing class?" Some kids move beyond the typical areas to more personal questions. "Who do you live with?" queries Keith, a kid who has not attempted nor participated in any activity up to now. I later learn Keith lives with his aged grandparents; his mother lives about a hundred miles away, and his dad never comes around. "Why do you like Will?" inquires Missy about Jolene's boyfriend. "Willy treats me like I'm somebody and he's always there for me," replies Jolene, the same girl who usually seems to be looking through me to the clock. "Does your family get along?" asks Lucinda, curious about whether everyone's family life is as disconcerting as hers.

Snippets of other conversations tell me a lot about my kids' life problems. Their candor adds legitimacy to the interview assignment. "It's important for me to do well this year at school 'cause I've already stayed back once," reveals Anita, who does good work when she's in school. Already old enough to work part time, she's often out late. Although she does know a high school diploma is important, "nobody in my family finished so I might drop out." "This school ought to do something for the kids who don't get any demerits for the whole year," complains Sean. This good-looking young man with nice manners and personality has learned the school routine and rules well. However, he has no strategies for generating and developing writing ideas or for planning his pieces, and he can't spell many basic sight words yet.

While the kids in this remedial writing class are quite diverse, their laughter and chatter reflect common interests and emerging bonds. Despite minor frustrations with this assignment, they are involved and seem to enjoy the interviewing. I, too, am immersed in the activity. The bell rings before we have rearranged the desks. I must pack up quickly if I am to reach my next class in an opposite wing on time.

Fourth Period: Supporting the Writing

After settling into this fourth-period class, I am pleased to find most students have prepared notes from yesterday's interview questions and are now ready to write their drafts. They know they will need rough copies to take to the computer lab tomorrow. While I couldn't have said this at the beginning of the year, I now understand how valuable it is that my classes have at least two forty-five-minute periods per week in a computer lab with individual word-processing stations. Computers are at the heart of my middle school remedial writing program. (See Figure 13–2, A, B, and C.) Knowing that revision would not require tedious rewriting, the kids have felt free to take risks and really explore refining their meanings.

Although we have been through the same preliminary steps as my second- and third-period classes, I start by displaying on the overhead a well-developed interview about a student named Jody. I distribute a dittoed guide to accompany this piece. Reading the interview several times aloud, students start to fill in questions on the guide, such as "What words describe how Jody looks and acts?" and "What sentences are included in the ending?". Most of the class contributes to the ensuing discussion because they have first jotted down some ideas and details and can confidently refer to them. For example, Alicia and Matt mention

Figure 13–2   The computer lab. A: Ricky involved in his writing. B: Kendrick using a dictionary.
C: Working partners.

A

B

C

"Jody's brown hair with a spike, blue eyes and tall height." Lester says, "Jody must be active because of all the sports he mentions, like swimming in his friend's pool and motor cross trail practice."

With their notes and other relevant resources to guide them, the students begin their own pieces. For the power of writing to take hold, my kids need the interest and confidence to start, which requires tapping into the energy of their lives. I move around the room, reading over students' shoulders and giving encouragement, pausing to help when a class member is not writing or seems frustrated. I try to give assurances that they all have something worth saying. I tell Dwayne, a slow but gentle kid hunched over his scrawling writing, that I like his second paragraph because he has shown how his partner feels about his family. He looks up with a broad grin. I move on to Steve, staring out the window, breaking the nub from the end of his pencil rather than using it. On being questioned, he says he learned that his interview partner "bikes a lot." I reply, "You know a lot about special moves on your skateboard yourself. Go back over to your partner and get him to explain his bike tricks for you so you can write more about that subject." I move among them—confirming, questioning, and suggesting—to keep them on task and trying.

I have come to see that the real reward of having conferences with the students is the environment we create. When learners are immersed in a process that is responsive to their interests and needs, they begin to follow the affirming and coaching lead. Some students use their neighbors as sounding boards: "Would you listen to me read my story?" Terry asks Susan. Although unsure of their abilities to help one another, both of these girls find real help and comfort in working together. During the reading of her "Childhood Memory" piece about a trip to Six Flags, Terry is able to change a few verbs for consistency and add a line that clears some confusion about staying over for another day at the park. By supporting each other, these partners generate ideas and accomplish revisions that neither could do alone.

Other kids have become more confident through conferences, and they then begin to offer help, teach skills and strategies, and hold informal conferences among themselves. After Sharon learns how to punctuate quotations in her story about helping her sick mother, she slides her chair next to Angel's to show her how to write the dialogue in her piece about ordering and eating at Pizza Hut. Hardworking Ron shows the boys at neighboring terminals in the computer lab how he puts a question mark after a word he can't spell when he can't locate it in the Spellex. He goes further and transfers this strategy to the classroom, circling words that he is unsure of as he drafts. I share this helpful adaptation with all my classes. During such moments, the remedial writing class becomes both a writing workshop and a learning community.

Fifth Period: Working from the Kids' Interests and Needs

The eighth graders in my fifth-period class all know each other, having spent almost a year together in remedial math and reading; the interview assignment, then, would not serve much of a purpose. Instead, our first full writing-process activity is an opinion piece about a favorite song. The students are at different stages of their writing about selected songs. Those kids who have completed the assignment are now reading Xeroxes of other finished pieces in order to make a graph of the most popular class songs. We will then send a copy of the chart to other classes and publish one in the school newspaper. At the same time stragglers continue writing their rough drafts. A couple of kids, again without their materials, attempt to borrow song lyrics from classmates. Those students who haven't yet put their final copies on the word processor go to the lab to work as guests in another class. (A fellow teacher and I alternate taking in members from each other's class when there is room.)

Meanwhile, Michele lists on the board the song titles that are the subjects of the completed opinion pieces. Students come up and sign under the titles for copies of the ones that they like. Some want to give extra copies to friends and relatives. I reproduce fifty or more, and, for a couple of days, kids excitedly read and share them throughout the halls and lunchrooms. Remarkably, every student in this challenging class eventually does some version of this assignment!

All the kids *wanted* to participate. What's more, they made an effort to be accurate and correct. In fact, some students in other classes who found out about the song paragraphs worked on similar pieces during our after-school computer hour. Obviously, it was an assignment very much connected to my students' lives and *their* purposes for reading and writing.

 Sixth Period: Authentic Reasons to Write and Real Audiences

Sixth period, and although the growing fatigue of the day is catching up to me, I look forward to an enjoyable class. Because of several days of standardized testing for sixth and eighth graders, only four seventh-grade students are with me. Instead of starting the interview project without the full class, we are making a school guide for incoming sixth graders. The idea really evolved from a conversation during which we considered having the fifth graders as our pen pals. One of my perceptive and outspoken pupils, Deliah, had said, "There's too much to tell them about the school in a letter. We'd have to write our hands off." So, after some discussion, we decided to make a handout for them and include it with our letters.

We meet in the computer lab. Each seventh grader in this miniclass anticipates drafting a section for the guide based on one of four subjects raised during our brainstorming sessions: building, schedule, rules, or activities. Having already learned the basic functions of the word processor through the use of a commercial sentence-combining program, these kids are eager to get started. They jump in with little hesitation, even though they are not fluent typists. The process enables them to discover ways of both organizing their notes and learning more about the practical functions of the word processor. The paragraphs develop quickly. The ease of revision delights them.

Tony, a repeating sixth grader who often dozes in the classroom, never wants to change or cut anything from a draft. Suddenly, he begins to understand the power of the word processor and becomes alert and interested. He questions, "You mean I just press delete and it's clear? It takes my mistakes away? It will make a space for me to add that right in there and won't mess up the rest?" Ashley, thinking that she wants her piece to be good if other kids are to read it, chimes in, "If I think of something I want to change tonight, it will still be here and I can write it the next time we come, right?"

The kids are free to concentrate on their content because they know they can fix the errors later. By the end of the period each student has a draft printed out that we will respond to tomorrow. But, excited and satisfied with these first attempts, they snatch their pieces from the printer and immediately share with each other before being reminded to slip them into class folders. Then they clamor for copies to take home.

Deliah's rough draft shows the organizational planning she did as she helped her classmate who was working with the activities topic. Portions of her finished copy are very readable and cohesive, with a strong voice and unity (Figure 13–3, A and B).

Figure 13–3   Deliah's work. A: Rough draft. B: Finished copy.

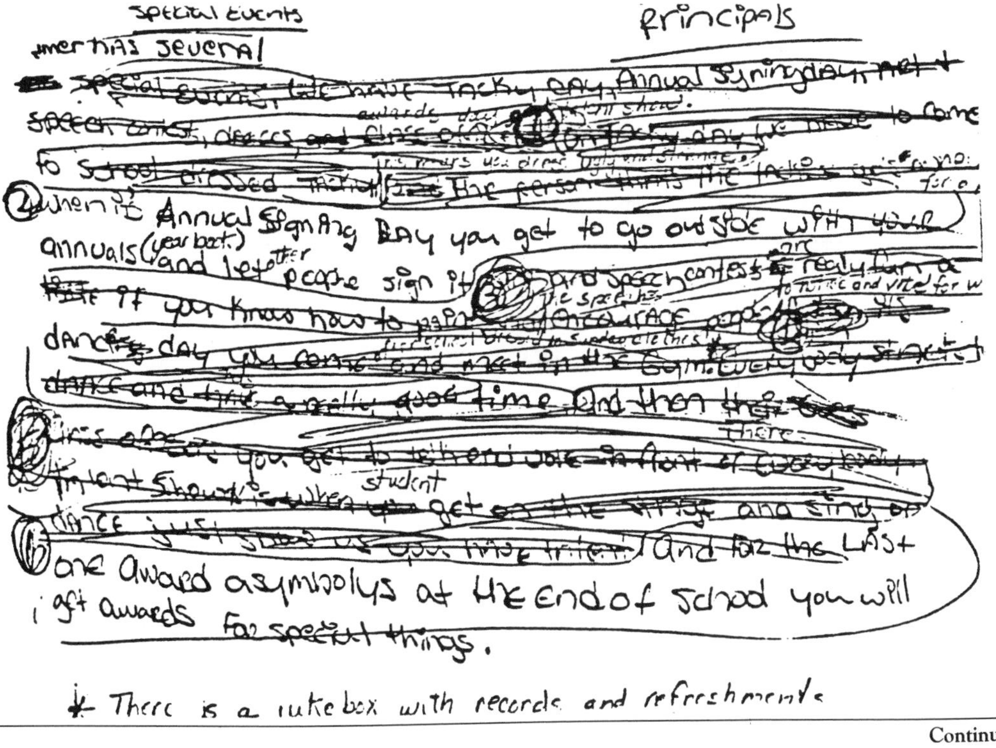

A

Continued

Figure 13—3   Continued

RULES·

This school is stricter than ever with more kids in the teenage years
They try to do more things like smoke, steal,do drugs and more.

We no longer have stay-in's. We have the demerit system — as many as the
teacher wants you to have depending on what you have done. Also in this school
we have In School-Suspension and Out Of School- Suspensiondepending on how many
demerits you get. In School Suspension means you don't get to go to any other
classes,you only have to be in one room all day even if there are special
events. Your class work and extra drill practice is sent there. You even
have to eat in there. Out Of School Suspension means you get kicked out of
school and it's hard to make up all your work and you can't participate
in activities.

Our school may sound strict but they need the rules because of what some
students do. Our school isn't bad after all .

When it's Dancing Time you come after school dressed in your
Sunday clothes and meet in the gym .There is a jukebox with records and
refreshments.Then everyone starts to dance. Now on Tacky Day we have to come
to school dressed "tacky". This means you dress ugly and strange. And the

B   person that is the tackiest gets money for. a prize.

The school guide the four seventh-grade students make is terrific. Their
articles are accurate and interesting. Their special cover and the graphics they
have embedded in their booklet make for an inviting text. Instead of including
them in their pen pal letters, the counselor has decided to run off 225 copies and
distribute them to all fifth graders during their orientation visit to the middle
school. Quite an audience and a lot of author pride!

The Computer as Support

As I think about today's experiences, I realize again how I initially under-estimated the impact the computer would have on our curriculum. The computer prompted me to focus on my students' work, interests, and needs. It also helped the students focus on their work: its features and processes enticed them to start; it matched their varied paces; it worked with them without stress or hostility. It made their work legible and helped them correct their errors. The hand and eye activity calmed the active kids and engaged the lethargic ones. Once drawn in, they frequently became aware of their own ideas and thinking. For some kids it seemed to be the start of controlling their own thoughts and of planning when writing. The word processor carried these writers through the hard parts so they could participate in the success of publishing and sharing.

The computer has also made a positive impression on the parents of these remedial students. The adults think it is wonderful for remedial kids to have access to new technology and to learn how to use computers. It is more important to me, however, that the shared printouts have increased parents' awareness of their children's writing efforts and of their feelings and ideas. Now, because mothers and fathers can easily read the neat print, they pay attention to their students' thoughts. At PTA conferences many parents are visibly impressed with the competent look of the final texts in their children's folders and the number of rough and printed drafts. Parents begin to notice their children's success. A few parents have asked for copies of special pieces to send to relatives; several mothers were touched by family stories.

> I admire my mom because she is so loving and strong. What I mean is that when I am sick she take's care of me and gives me love. When I said she was strong I ment that she can have the most bad luck and she still does not give up. That's why I admire my mom.

> The person I want to write about is my grandfather. My grandfather is the best carpenter I have ever seen. Only a pro carpenter could be better than him. My grandfather has a work shop that has a lot of tools and when I work on my bike I use his tools. He sometimes gets mad at me because I do not put his tools back in the same place. But when my grandpop gets mad, he does not stay mad. After that, him and me will go out for looking for cans for me to sell. My grandfather and I get along real well.

> There are some things about my uncle that are special. His name is Uncle David. He lives in Charlotte. I only get to see him much in the summer. These are some things I like about him. When I need some hugs I write and tell him. Uncle David is the only one that said he loves me. In the summer he comes and talks to me about my problems. Uncle David comes if I have any more problems on the weekend. My uncle is the nicest one on earth that is in my family.

> I didn't like the two days I spent in Richland Memorial because grandma was very sick. I hated those two days because they were lonely and dark. My grandma looked so

helpless lying there on the bed. Her hands and feet were cold. She couldn't move because she hurt....I wished that I were in the hospital instead of her. I wished it could have been me instead. She looked like she was close to death, but later we learned that she wasn't....On the third day the doctor told me and daddy she could come home, but she needed someone to stay with her. And I did.

Personal Reflection

A year ago, when I met my first class of rowdy, uncooperative, "at risk" students, I felt like an outsider. Glancing at their writing samples left me with an overwhelming feeling of helplessness. I doubted that anything positive would grow from this teaching situation. I might have been done in by all the problems connected with remedial learners and by my itinerant schedule. But my introduction to whole language offered an intimacy and meaning that was real for all of us. When I provided authentic language experiences, some of my students seemed to float a little freer, and some even ventured out on their own. As I learned about my students' lives through their writing and our conversations, we were no longer strangers. We had touched each others' lives. Rather than impossible, the job proved to be rewarding.

References

Olsen, M., D. Kirby, and G. Hulme, eds. 1982. *The Writing Process.* Boston: Allyn and Bacon.

14

"I Have Never Read Five Books Before in My Life": Reading and Writing Naturally in High School

DONELLE BLUBAUGH

This chapter is the story of how B. J. and Helen became poets, how Ella's curiosity was satisfied, how Eric got to be marvelous, and how Marianne killed the grade grinch. It has several endings, not all of them happy: Adam never fulfilled his contract, I think Rob is *still* in internal suspension, and Deke never did write an opinion about the legalization of drugs. All the same, we got to June without manufacturing a single pop quiz or teaching the five-paragraph essay. If Middlebury Union High School were a Hollywood movie set, the alumni of Marianne Dalton's third-period 10B English class would be filling out Ivy League college applications. In real life, they read some books. Wrote some stuff. Big deal. You bet.

The Setting

MUHS is a small high school located in Middlebury, Vermont, with about seven hundred students in grades nine through twelve. It's a union high school: its students come from five separate rural communities with independent elementary schools and junior high schools. They are the sons and daughters of Middlebury College professors and town professionals, and the sons and daughters of the dairy farmers and loggers of the surrounding Green Mountains. It's two schools, really: one offers the "A," or college preparatory, curriculum for academic go-getters, with their sights set on Ivy League careers; the other provides the "B," or general, curriculum for students who might have been up at 4:00 A.M. to work on the area's dairy farms, who might be the first members of their families to earn high school diplomas. This dichotomy operates in a context common to most high schools in the country: limited money, limited time, limited space, and the almost overwhelming facts and vagaries of adolescence.

What happens in Room E-1 between 10:10 and 10:50 for twelve tenth-grade "B-level" students is the product of community demographics, the realities of high school, and the efforts of Marianne Dalton to give the lie to limits, overcome the forty-minute-barrier, and invite a disparate group of sophomores to become readers and writers on their own terms. My contribution as a reading consultant is to help Marianne design reading and writing activities that make sense for her students, that help them to develop habits common to people who are good readers, and that allow them to realize the personal and social functions of print.

The physical and temporal environment that supports literacy for these students is difficult to describe. There is no ownership of space in a high school. The room that houses twenty Shakespearean scholars during one period is an American studies classroom during the next, and a study hall following that. In her room, Marianne teaches four different courses and monitors a study hall. The learning stations and activity centers that help many elementary school teachers organize individualized programs are impossible in a room through which perhaps more than a hundred students and several teachers will pass at forty-minute intervals. Teachers, students, computers, and materials must all be portable.

One day I walked into E-1 to find only two students present. Jo sat in her corner between the bookshelf and a file cabinet reading a novel. Deke was perched on the heat register with a *Time* magazine on his knees. Neither student heard my "Where is everyone?", so intent were they on their reading. Once my voice penetrated, I learned that Marianne was in three places at once: after setting up one group of students for a revision session in the computer lab and seeing Joy off to the nearby elementary school for her read-aloud project with a third-grade student, Marianne had taken another group to the local bookstore to buy books. One each. To read. To keep. Or share.

On another day I might work with some students in the classroom while Marianne takes the fishermen and carpenters from our group to see a display of boats and decoys at the Vermont Folklife Center. Or I join students in the computer lab who are collaborating on a letter to the principal requesting funds for a field trip (the students have developed the budget) while Marianne confers with Rod about his reading of *The Loneliness of the Long Distance Runner* (Sillitoe 1959).

We lose some days to accident and circumstance. The portable computer arrives on time, but the printer doesn't, and by the time it's located we discover an absent-minded student left the data disk at home. B. J. and Helen are ready to publish their poetry collection at the same moment the photocopier issues its death rattle. Ron has just finished reading *Heart of Darkness* (Conrad 1981) and asks the kinds of questions about Kurtz that make an English teacher's heart sing. Neither Marianne nor I have read the book for years. When we suggest he arrange a conference with another teacher who recently taught the novel in a world literature course, Ron asks if Marianne really has a degree in English.

My Role as Reading Consultant

I teach three classes of my own, work individually with several students on a regular basis, others per request, and help other teachers in the building plan for students with special needs. I'm not able to attend Marianne's third-period class every day. She and I examine a student's writing in the three minutes between lunch and someplace else, discuss appropriate books for Eric in the hallway while I keep one eye on my study hall. A five-minute discussion in the faculty room on the use of fairy tales to promote knowledge of story structure leads to a two-week unit on Arthurian legends. I leave a poem that connects to themes in the novel *Walkabout* (Marshall 1984) in Marianne's mailbox. During faculty meetings, we pass notes about how to get Jo to the New England Young Writers' Conference.

Marianne fosters our working relationship by asking the right questions. Not once has she asked me to administer tests to students to determine reading levels or to apply readability formulas to a text. Her questions are guided by her close watch on her students' reactions and responses: How can I help B. J. get more involved? I think Eric is ready to try a novel. Can you think of a title he might like? When is the right time to help Jo edit her poems? My role has become one of supporting Marianne's efforts to provide a curriculum informed by the needs of her students, in spite of the expectations of the school structure.

One day toward the end of a marking period she came to me, grade book in hand. "Look at this. What am I going to do? There are no grades to average. They've been reading and loving it. I don't want to ask them to do book reports, but what am I going to do about grades?"

In the twenty seconds I have to consider the beautiful irony of Marianne's dilemma, I think of Nancie Atwell's descriptions of her efforts to create in her classroom the same environment that invites friends and family to discuss books around the dinner table (Atwell 1987). I ask, "What do you and I do after we've read a good book?" An authentic curriculum emerges as Marianne considers how to invite her students to respond to their reading in natural ways. Their responses won't be graded according to a number of correct answers, but evaluated according to each student's efforts to share an experience.

Marianne didn't start the school year with individual or small groups of students working on separate projects in various parts of the building. She began with the common reading of the novel *Walkabout* (Marshall 1984) and a project—designing and producing a school activities calendar to be distributed to students and their parents—that required each student to share in its creation. It takes time to develop the trust that makes it possible for a teacher to be three places at once.

The year-end examinations for this group of twelve students provide the best illustrations of ways students can be encouraged to involve themselves in reading and writing. Because Marianne and I are concerned with helping students demonstrate their learning through activities related to their classroom experiences, a test on course content is inappropriate. During most of the fourth marking period students have been involved in a variety of individual projects. The only thing to do is personalize the exam—use the scheduled examination period to invite students to tie up loose ends, reflect on their learning, and perhaps share the products of that learning with their classmates. Twelve students. Twelve exams.

Eric

This is Eric's exam:

> You are a star. I can't tell you how proud of you I am. What is more important is that you should be proud of yourself. You committed two periods a day to English and reading. Wow!!!! Have a great summer and let me know what you read. If you run out of things to read, please write or call me at home. —Mrs. Dalton

> 1. Finish your page for the class book. What you need to do is polish the writing you have already done and explain why you like to read books about friendship, good times, bad times...
>
> 2. Pick your two favorite characters from two different books. Have them meet each other on the street and imagine what they would talk about. What questions would they ask? What words would they use?
>
> 3. Write a letter to me explaining what you have really enjoyed doing this year. What have you learned about yourself? What have you learned about others? Talk about your reading, the class trips, the class discussions...
>
> 4. Write a page about being an outsider.

Marianne's invitation to Eric to continue to talk about his reading with her during the summer typifies their exchanges throughout the school year. Eric is a quiet, some would say brooding, boy. A loner, and sometimes the object of derision among other students in the school, he found it hard to communicate his thoughts and feelings in writing or speech. When asked what he thought of a story, his usual response was, "It was boring." Why? "It just is." When told that something he wrote was good or interesting, he would deflect the compliment with "No, it isn't, it's stupid."

We knew that Eric, like most of his classmates, was capable of reading and responding with feeling to that reading. But he was reluctant to involve himself and bring his opinions to public attention in the classroom. We knew that if we could match the boy with a book we would be on our way to helping Eric develop the habit of reading. By asking the right question—What have you read before or heard read aloud that you really liked?—we were able to make a match that kept Eric on automatic pilot for nine weeks. He asked for books about gangs and fighting. We dusted off worn and, to us, dated copies of the S. E. Hinton novels and gave him time to read.

Eric frequently spent two class periods a day in Marianne's classroom. During third period he participated in class activities and assignments. Later, when he would ordinarily attend a study hall, he came back to read. He was not asked to keep a journal or comment formally on his reading. We monitored his involvement through casual conversation—How far did you get? Do you like it? How'd it go today? Eric needed to develop a personal relationship with print before he could be pressed to bring his responses to the social arena of the classroom.

Later, when Eric began asking for more books like *The Outsiders* (Hinton 1967), we began asking him to write brief reactions to his reading, then to venture explanations for his opinions. By the end of the school year Eric is still reluctant to voice his opinions to anyone but Marianne. However, she invites him to take one more risk by asking him to revise a piece of writing that will be included in a booklet containing examples of the work of each student in the class to be published and distributed to the class. She quotes words from his rough draft (friendship, good times, bad times) to get him started. Eric's page for the class yearbook is full of humor and honesty: "Over the last eight weeks, I have been reading books called *Snow Dog*, *Rumblefish*, *The Outsiders*, *That Was Then*, *This Is Now*, and I'm reading a book called *Hot Rod*. The things that the books meant to me are a good grade in class and knowing that I have never read five books before in my life." He signs his final exam "The Marvelous One (Eric)."

Ella

Ella's final exam acknowledges the challenging reading choices she made and her efforts to deal with difficult questions and issues through literature:

What can I say? You have done a wonderful job this year in English. You have pushed yourself and me! There is hardly anything left to do except applaud your many accomplishments. Call me at home if you run out of books to read over the summer.

1. Imagine that Elie Weisel and Anne Frank meet. Create their conversation.
2. Write a letter to Ms. Blubaugh explaining all you have done, learned, and thought about this year.
3. Write a letter to the world explaining your feelings about prejudice. Base this on your reading this semester. The people of the world are selfish and egocentric. Make them feel prejudice, loneliness, fear . . .

We did not have to coax Ella into books. The challenge was to find ways to indulge her curiosity about titles usually reserved for "A" curriculum reading lists and help her develop self-confidence to match her curiosity. After a class reading of Elie Weisel's *Night* (Weisel 1982) Ella became interested in issues of civil rights and human suffering. At the same time, she became ready to progress in her writing from personal response toward exposition. How could we help her maintain her interest in reading, take on the challenge of longer, more difficult books, and examine the meanings of those books through her own writing?

Help came in the form of Whitman Knapp, a volunteer tutor from Middlebury College who met with Ella at least once a week to work with her on a close reading of *The Heart Is a Lonely Hunter* by Carson McCullers (1953). Since Ella read every day but saw the tutor only once a week, letter writing emerged as a natural vehicle for communicating about the novel and related issues. Through letters, Ella could record her immediate concerns about her reading—confusing passages, difficult vocabulary—as well as share her reactions and feelings with an authentic and trusted audience. Whitman monitored Ella's understanding and provided contextual information to ease her struggle with the dense text.

When the tutor returned to his home at the close of the college semester, his correspondence with Ella continued. His letters provided an excellent demonstration for Ella about how to write about literature (Figure 14–1).

The letter in Figure 14–1 acknowledges the validity of Ella's sometimes unsophisticated observations (Scout does not act like a "normal girl") while inviting her to think harder and deeper. (What are the similarities between *To Kill a Mockingbird* [Lee 1982] and *The Heart Is a Lonely Hunter* [McCullers 1953]?) In her response (Figure 14–2), Ella accepts the challange and works hard to emulate the tutor's analysis while maintaining the informality of a letter.

For her page in the class yearbook, Ella contributed quotations from her letter to the tutor with scenes from both novels illustrated by a classmate.

Figure 14-1   The tutor's letter to Ella

June 2, 1988

Dear Ella,

I am very glad to hear that you are enjoying <u>To Kill A Mockingbird</u>. It is a super book and, if you ever get the chance to see it, the movie is really good too. Harper Lee's novel raises many of the same issues as Carson McCullers' <u>The Heart is a Lonely Hunter</u>.

You said that you really like Scout, so let's take a look at her — and ask more of those bizarre questions that I usually write in the margins of your papers: You observe that Scout is not considered a girl — and that she does not act like a "normal girl." This seems to be an important aspect of her character. Why does she not want to act or be like a girl? What might change (her image of herself, her ability to behave in certain ways) if she were to act like a girl? Perhaps most important — and you can look for this as you read — is the way that Scout changes between the beginning and the end of the novel.

I am interested in the similarities between McCullers' and Lee's books. Maybe you have already noticed some

Continued

Figure 14–1   **Continued**

of these. The most important similarit
is the way both novels deal with
racism. How does each author look
at this? A tough question: what are
the similarities and differences
between the two approaches?

One way to compare the two novels
is to look at the characters. How are
Scout and Mick Kelly similar, for
example? How are they different? Can
you compare Boo Radley to anyone in
The Heart...? Which of McCullers'
characters would sympathize with Boo,
and why? Last question (but important)
would Atticus side with Jake or Dr.
Copeland in their argument (McCullers
pp. 258-262) about the best way to achieve
equality for blacks? Why?

How is that for a million questions?
You certainly do not have to answer
them all, but if you keep them in
mind while you are reading, you might
reach some interesting conclusions!

Thank you for writing. I really enjoyed
reading your observations about To Kill A
Mockingbird. I would like to say, again,
what a pleasure it was to read Carson
McCullers with you this spring, Ella.

I hope you have a wonderful (reading)
summer.
                  Sincerely,
                     Whitman.

Figure 14-2   Ella's response

Whitman,   June 6, 88

   I don't really like to write letters
with, Hi, how are you?, ect. so I will
just go into answering the bizarre
questions you asked.
   Scout doesn't want to act like a
girl because Jem picks on her about it.
She hates to be picked on or made out
to be a Fool. there's one thing that I
could add that she might agree with,
that girls can't do as much as a
boy all dressed up in dresses all the
time. If she where to act More like
a girl she wouldn't be able to wear
pants as much, Fight with Walter Cunningham,
or play boyish games with Jem and Dill.
She would have to act more like a young
Lady not a tomboy.
   Racism is a big thing in both books. The
Negros. in To kill A Mockingbird, are well as In The Heart....
at the bottom of the heap As. The
Differences on the approach of racism are
very much the Same, they both seem to say
Negros are dirt or just about that low.
The Similarities on the approach of

Continued

Figure 14-2   **Continued**

racism are so great that I'm only going
to say a few. Like you can do just about
anything to a r   . and not have to
be bothered by the law, (that's only if your
a white person going against a Negro).
On the other hand if a Negro where
to do something to a white person, He/
she would be shot or thrown in jail.
Scout Finch and Mick Kelly are similar by
the way they are girls acting like tom-
boys. Doing everything a boy would do.
wearing pants and playing with boys not
girls. Scout doesn't really have any girls
to play with at home. kelly has two sisters,
but they were older and to grownup to play.
   Oh, Boo Radley: He can be compared to
two people, Singer and Biff (the Bar tender).
With Singer because he's quiet and somewhat talks with body Motions. With Biff
because he comes out at night. And is alone most of the time.
They each like the night time. They each
Feel More Comfortable in the dark and
alone. that's only because Boo was
shut up for so long by himself in the
dark, that he has gotten used to it.

Figure 14-2   Continued

I would call your last question a mind bender. I would think Atticus would agree with Dr Copeland because he said that you should go with Morethanyourself. (If your goiin to help a Negro He would or should go with the Idea of Copeland because at the result, of what happened in the trial. He tryed to go in to the trial by himself and lost. (I think he would have won, if Tom hadn't of tryed to run away and gotten shot).

I like your letter it was full of things that I could actually think about. Oops! I answered all of your questions. I think I should have told you that I finished the book 2 days ago, and watched the movie today. I'll keep the questions in my thoughts as I also answer Questions from Dalton.

Thanks for your letter, Most college helpers would have just forgotten to answer a letter sent to them. Not you. I like that. I got to go and answer some of Mis. Dalton's Questions.

Ella T.

Helen and B. J.

I am hard-pressed to explain how Helen and B. J. became poets. I asked them, but they couldn't tell me. It might have been an outgrowth of some indolent browsing through books I brought to class, appreciation for a shorter form, divine inspiration, or the influence of Jo Billings, an award-winning student poet in the class. I tend to think it was a combination of all of the above—and Marianne's refusal to give up issuing invitations to write poetry in response to in-class or personal reading.

Helen's attitude toward school is generally one of limited tolerance. She has applied to attend our district's alternative high school program. While she is a competent reader, her preference is for real-life drama rather than fiction, and until recently writing was an academic exercise to be endured. B. J. has experienced little graded success in school, is not a fluent or enthusiastic reader or writer, and was reluctant to leave the safety of factual questions and answers behind. Helen's lack of participation and B. J.'s problems with reading and writing were frustrating. When other students in the class were able to generate their own projects and assignments, these two hung back. Attempts to match them with books as we did with Eric were futile, and efforts to satisfy their curiosity through literature, as we were able to do with Ella, got us nowhere.

Then, almost overnight it seemed, Helen developed an interest in copying bits of poetry and prose that meant something to her—song lyrics and passages from a contemporary interpretation of the Bible. Marianne and I tried to take advantage of this interest by suggesting, ever so casually, poets and collections that might be appealing to a sixteen-year-old girl about to develop a personal relationship with print: Nikki Giovanni, Hugh Prather, *Reflections on a Gift of Watermelon Pickle* (Dunning et al. 1966), *Some Haystacks Don't Even Have Any Needles* (Dunning et al. 1969). Again, our invitations and inquiries were informal and undemanding: You might like to try this; What did you think?; You can write poems as good as these, you know.

Helen browsed for days. And since she and B. J. usually sat together, they browsed together. Their careers as poets were launched when Marianne gave them a collection of depression-era photos and asked them to consider the possibility of doing some descriptive writing, perhaps cinquains—a form they were familiar with from descriptive writing practice in the fall. Something in those photographs of weathered faces and hungry children struck a chord and inspired probably thirty short poems.

> Sitting in the open field,
> On my blanket near my car,
> I play my guitar to the sound of the birds.
> As my friends listen to me play,
> I start fading away.

Figure 14–3   Helen and B. J. collaborate during a poetry-editing session

One weekend Helen went with her family to Connecticut to see the circus. She came back with brochures and posters, chattering about the color and excitement and fun. This time when Marianne suggested a poem there were no groans.

Circus

Bright colors,
Excitement,
Laughter,
Death defying,
So much to see,
But not enough time.

Huddled at their desks or at a computer terminal, their collaboration was complete (Figure 14–3). I overheard them conferring about word choices, reading aloud to test the sound of a line, discussing the merits of a comma here or a period there. Their joint final exam validated and celebrated their partnership.

You are a dynamic duo. I am so impressed with the poems that you have written this quarter. So many and so wonderful.

1. Finish your page for the class book.
2. Finish your poetry book.
3. Write a letter to each other about your poems and writing them. What has this meant to you? Why are you so successful at writing poems?

Here is B. J.'s response to the exam:

Dear Helen,

I had fun working with you on the poems. I thought that once we strared going on them we really did something with them. I think that we should try and keep up with the tring to write poems. I learned alot about how to get along woth one other when you are trying to work together. I know that when we got where it did't make any sences you could always help get out of that prouble. I think that you and I could always agree on the words that we would use and if we didn't like it we would just say so. Think that when one of was out sick we wouldent do anything because we would think that the other one would get made at what we wrote so we didn't do anything at all. Again I really had fun working with you on this.

Hanging form the clothes line looking at the ground,
I laugh and laugh because I think that Iam going to fall down.
Waiting there for someone to take me down,
I wait there for hours.
After waiting for hours I finily fall down,
I stand up and say "is any one going to come around".
As I wait for someone to come around,
I keep waling the ground.
When Iam walking the ground I look up and see people coming around.
I say to them "that it is about time someone comes around".
I told them what had happen,
Then they hung me up side down.

Helen's letter to B. J. (written on the word processor) expresses her pleasure with herself and their joint effort.

Hi BJ

Well another year is gone and this english class has been a good one. The poems were good exspecially the one about sitting on the porch and sleeping. This second half of the year has been great I loved writing poems, maybe we were meant to write poems. Well next year I won't be in your English class unless I stay in regular school I'm thinking about it I have the summer to decide. If I do we will have to get together to write some poems. Well thats all have to write, but this year has been great and meant alot to me and I'll remember this year. The poems were great they have meant alot to me.

Your friend always,
Helen

Donald

Helping students become readers and writers on their own terms often means accepting what our students view as valuable, even when they contradict our own beliefs. A biologist invited to speak to the class about the problems she faced as part of a team of scientists working to track polar bears in the Arctic challenged Donald's notions about the purpose of hunting and elicited this not-so-tongue-in-cheek letter:

Ms. Sheldon:

I think there should be a hunting season on polar bears. I would be first in line because I could use twenty thousand dollars for each hide. I would appreciate it if you would stop putting paint on their fur because it makes their value go way down. You should also stop putting transformers around their necks because it dulls a knife when you have to cut it off. If you think that the polar bears are going to be extinct, I should be able to kill them. Then you won't have to go and freeze your butt off studying them. If you let me shoot five or six a year for ten years I will pay your way to Florida each and every year. Thank you.

From soon to be unbearably rich,
Donald

When Donald wrote this he fully expected to receive some argument from Marianne or me about the ethics of its content. His final exam reflects both Marianne's acceptance of Donald's values and her acknowledgment of his way with humor.

I am most impressed with the work you have done this quarter. You have taken responsibility for assignments and as a result have met with considerable success. I hope that you will continue with your reading this summer.

1. Edit and polish your letter to Sally Sheldon. Check the handbook that I gave you for the format of a friendly letter.
2. Reread "To the Open Water." Rewrite part of the story to give a more accurate picture of hunting in winter.
3. Read "The Big Two-Hearted River." Select the phrases that you feel accurately describe trout fishing. Comment on the accuracy and relate it to your own fishing experience.
4. All year you have kept me on the edge with your stories, or maybe I should call them your whoppers. Tell me the biggest one yet; I can take it.

Personal Reflection

I haven't told the stories of Michelle's incredible coincidence, or Ron's encounter with three dead authors, or Jo's startling poetry, or Joy's plans and journals. Their stories, like those of their classmates, reflect the belief that students will learn to use language in an environment that supports risk taking and takes into account what students tell you—through reading, writing, and talking—about where they need to go. The twelve reluctant students in Marianne Dalton's 10B English class are not reluctant learners when the school agenda is kid centered, when they are given time to read and write about things that matter and for authentic audiences, when they are provided with realistic language models, and when their voices are as important as our own.

A few weeks ago during a planning session for a new heterogeneously grouped, interdisciplinary tenth-grade course to be offered next year, I heard Marianne say to a colleague, "I'm not going to worry if we can't make detailed plans beyond the first month. We have to wait until we see how the students respond to these initial activities. That's where the curriculum will come from."

References

Atwell, Nancie. 1987. *In the Middle: Writing, Reading, and Learning with Adolescents.* Portsmouth, N.H.: Boynton/Cook.

Conrad, Joseph. 1981. *Heart of Darkness and The Secret Sharer.* New York: Bantam.

Dunning, Stephen, et al. 1966. *Reflections on a Gift of Watermelon Pickle . . . and Other Modern Verse.* New York: Scholastic.

———. 1969. *Some Haystacks Don't Even Have Any Needles.* New York: Scott, Foresman.

Felson, Gregor. 1950. *Hot Rod.* New York: Dutton.

Ford, Jesse Hill. 1972. "To the Open Water." In *Man in Action.* Evanston, Ill.: McDougal, Littell.

Giovanni, Nikki. 1979. *The Women and the Men.* New York: Morrow.

Hemingway, Ernest. 1925. "The Big Two-Hearted River." In *In Our Time.* New York: Charles Scribner's Sons.

Hinton, S. E. 1967. *The Outsiders.* New York: Dell.

———. 1971. *That Was Then, This Is Now.* New York: Dell.

———. 1975. *Rumblefish.* New York: Dell.

Kjelgaard, Jim. 1948. *Snow Dog.* New York: Bantam.

Lee, Harper. 1982. *To Kill a Mockingbird.* New York: Warner Books.

McCullers, Carson. 1953. *The Heart Is a Lonely Hunter.* New York: Bantam.

Marshall, James Vance. 1984. *Walkabout.* Littleton, Mass.: Sundance.

Prather, Hugh. 1970. *Notes to Myself: My Struggle to Become a Person.* New York: Bantam.

Sillitoe, Alan. 1959. *The Loneliness of the Long Distance Runner.* New York: New American Library.

Weisel, Elie. 1982. *Night.* New York: Bantam.

15

We Call It Good Teaching

DIANE STEPHENS   REBECCA HUNTSMAN

KATHLEEN O'NEILL   JENNIFER STORY

VIRGINIA WATSON   JANINE TOOMES

D r. Moira McKenzie tells the story of some Americans who came to visit her school in Great Britain. They were impressed with what they saw and wanted to know what she called it. (Dr. McKenzie here notes that Americans always seem to want to label things.) She informed them she didn't call it anything. The Americans, however, pushed for a label. Finally, she conceded and responded, "We call it good teaching."

About the Learners

The Ed Lab at the University of North Carolina at Wilmington provides undergraduate and graduate education majors an opportunity to work with individuals who are experiencing learning difficulties. A mathematics professor may ask that all the students in her class work one on one with a child having difficulty with math; a special education professor may want her students to identify and plan for specific learning problems; a reading professor may want her students to spend time reading and enjoying books with small groups of children. Individuals of all ages call the Ed Lab to ask about receiving tutoring services. Sometimes individuals call to get help for themselves; sometimes parents want help for their child; sometimes teachers or principals want help for children they see at school. Forms are sent out and, when they are returned, interviews are scheduled for the individuals and, if applicable, for parents. After the interview, the needs of the individuals are matched with the needs of college students taking methods courses. Tutors and tutees are scheduled to meet at least once a week for a semester, and it is not unusual for tutees to return for a second semester.

In reading education, teachers who are graduate students assess the needs of individuals and often provide the first semester of instruction. Undergraduates work with children in subsequent semesters as well as provide first-semester instruction to some children. Teachers enrolled in their final reading practicum assist in the Ed Lab by working with the undergraduates. In addition, one graduate student works with the director of the lab as a teaching assistant.

The Setting
DIANE STEPHENS, DIRECTOR, ED LAB

There are some places that live in my mind as visual vignettes. The Ed Lab is one of those places. It is a large room, carpeted, warm, and inviting. Near the door a former bulletin board has been converted into a message area; students and teachers have folded and decorated cardboard to make mailboxes. The different styles of mailbox decoration reflect the diversity of participants. Noel Jones, who is on the faculty, has written on his mailbox "Good News Only"; James, his young tutee, liked that idea so much that he has put it on his mailbox too. Sam, an undergraduate with a quiet sense of humor, has two mailboxes connected by a piece of string, one several feet below the other. The lower mailbox simply says "Mail" while the higher one reads "Air Mail." Kate, the graduate assistant assigned to the Ed Lab, also an art teacher and a sailor, has sketched a lovely sailboat on her mailbox. Horses, football players, kites, sailboards, and dinosaurs identify the interests of their owners.

A couch has been placed against the wall under the mailbox area, providing a place to read mail and something for shorter learners to stand on in order to reach the higher mailboxes. A small bulletin board rests against the far end of the couch. It displays the invitations students have made for each other. At semester's end, a few invitations remain.

> Everyone would please read my book.
>   Scott Catone
> It is about cars.

You are invited to help sort new/old books. Look in Kate's space for the box marked "To be sorted."
Kate

Six-year-old Mark's narrative visually dominates the small board (Figure 15–1).

Figure 15–1 **Mark's narrative**

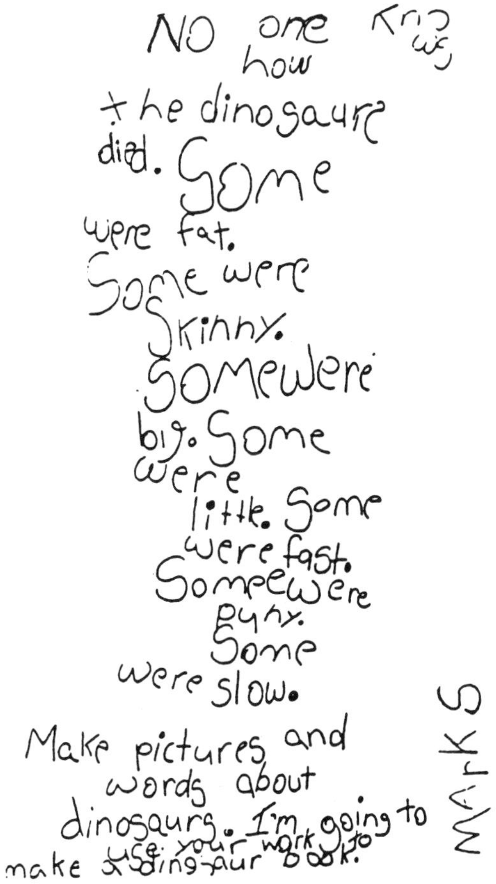

NO one Knows how the dinosaurs died. Some were fat. Some were skinny. Somewere big. Some were little. Some were fast. Somewere funny. Some were slow.

Make pictures and words about dinosaurs. I'm going to use your work to make a dinosaur book.

Mark S

During the semester, tutees sometimes choose to send invitations to each individual rather than collectively invite others via the invitation board. When this happens, invitations are dittoed off and placed in the mailboxes. For example, one day, Jay invited everyone to join a literacy club; another day, Casey solicited stories for his book about the lab; and on yet another, Randy asked students to circle the teams they were hoping would win each round of the NCAA tournament, while Brad asked lab participants to vote for their favorite inventions.

Just past the couch, mailboxes, and invitations, the room opens up. Bookcases hold materials and create smaller spaces within the large room. In the back left corner, they conceal the area that houses, among other things, a lawnmower engine, which Wally Story, the Ed Lab secretary, and Jennifer Story, last year's graduate assistant, cleaned up, painted, and mounted; a craft supply area for which Kate bought and scrounged materials; assorted games like Concentration and Scrabble; and my son's sixth-grade science project on electromagnets. I'm a bit of a neatness freak, and for me the bookcases serve as a lid on a toybox — everything remains accessible, but I don't have to deal with the messiness of projects in process.

The shelves of the bookcases hold different materials. Books have been categorized by children: "Dogs," "Jokes and Riddles," "Poems," and "Books about People." Thematic units, created by undergraduates, boldly advertise their themes: Dinosaur Land, Weather, The Sea, and Space. Handouts for my graduate classes occupy a small bookcase by my office door; in another bookcase we celebrate the authors in the room—"Our Authors Publish!"—by displaying books and articles that lab participants have written.

My office adjoins this lively space. One day last fall I glanced up from my desk to see Laura, a tutor, standing on a chair in the back of the room, holding open a Big Book and laughing gaily. In front of her, Paul, a nine-year-old who came to the lab labeled as a "nonreader," appeared to be reading the text and acting it out at the same time. He gestured intensely, his eyes glued to the text, his body moving around energetically.

Probably that scene stays in my mind so clearly because in order not to disturb others, Laura and Paul were keeping their voices low; from my office it appeared as if someone had turned the sound off. Disconcerted by the silent movie, I glanced around the room and was struck by the fact that no one else was noticing the scene. There were seven other tutor-tutee pairs that day, and each pair was so engrossed in its own activity that the "mime" at the end of the room went unnoticed. I had a visitor that day who also noticed Laura and Paul having such a wonderful time with a book. Looking at me, the visitor asked, "What will this be like when you are gone?"

I'd like to think that the lab was only begun by me and that the play will continue to unfold yearly as it now does daily. Thirty individuals are players every week and with their thirty tutors, four supervising teachers, one graduate assistant, one secretary, and one director (plus assorted parents, siblings, visitors, and students who sometimes "hang out" in the lab), rich scenes get acted out every day. The lab is open from 2 to 5 P.M. and the actors differ from hour to hour—some students come twice a week for an hour each; others participate once a week for an hour or an hour and a half. Some are there in small groups; others work within a whole rather than as a part of a specific group. Every day, every hour, a different scene, and yet each scene part of a whole.

I've shared my mental videotape of Laura and Paul. There are many others. . . .

Brandon's mother, sitting in my office, looking relieved and at home, telling me that over the break, Brandon, a seven-year-old, couldn't wait to get back to the Ed Lab. He had asked every day, "How many more days?" One day he remarked, "At the Ed Lab, I don't feel stupid. Dr. Stephens knows I'm not dumb."

Robbie, initially reluctant to leave his mother's side, circulating through the lab, conducting a survey to find out who wanted which kind of cupcake.

Grace, recently adopted from the Philippines, precise age unknown, shy and frightened at first, giggling over a story with her tutor Karen, concealing from me in a wonderfully privileged sort of way a joke they are sharing.

Charles, an adult participant who had been told he could never read, explaining to me about how he managed to take his dates out to dinner: he'd ask them what they wanted and then tell the waiter, "Make that two." "Sometimes," he explained, "I'd eat some pretty strange things!"

Heather and Tara flying paper airplanes in the hall, recording distances on a chart.

Christine and Kele counting off dinosaur lengths using paper models of dinosaur feet. Later, a university hallway with dinosaur feet walking the walls from the Ed Lab, down the hall, across classroom doors, and around corners.

Brent, another adult participant, complaining to me about *their* and *there*. "Look at this!" he nearly shouted, vehemently pointing to the text. "This," he indicates the word *there*, "says /ther/, I know it does! I read it over and over. But look at this." Here he points to *their*, which appears in the text directly underneath *there*. "I figured out this says /ther/ too. But it took me ten minutes to figure that out. Why do they do that? I figure this one means like where something is and this one is like it's someone's. But why do they do that? It took me *ten minutes* to figure that out. Why do they want to make reading so hard?"

There are smells, too. The motor on the popcorn machine when yet another child does not carefully follow the directions and overloads the machine. (Miraculously it suffers patiently—never burning out—just giving off burnt odors that signal it is overburdened.)

Popcorn, popcorn, popcorn. Many children come right from school and arrive hungry. It has become almost a ritual. "If the hallway smells like popcorn, the lab must be open."

Pumpkin. Fresh. Pumpkin seeds. Roasting. Jason squishing his hands inside his pumpkin and everyone else's too. Nine years old, he's never carved a pumpkin before and wants to clean them all out. (Later we find out that he's never seen the ocean. The university is three miles from it. We take him to the ocean.)

Smells, sounds, and images. Children and adults. Learners understanding how graphs are made or how books work; other learners understanding about teaching. I suppose it could be called a nested design. Inside: children and adults from the community who are experiencing learning difficulties. Next circle: college students learning about teaching by teaching. Next: master's degree students learning about teaching by helping teachers. Finally: me, college professor, not staying in my circle, and working for others to move beyond theirs — helping children, undergrads, graduates. We all help each other and help me, all of us weaving in and through each others' learning.

Scene One: Monday Afternoon
REBECCA HUNTSMAN, MASTER'S DEGREE CANDIDATE

Ten-year-old Jeremy comes running up to the Ed Lab as if pulled by the three helium balloons he carries. Under his arm are packages of party hats. Another birthday party? No, it's an "after the CAT test party." Jeremy, along with most of the county's elementary-age school children, has just recently completed taking the California Achievement Test (CAT). The children are thrilled that the test is over and they can now get back to their regular school routines. So we at the Ed Lab celebrate with them. As Jeremy's tutor, I am especially excited. Jeremy's done the planning for this party and is carrying through on his plan — no small feat for Jeremy. He is notorious for beginning projects that he later decides not to finish. He also has an aversion to writing, usually finding an excuse why he shouldn't. But this time it's different: he has seen his plans the whole way through and has done all the writing. He created the invitations (Figure 15–2, A) and distributed them to the others who come to the Ed Lab. He even wrote out a list of party necessities for us to use in planning the party (Figure 15–2, B). Jeremy feels good about finishing this project. He and I go to the kitchen to mix the lemonade and bake the cookies — a perfect time to understand the importance of following directions and to talk about fractions and abbreviations.

Meanwhile, over in the corner by the window, Amanda, a seven-year-old reluctant reader, and Kim, her tutor, are covered with dirt. Working since 3:30, they now have newspapers spread all over the floor as they plant carrot and radish seeds.

AMANDA: Look at how little they are. Will they really grow into something?

KIM: They did in the book we read, remember? We'll take good care of them the way the book said to and when it's time, we'll pull them up and see.

Although Amanda enjoyed listening to others read stories to her, she came to the Ed Lab not seeing any reason to read for herself. Kim thinks that one way to make reading fun and purposeful for Amanda is by a *real* follow-up activity.

Figure 15-2   Jeremy's "After the CAT Test" party. A: Invitation. B: List.

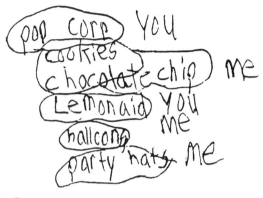

Jeremy after C.A.t. test Party
avery body is in invited. The Party
is on Monday.

A

B

Therefore, after Kim and Amanda finished reading *Growing Radishes and Carrots* (Bolton and Snowball 1986), Kim casually mentioned the idea of planting a minigarden; Amanda latched onto the idea, enthusiastically making plans. She made a list of what they would need and, of course, engaged in reading as she wrote.

As Kim and Amanda continue their planting, Luke, age ten, and Michael, his tutor, begin to work on Luke's math homework. "I just don't get this stuff," Luke complains. Luke has been doing poorly in school and reportedly does not like math. He is currently having trouble telling time on a "real" (not digital) clock. Michael gets out the Ed Lab's play clock to help Luke understand the relationship between seconds, minutes, and hours.

Ten-year-old Cindy and her tutor, Barbara, are too thirsty to wait for the lemonade, so they walk downstairs to the drink machine. They always carry pencil and paper with them when they go for a walk, and today is no exception. Partway down the hall, Barbara stops, holds her paper against the wall, and writes, "What are you going to get?" She hands the paper to Cindy. They walk a few steps further, then Cindy stops, positions her paper, and writes back, "I don't know. What are you thirsty for?" She hands the paper back to Barbara who, after they turn the corner, answers, "Oh, maybe a Coke or a Sprite." On the way down the steps, Cindy pauses and writes, "I'm going to get a Coke." Barbara's turn: "Yeah, I think I will too. A Coke sounds good."

Cindy and Barbara have these written conversations almost as often and as effortlessly as most people have oral conversations. Because of Cindy's reluctance to read and write, she's been having trouble with both in school. Barbara has been trying to help Cindy understand that writing has meaning and is meant to be read. She wants Cindy to realize that there is a purpose behind the written word, whether it is in a book or in a note.

Back in the lab, twelve-year-old Randy and his tutor, Gina, are working on directions for a snake hunt. Like Jeremy, Randy finds many reasons not to write and not to complete tasks. This has caused him some difficulties in school. Through conversation, listening, and observing, Gina has discovered Randy's interests and capitalized on them to help him as a learner. Earlier in the semester, for example, she noticed his love of basketball and so encouraged him to invite others to vote for the team they thought would win the NCAA tournament. Randy followed the games, kept track of the winning teams, and posted a huge chart on which he recorded each game's score and noted its winner.

Today, having discovered Randy's interest in snakes, Gina encourages him to create a game based on snakes.

GINA: I bet there are other kids here who like snakes too, Randy. I wonder if there is something we could do with snakes that would involve some of them?

RANDY: Play a game.

GINA: What kind of game? [*Pause*] Are there any games in here having to do with snakes?

RANDY: I don't know.

GINA: Let's go and see.

[*There are lots of games, but none dealing with snakes.*]

RANDY: Nope. Oh well.

GINA: Well, could we do something else? How about making up a game?

RANDY: I could, I guess. I could hide a snake and they'd have to find it.

GINA: How would they know where to look?

RANDY: I'd give them clues.

GINA: Could you write them down and then the other kids could read them as they went along looking for the snake?

RANDY: Okay, but we'll need a snake!

Gina and Randy settle on a paper snake, which Randy designs. They hide it downstairs on the first floor, and then Randy comes upstairs to the Ed Lab to write his clues.

Meanwhile, Max and Stacey are enthusiastically writing about Max's future fishing pier. It wasn't too long ago that Max, a fourteen-year-old, was not very interested in either reading or writing. He thought school was a waste of his time and wanted to drop out when he was sixteen. Stacey discovered Max's love of fishing and his desire to build his own pier. Although Max subsequently wrote and illustrated his own story, "A Day on the Boat," and compiled stories from other lab participants into a book called *Exciting Fishing Stories*, he was still not convinced that reading and writing were really very useful. Stacey wanted Max to realize they were. She capitalized on his desire to build his own fishing pier, and they began their pier project.

STACEY: You know, Max, it won't be too much longer until you're in high school and then graduated and you can make real plans for your fishing pier. If you're going to build one, would you like to begin finding out how to do it, how others have built theirs, or what's involved in planning one?

MAX: Sure, but I don't know how to find out any of that stuff.

STACEY: Well, I'll help you. We could find out together.

They began by listing the information Max wanted to know and then researched it in the university library. They wrote to and subsequently visited the owner of a local pier. After gathering all the necessary information, Max and Stacey read and discussed the material together. As a result, Max developed an idea of how he'll build his pier and what it will actually look like. Today he's designing it and writing about it (Figure 15–3).

His motivation to see the project through and his comment, "I'll have to go to college to get a good job to earn enough money to build my pier," have convinced Stacey that Max is beginning to see reading and writing as a way of learning.

By now Jeremy and I are finished in the kitchen, and he begins filling glasses to serve lemonade to everyone. It is enjoyed by all as tutors and tutees remain engrossed in their own special activities.

Scene Two: Tuesday Afternoon
KATHLEEN O'NEILL, GRADUATE ASSISTANT, 1987–88

Keith's brown-haired head appears through the doorway. As we exchange smiles and greetings—"Hey, dude"—Keith enters the room and heads toward his mailbox. Retrieving his mail, he sits on the couch to read the riddles that Suelynne, his tutor, has left for him. Watching him pore over his mail, it's hard to believe that seven-year-old Keith came to the lab a few months ago as a nonreader and nonwriter. From the couch, his eyes scan the "Is It Hot or Not?" book chart. Students use colored circles to rate the books they have read: a red circle means don't miss this; gold, very good; and green, pass this one by. Since he's early today, Keith uses the ratings to select a new book and moves to a large pillow on the floor to read while waiting for Suelynne.

Tom comes through the door next, clutching his personally made tie-dyed pillow and, like Keith, heads immediately for his mailbox. His tutor, Natalie, always leaves colorfully decorated notes for him. In today's mail she's left him drawings of the solar system and an invitation to join her for a "Visit to the Stars." Before his arrival, she'd created a display of books and materials about space. Together she hopes they will "explore the heavens" and write a book on the solar system. An artist at seven, Tom enjoys making and illustrating his own books. A few months ago, he was often unwilling even to write his name; now his

Figure 15—3   Max's writing about the pier

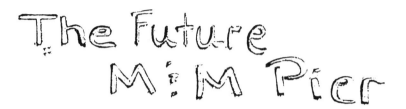

The Future
M:M Pier

1. 1050 feet long

2. small snack bar boit shop tackle shop (clean) bathrooms

3. 7 fiam en$

4. 40 feet wide

5. At T 75 feet wide

6. season pass $70

7. 1 day pass $ 2.50
   open 04 hours a day

8. Location. At shell Island

The reason the peir is named the M+M peir is because my friend Mitch Fuller + I are going to run + own the Peir M+M Stands for Mitch and Max.

numerous publications are proudly exhibited in the area labeled "Our Authors Publish."

Behind me, I hear Kele running down the hall with his characteristic exuberance. He begins telling a story before he's even through the door. Rushing to his mailbox, he finds dinosaur stickers and a note. "Wow, look at these!

Wonder where they came from." Christine gently suggests he read the note, which explains that she has brought materials to make brontosaurus finger puppets. Kele immediately settles in to read the directions for making the puppets. His progress over the past eight months has helped him understand the usefulness of reading and writing. His previous experiences with print were not meaningful ones and he often felt frustrated. He now glows with enthusiasm and is pleased with his newly discovered ability to use reading and writing to learn.

Jason arrives next, flashing his report card. Once thought to be retarded, unable to read or to communicate well, Jason's progress in reading is evident in today's report card, which even cautions, "Jason is beginning to talk too much in class." Laughter and hugs abound as he shares his report card with the other tutors. Jason laughs shyly, almost as if he had been fooling everyone all along. He returns the Sorry game he had taken home to play and charts the books he's read at home. His tutor, Connie, has suggested a trip to the ocean and to the aquarium, and they have been preparing for the trip by reading from the "sea" collection.

Brandon is usually a ray of sunshine entering the lab; today he arrives last and stays in his mother's shadow. His day started fine, but now he's missing his two front teeth and, like many first-grade students, he has spent most of the day struggling through standardized tests. He remains tight-lipped until he notices that Melissa, his tutor, is prepared to tie-dye the shirt he brought. Smiling, he begins to make directions for tie-dying that will hang in the kitchen next to those for playdough and popcorn.

With these five settled in, I pause for a moment and glance around the lab. Robbie is coming out of the kitchen with a notepad, taking orders for custom-made paper. Four months ago he struggled with sound-symbol relationships; now he circulates around the room, using invented spelling to keep track of the size and color of paper ordered. Cindy and Barbara are in the back corner, hunched over writing and drawing paper, editing Cindy's stories about horses. A few weeks ago, Cindy was nearly in tears as she apologized, "I can't draw horses." Today, she is giggling as Barbara sketches her best rendition of "Lucky." These two switch roles as the need arises. Their completed story becomes a five-foot-high illustrated panel about horses. Previously unwilling to take a risk, Cindy now blooms as an independent learner.

Crystal and her tutor, Tina, are painting a thunderstorm. Speaking in a whisper, Crystal describes her techniques as she expands her expressive brushstrokes and color choices. She and Tina have been exploring the world of illustrators, and Crystal is proud of her artwork. Jay and Lisa are making membership cards for the literacy club they have organized. Invited to join by signing up on a large sheet of tagboard, Tom signs his name and receives his personalized membership card (Figure 15–4, A and B).

Laughter from the kitchen turns out to be from Brandon, Abby, and Jeff, who are making "Jiggle Hearts," following a recipe from *Vicki Lansky's Kid's Cooking* (1987). Thursday they mixed sugar-free Jell-O and poured it into a mold.

Figure 15–4   The literacy club. A: Tom signs his name. B: Jay's acceptance and card.

A

Thank you for Join the literacy club.
I hope you will wright
by Jay Cattera

Literacy Club member Card

B

Today they are unmolding the Jell-O at the same time they are brainstorming, laughing about, and revising their story about the Jell-O monster (Figure 15–5).

As they finish up and Brandon gets ready to leave for the day, he puts something into my hand: "Here, Kate, for you." I open my hand and, with a lump in my throat and tear in my eye, read Brandon's note, "I love you."

That's what it's all about.

Figure 15–5 Brandon, Abby, and Jeff's "The Story of the Jell-O Monster"

The Story of the Jello Monster

It started out as Jello disaster
and turned into a monster.
It looked like blood!
The Jello was big. The Jello
monster is wiggly.
It tasted like something wiggling
in.
The hearts on it were good.
The hearts had words on them.
The Jello felt like plastic—but
was FANTASTIC!

Intermission: A Look Behind the Scenes
JENNIFER STORY, GRADUATE ASSISTANT, 1986–87

To look at the lab as it is now, you would think an interior designer had planned it. The centers seem so fascinating and useful for the students who come to the lab. But no one planned it; it evolved.

One of our most surprising discoveries was that the centers *had* to evolve, had to change according to the interests and interactions of the tutors and students. Consider the lawn mower engine, for example. A tutor could learn a lot about a child's approach to problems by watching the child persistently try to remove a Phillips screw by brute force with a standard screwdriver, or by observing a child try smaller and smaller wrenches to find the right fit for a bolt. So we tried to devise activities that drew on interest in the engine, like a memory game for learning the parts of the engine. No one ever played it twice. Diane and I had thought it up, not a student and tutor, and there was something missing in it, that vitality that draws people back again and again.

We had also set up a saltwater aquarium, and the life-and-death struggles played out in the tank daily were a source of fascination for everyone. A whole collection of activities based on the animals went untouched, but children often wrote and drew about the aquarium. I provided a log book for making observations about the tank but only an occasional tutor, Diane, and I wrote in it. Then one day Diane wrote and illustrated a letter denouncing Terry, my tutee, and me for opening up the pet clam's shell and cutting up the clam to feed the crab. (We had run out of frozen shrimp.) That letter drew a response from Terry and others and grew into a scroll of observations that crawled up the wall and across the ceiling. While the scroll was identical to the log in intent, it differed in purpose: the log was a contrived means of getting the children to write, the scroll a genuine communication about things that mattered.

Dinosaur Land is one of the most popular centers in the lab and is a good example of how the centers grew of their own accord. It occupies a corner five feet by eight feet and borders on the secretary's desk. Dinosaurs sometimes wander away to be found under the computer and printer tables. Books, puzzles, inflatables, games—all kinds of dinosaur-related activities are available to anyone willing to sit on the rug and get involved. Children, parents, tutors, and even lone college students can often be found playing and learning in Dinosaur Land.

Dinosaur Land began inauspiciously. In one of the first graduate reading courses Diane taught as director of the lab, she introduced the students to skinny books. These are books in which the student is editor and cuts out materials from other sources (such as old basal readers) and organizes and publishes them in an edited volume. We used small plastic rings called Chinese jacks to bind the books so we could add more stories later. My book was on dolphins, Evelyn's was on activities for a rainy day, and Diane's was on dinosaurs.

Diane hung her book near the bookshelf that at that time housed our small but growing library. Hers was the only skinny book that continued to flourish as Diane got manic about adding stories. An article about dinosaurs in *Learning* would send her leaping to the Xerox machine. She began to profess to love dinosaurs, and friends stayed on the watch for prospective contributions to her book. A first-grade teacher sent her copies of dinosaur poems her students had written; an undergrad gave her a clipping from the newspaper about new theories on the death of the dinosaurs.

Soon the dinosaur virus spread beyond the book. We started putting poems and pictures on the wall beside the book. Children in the lab loved to look at Diane's book and drew and wrote stories about dinosaurs, which also decorated the walls. Diane's husband sent her a large inflatable apatasaurus (which used to be called a brontosaurus) and stegosaurus. These were ridden and hidden all over the lab and could be found peeking out of doors or out of drawers. Almost any young learner who was fearful about individual reading instruction loosened up upon meeting the dinosaurs.

A collection of little plastic dinosaurs had to be purchased when first grader Nick decided to make a dinosaur game. After laboriously drawing large squares around the edge of the gameboard, numbering them from one to fourteen, and illustrating a couple of the squares, Nick began writing the cards. Upon playing the game, it became obvious that more cards were necessary because the same ones kept turning up. Nick gave blank cards to Diane and Wally, the secretary, and put one in each tutor's mailbox along with instructions. I was also asked to accost passersby and entice them to make cards. This resulted in a strange collection of cards, from adult-made standard types ("Tripped on a log, lose one turn") to adult-made nonstandard types ("Go back to New York") to invented-spelling kid types ("Go bak to the swop") to one written by the four-year-old brother of a tutee ("Wkntmud" [went in the mud]). The rules were written on the game: "Whoever gets to number 14. Wins." They turned out to be rather ambiguous, however, and had to be renegotiated every time the game was played.

Once we recognized the universal fascination with dinosaurs, we made a concerted effort to get more books on dinosaurs. These were hard to come by at the time, especially ones for the youngest readers, and we were grateful when tutors and tutees chose to write books to add to the collection. Terry and I photographed the inflatable dinosaurs in order to write and publish a book, first plotting the story and planning the pictures before actually doing the photographing.

Cindy, a very reserved third grader, delved into the book collection for a different purpose. Prompted by a letter to Diane about her favorite dinosaur, she decided to do a survey on everyone's favorite dinosaur. At my suggestion, she first made a chart with directions for respondents (Figure 15–6). On each page she listed two dinosaurs and left space for names. On the last page she wisely allowed

---

Figure 15–6   Cindy and Jennifer's chart

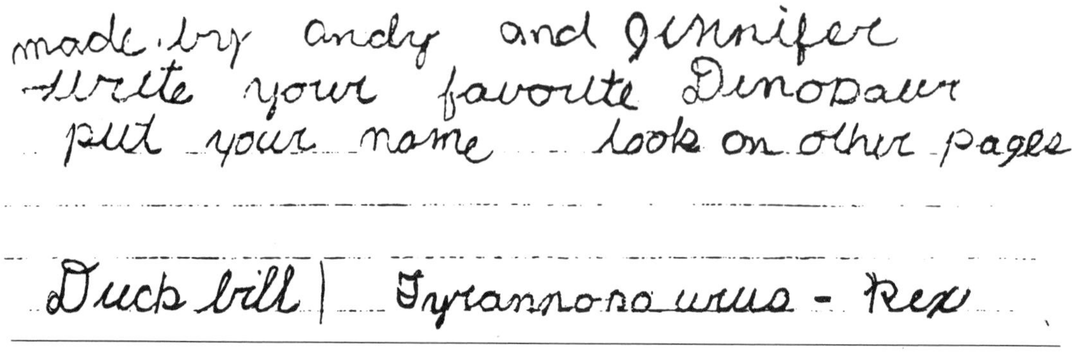

made by andy and Jennifer
write your favorite Dinosaur
put your name . . . look on other pages

Duck bill | Tyrannosaurus - Rex

for the possibility that she might not have listed everyone's favorite, and she wrote:

> if we didn't write down your favorite Dinosaur write it down with your name

Armed with clipboard and pen and several dinosaur books to prompt the memory of those who couldn't remember the names of their favorite dinosaurs, Cindy and I first took the opinions of students and tutors in the lab, parents as they came by, Diane, and long-suffering Wally. Dissatisfied with the meager number of responses she had collected, Cindy asked who else she might solicit. I suggested asking the professors in the rest of the education department.

This was intimidating to Cindy, but I helped her cope with the task by trading off responsibilities. First I would introduce Cindy and our project and ask for the respondent's favorite dinosaur, and Cindy would record the answer; then Cindy would turn over the clipboard and bravely whisper the questions. We left an invitation at the lab for others to answer during the week, and when Cindy returned, she and I made a bar graph to display the results of the survey. (In case you are wondering, tyrannosaurus rex was an easy winner, but apatasaurus came in a clear second.)

A group of undergraduates who chose dinosaurs as the topic of their thematic unit project in a large growth spurt initiated Dinosaur Land. They collected games, books, and many activities, and they organized the center. Another group of undergrads in an art education class donated their dinosaur mural to the center.

Dinosaur Land seems pretty complete now, and you would suspect it would stay the way it is, but we know from experience in the Ed Lab that nothing is complete and nothing stays the same. The kitchen, the space center, the store, everything is in flux, elements mixed in a cauldron reflecting the needs and interests of the children, adult students, graduate and undergraduate college students, parents, and professors who care to get involved.

Scene Three: Wednesday Afternoon
VIRGINIA WATSON, MASTER'S DEGREE CANDIDATE

Most Wednesdays I work with Robbie, a seven-year-old, and help supervise the undergraduate tutors. Today Kate, the graduate assistant in the lab, is out of town at a conference and has asked me to be available if Brad or Shawn, her tutees, should need help. They're working on projects and have asked to come to the lab even though they knew Kate would not be there.

As I wait for Robbie, Brad, and Shawn, I happen to notice one of Brad's publications and I am reminded of how far this nine-year-old fourth grader has progressed since he was referred to the Ed Lab last fall. His first attempt at real writing hangs on the bookshelf labeled "Our Authors Publish." Last year, Brad witnessed a plane crash while on a family vacation trip to Fort Bragg. Shortly after, during one of his first visits to the lab, he noticed the headlines "C-130 Crashes at Bragg" boldly printed in the newspaper. "I saw that!" he cried. "I was there! I even have some pictures!" Recognizing a good opening, Kate, his tutor, invited Brad to write his eyewitness account of the event. Brad willingly told his story to Kate, but was hesitant when she asked him to express those same thoughts on paper.

Kate suggested to Brad that they make a first draft of his story together, not worrying about conventional spelling or punctuation, a form of writing we refer to in the lab as "kids' spelling." Brad gave it a try and published his first news story for the lab. He asked Wally, the lab secretary, to edit and type the story (Figure 15–7).

For the past four weeks, Brad has been asking questions about machines and how long they have been around: "When was the computer invented? Who thought of it? How does this lock work? Who thought up staplers?" He and Kate chose a book in the lab, *Small Inventions That Make a Big Difference* (1984), to help answer some of those questions. After reading that book, Brad decided he wanted to make a book. He and Kate took a discovery walk around campus and Brad wrote on a three-by-five-inch card each invention that interested him. His finished set of twenty-five included window locks, Coke machines, fire alarms, and televisions. He chose twelve and posted an invitation asking others to vote for their favorites. When the ballots came in, he used the votes to narrow the field to six. Today he is going to be organizing the who, what, where, when, why, and how of each invention. As he arrives, he eagerly grabs his resource book and several encyclopedias from the bookshelf and begins documenting his findings on notecards.

Shawn arrives next, bounding through the door inquiring about cardboard, trivia, and an alien named Alf. He's planning to add game cards to his version of Trivial Pursuit entitled Space Trivia. As he goes to various corners of the lab to gather the supplies he needs, I glance around the room to see what the other participants are engaged in. Paula gives me a big smile and holds up the note she

Figure 15—7　　Brad's first news story

Brad Johnson was there!

"My cousin took me to Fort Brag. I saw a plane crash. We had to leave at 4:00 a.m. in the morning. We stopped to eat at 6:00 a.m. with some Marines. We got there at 7:00 a.m. I got to get on a Super Attack Cobra. I got to play with a Machine gun. I did not think it was going to crash."

My cousin took me to Fort Bragg. I saw a plane crash. We had to live at 4:00am in the morning. We stopped to eat at 6:00am with some meranies. We got there at 7:00am. I got to get on a super atteat crobba. I got to play with a chane gun. I did not think it was going to crash.

is writing to Dr. Stephens. Notes are frequently being left in mailboxes, and I notice that Kate's is getting full of "Thank you" notes as the children write about the balloons and pencils that she'd placed in their mailboxes the day before. I overhear Tom say, "How do you spell *balloon?*" to his tutor, Natalie. "Where can we find out?" she responds. After a moment, he replies, "On Kate's desk in the back where the bag of balloons is!" A short time later this note appears in Kate's mailbox:

> Thank you for the balloon and pencil.
> Kate　　　　　　　　　　　　　　　　　　Tom

The smells from the kitchen remind me that Carrie and Daryl have brownies planned. A quick peek into the kitchen confirms what my nose suspected. It is always amazing to see what our small "kitchen," a room equipped with only hot plate, toaster oven, and popcorn popper, can accommodate.

As I stand in the doorway hoping someone will offer me a taste, Robbie appears. Grabbing my shirt, he asks, "Can we make playdough today?" Since

Brad is engrossed with his notecards and Shawn with game cards, I say yes. While we read through the directions together, we talk, and Robbie, who is six and labeled a nonreader, becomes familiar with the words and concepts *teaspoon, tablespoon, cup of flour, salt, liquid,* and *solid.* As we mix the various ingredients, Robbie announces, "I want green and yellow coloring for this batch of playdough." However, after he mixes those two colors, he reaches for the bottle of red coloring and then the blue. He keeps adding drops of color until the bottles are empty.

The mother in me tells me to interfere and put a stop to this mess. But the teacher in me tells me to wait and let Robbie experiment with the colors. "This looks like green slime," comments Robbie. "What do you think?"

"It looks like lava rock to me," I respond. Wanting to nudge Robbie toward even more reading and writing, I add, "I wonder what Daryl and Connie think?"

Robbie decides to question the other tutees about our greenish-black glob of playdough. As he circulates through the lab he invites others to guess which colors have been combined to create this odd hue and records the comments onto a chart. He leaves the chart alongside his creation for others to respond to later in the week.

As the hour draws to a close, learners begin to put away supplies and gather their various projects together to carry home. Daryl grins as he emerges from the kitchen toting a plate of brownies to share with his sister at home. Brad has a stack of notecards ready so that he can do a first draft of his favorite-inventions book next week. He drops his cards into his lab drawer before leaving. Shawn puts his Space Trivia game back into a box along with the directions he's just written. Paula sticks her note in Dr. Stephens's mailbox and comments to me, "I hope she writes back."

As I watch the last tutee leave, I turn my attention back to the lab. Tutors are cleaning up for the day and beginning to make a written record of the day's events. This is when we tell stories: "Did you see Daryl mixing those brownies? He even showed Carrie how three teaspoons make a tablespoon!" "What about Robbie and that green blob? Look at how well he designed that chart!"

And the stories go on . . .

Scene Four: Thursday Afternoon
JANINE TOOMES, MASTER'S DEGREE CANDIDATE

It's 3:45 and already nine-year-old Scott and his tutor, Joy, are hard at work, heads bent over a book in front of them. Scott is a pleasant, easygoing child who has a love affair with vehicles of all kinds. On Monday, the pair read several books about cars and trucks. That experience prompted Scott to ask about writing his own version to share with the other kids in the lab. Joy, an undergraduate majoring in special education, readily agreed. She had discovered that while

Scott seemed to have developed several reading and writing strategies—such as using information from the context, substituting a word for an unknown word that retains the same meaning, or referring to pictures—he didn't seem to reflect enough to use those strategies effectively. She hoped that the writing project would be a way to increase Scott's awareness.

As it nears 4:00, other children and tutors begin arriving for their hour together. There's Carol, a blonde, bubbly eight-year-old, and Jennifer, another special education major who will be student teaching in the fall. Usually the tutors are a mixture of elementary and special education majors; however, today they all happen to be special education majors. As usual, Carol enters the lab with mother in tow, talking excitedly about a million things. Her chatter flits from one topic to the next as she pauses only momentarily to catch her breath. It's as if a whirlwind has blown into the lab. As Carol's mom waves good-bye and slips out the door, Carol runs to greet "Miss Kate" and me before settling in with Jennifer to review the day's itinerary.

Next comes Marty, a sixteen-year-old young man who was referred to the lab for help with content area reading. In contrast to Carol, he enters quietly, giving everyone who greets him a shy smile. "Hey, Marty, how are the Mets doing?" Marty, a real sports nut, grins and gives the latest update on the baseball standings. His tutor, Janice, who is an older, nontraditional undergraduate, has been waiting. The two check his mailbox and head for their favorite spot—the table in the kitchen.

Finally comes Casey. Like Carol, he is a second grader. He pauses a minute to look for Lenize, his tutor for the hour, who is sitting at one of the many large, round tables in the center of the lab. Lenize gathers their materials and they retreat to the carpeted area in the back corner. With the cast of characters now complete for the hour, the action begins full tilt!

Last week Carol discovered *Air and Flight* (Ardley 1984) on a trip taken with Jennifer to the children's section of the university library. Through a series of written notes, Carol invited my son, Brian, to participate in several science experiments she had chosen from the book. Today, with Jennifer's help, the children choose two experiments: one that calls for making paper airplanes and a second that shows how to stick a straw through a potato. As Jennifer watches, the noisy pair quickly gather the necessary materials from the supplies kept on the bookcase and decide to conduct these two experiments outside on the large grassy area surrounding the education building.

Meanwhile, the other tutor-tutee pairs seem oblivious to the commotion, for they are all engrossed in their own activities. Marty and Janice are busy reading together from his ninth-grade civics book. Because this particular subject has given him a great deal of difficulty in school, Marty has asked Janice to help him study for an upcoming test. They pause frequently to discuss the meanings of the specialized terms in the text.

Casey is busy stuffing the mailboxes with invitations for the other lab participants to write about themselves (Figure 15–8). He accepted an invitation from

Figure 15—8   Casey's invitation

TO All Lab students,
you're invited tO make a book
all About You Thing you might
want to include: What you do at
home, What you do at school what
you look like, What you like to read,
Your favorite animal, your · · favorite
sport, and whatever else you want to

tell everyone about you.

Diane (Dr. Stephens) to compile this semester's lab book — sort of a "Who's Who" collection about the students and their tutors, complete with photographs. Lenize has helped him draft a letter and duplicate enough copies for everyone in the lab. The chance to be independent while engaging in purposeful reading and writing activities has been very important for Casey, as for the other children, for when he first came to the lab he relied heavily on his tutor to do all of the reading and writing.

Figure 15—9   Scott's invitation ·

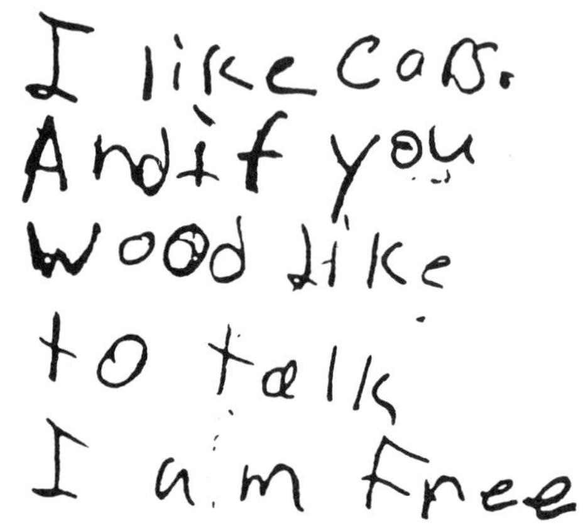

> I like cas.
> And if you
> wood like
> to talk
> I am free

I notice that Scott and Joy, who began early, are finishing up for the day. Scott comes over to show his completed book.

"Would you like to read my book about cars?" he asks shyly. "Please sign the page in the back, too. I want to know who read it."

"Sure! I'll be glad to!" His book, *This Is All About Cars*, shows just how knowledgeable Scott is about different kinds of cars. I notice that he has even included a page in the back about the author, complete with an invitation to discuss some of the finer points of automobiles (Figure 15—9).

Scott continues to circulate to the others in the lab, proudly sharing his creation with each one. "Great job!" "You sure do know a lot about cars!" Each reader makes positive, supportive comments, which are critical to Scott's growth as a reader and writer. Before leaving, Scott adds a note to the invitation board to encourage children who come to the lab on other days to read his book as well. His dad arrives and Scott greets him at the door with a huge smile on his face. We all know that at that moment he definitely feels good about himself.

As they leave, the experimenters return, enthusiastic about their discoveries.

"Miss Jan, we stuck a straw through a potato!" Carol exclaims excitedly.

"Yes, and my airplane beat Carol's," Brian chimes in.

Together they recount how air pressure helped fly the paper planes they had made and also enabled them to stick a drinking straw through a potato. Before long a small crowd of other students and tutors have gathered to see the two repeat the potato trick and to hear them explain that by pinching the straw and trapping air inside, the straw becomes stronger and pierces the potato. Before long, the potato has dozens of holes all over it.

Figure 15–10   Brian holds two apples while Carol blows air between them

Following this sharing session, the children consult the book again and read the directions for doing the next experiments. Brian holds up a ruler, from each end of which two apples are suspended by strings; Carol blows air between them with her straw (Figure 15–10). Much to the children's surprise, the apples move together.

"Why did they do that?" Carol queries. "I thought they would go apart."

"Let's see what the book says is happening," Jennifer responds.

The trio consults the book and finds out that by blowing air between the apples they had caused the air pressure to become greater on the outside of each apple. When this happened, the two apples swung toward each other. The children repeat this experiment several more times and then dash off to the kitchen to perform one final activity dealing with water pressure.

Once the last experiment has been done, Carol and Jennifer settle in on the floor in the back corner of the lab. Carol confidently explains to Jennifer all that she learned from the day's activities. As they talk, Carol also makes a written summary of the day's proceedings (Figure 15–11).

To the unknowing eye, Carol's activities might seem typical for any second grader with an interest in science. In reality, the scene is far from it, for just a few

Figure 15−11   Carol's written summary

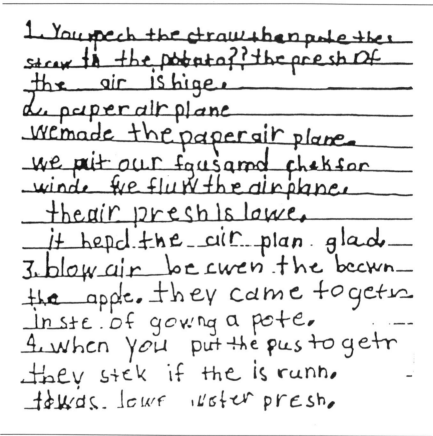

months ago she had been a child who was severely crippled by her reluctance to take any risks whatsoever. She avoided everything—reading, writing, listening to stories, speaking to another person, and even walking across the room alone to get a book or supplies! We have all marveled at how much she has changed.

As 5:00 nears, parents begin arriving and happy children eagerly rush to explain what new experiences they had as language users today. Tutors also pause on their way out. They share with me discoveries made about their tutees as learners, plans being formulated for future lab sessions, and, often, reflections about themselves as students of the fine art of teaching. As the last one departs, the lab becomes quiet and the curtain closes on another busy afternoon.

Scene Five

The lab opens the first day of next semester. We've got a call out for participants. The scenery's in place. Tutors will design the rest of the props. Dialogue and action will emerge. In the theater, they call it improvisation. In the lab, we call it good teaching.

References

Ardley, Neil. 1984. *Air and Flight*. New York: Watts.

Bolton, Faye, and Diane Snowball. 1986. *Growing Radishes and Carrots*. New York: Scholastic.

Lansky, Vicki. 1987. *Vicki Lansky's Kid's Cooking*. New York: Scholastic.

McKenzie, Moira. 1987. Personal communication.

National Geographic Society. 1984. *Small Inventions That Make a Big Difference*. Washington, D.C.: National Geographic Society.

16

Whole Language: Starting New Conversations

JOHN McINERNEY   JEROME C. HARSTE

McINERNEY: Did I ever tell you the one about the first time my wife met my relatives? There were about fifteen of us at my Aunt Stella's house in Brooklyn and my grandmother was making a typical meal for my family, something like leg of lamb and lasagna. No connection to each other, but they were lying around the kitchen so she cooked them. So, we've got fifteen Italians sitting down, shouting across the table at each other, and here sits Carol, my wife. Now, she comes from sort of a Germanic background, a bit more reserved. She's waiting for everybody to sit down before she eats. My cousin, Dom, takes a few bites but then has to leave for a hockey game. My other cousin takes up where he left off on his plate. My grandmother's standing in the corner worrying that there's not enough food, and Carol sits there waiting. And I lean over and say, "If you don't start eating, it'll all be gone!"

HARSTE: I really love that upbringing of yours.

M: Now, am I stretching it to suggest that this is something like whole language? Don't hold back until it all falls into place, you've just got to do it.

H: That's a great place to start.

M: I felt like Carol when I first started teaching seven years ago. I heard the lectures, I read the books, I knew what whole language was about. But come the first day of school, here I am saying to myself, "Well, this basal isn't so bad." I couldn't decide how or where to begin.

It was weeks before I settled on journals as a starting point. Which brought up a similar problem—there's about a million ways to do journals. So I thought, "To hell with this handwringing." We just jumped in and hashed out the parameters as we went. And, like in a lot of whole language classrooms, one thing led to another.

H: Well, you would cast yourself as a learner then.

M: Right, because I'm uneasy projecting myself as someone who's the whole language expert. I'm a bit apprehensive when people visit my room. I know where my classroom *could* be and I know where it is now—not even close.

H: Well, you could talk about that discomfort—where you are and where you want to be—but it shouldn't paralyze you.

M: That's true, that's true. If you understand the basic principles and see them in action, I think the promise and rewards of whole language are too great a lure to allow paralysis to set in.

Yet there's no denying that many teachers, if not paralyzed outright, are wandering aimlessly. The desire is there but they do seem unacquainted with the realm of possibilities. And if no one in their building is doing whole language, if there's no role model, the problem may never be resolved. To me, that's the greatest benefit of support groups like Teachers Applying Whole Language—the exposure to original viewpoints.

That reminds me of when I first came here to Indiana from New York. When you grow up there, you have this attitude that there is "New York" and then there is "The Rest of the World." I was physically ill for weeks after I arrived because I thought it was the stupidest thing I had ever done. It took a year, but I finally discovered this other world of smaller towns that appealed to me. Now, I could never go back to New York.

It's the same for whole language. If you don't know it's out there, if you don't see it with your own eyes, you really can't make an accurate judgment, can you? You're not even aware that there is a decision to be made.

I guess that's how I see my function in the school. Not to proselytize, but just to be there—that some other teacher might look at me and say, "I didn't know you could do that."

H: You're just trying to involve more people in the conversation. That's the whole point. And when I teach teachers, I want to help them develop a voice, the same way that whole language can help them begin to hear from more children in their classrooms.

I like to think of the classroom as a readers' and writers' guild. I think the key question that teachers need to ask is, how can I organize my classroom so that each person is allowed to have a voice and join the conversation?

I think that means that instruction has to begin in life experiences. Students need to make connections between their own lives and what is going on in school. Instead of reducing the world to problems for them, we need to begin with their concerns. For me, this boils down to using the child as your curricular informant.

M: Right. What works for you as an adult can also be applied to your elementary or secondary classroom.

H: And when you hear all these different voices, *new* conversations begin. That's the foundation of strong communities — difference, not like-mindedness. If everybody thinks the same, then there's no basis for a conversation. Well, we don't want everybody to be the same. We don't want all whole language classes to look the same. It's the differences that can transform our thinking.

Remember that article you wrote last summer — "Are We There Yet?" That spoke to whole language teachers. No whole language teacher I know feels he or she has arrived. Your point was that you learned that getting there is all the fun.

Now, that topic was not one I would have picked. You did. If I had forced you to write about topics that interested me, I would never have come to understand this very real feeling that so many whole language teachers have.

I heard a new voice, I gained a new insight, I began a new conversation.

M: Jerry, that's fairly profound! That's a wonderful way of interpreting a community. It's like when I was the recreation director for the Speech and Hearing Clinic. These six- to twelve-year-old kids had such severe problems, they lived on campus all week long and their parents picked them up for the weekends. Their differences really forced me to confront issues that I never had to deal with before. And it seemed the thing to do — the *only* thing to do without being overwhelmed — was forget about the handicaps and treat them like people, first. Their disabilities would certainly surface, but my starting point had to be their abilities.

Now, I know this is pretty basic for anyone who is in special ed, but for me, it was a revelation. And that's something in whole language that really clicked with me — this idea of respect for the learner.

H: I like that: whole language as learner friendly. That should be our theme. If we get this message across, the specifics will fall in place. I see the real contribution this book will make is dispelling the notion that there is one right way to do whole language. Each chapter has demonstrated alternate paths that teachers have taken to make their rooms user friendly.

M: That's right. Exactly. I think that most whole language teachers intuitively pursue those different paths because they feel right for them. By the same token, I think that most people intuitively understand whole language. They have it inside them. It's not so much a question of converting these people to whole language as it is simply opening a door.

H: Let's just pick up on this question of how *you* got there.

M: I thought you'd never ask. It was in Karen Feathers's reading methods class. Remember her? I was teaching kindergarten at the time. For the first three weeks of that class, I came home to Carol ranting about this lunatic who was telling us to teach reading by *not* teaching reading. Then—and I remember this vividly—it was like a slap in the face when I suddenly realized that what Karen was saying was *precisely* what I was striving for in my class.

It also helped that I was taking another reading methods class at the same time from a strict behaviorist perspective. The "rational" approach seemed like just so much voodoo, I couldn't take it seriously.

H: After the first three weeks, right?

M: After the first three weeks.

H: Well, for me, whole language has always been a practical theory of language and learning, developed from watching real readers and real writers, and the theory is continuing to change as we do this observing.

M: That's a key point, this developing nature of the theory. If more teachers could understand that, I think they'd see that whole language isn't some ivory tower, but an open invitation to participate as an equal in the actual development of the theory.

H: The thing that concerns me, though, is if people look at us, for example, and say, "Well, Harste is strong on theory and McInerney is strong on practical activities." I'd like to have teachers understand whole language in a different frame.

M: That the theory *is* the practice and the practice *is* the theory.

H: Right, right. Ken Goodman is the perfect example of this. Whole language really started with him. What he did was look at what real readers did when they read whole stories and, from this, he culled some principles of language. For example, one principle was that all of the cue systems in language work together in reading. He saw that children simultaneously use their knowledge of the flow of language (syntax), their knowledge of the world (semantics), and their knowledge of letter-sound relationships (phonics). So, every miscue a child made had to be evaluated in terms of whether or not it made sense in light of the story, to what degree it did or did not sound like language, and to what extent it showed letter-sound relationships between the expected response and the observed response.

M: We're talking about the late 1960s, right? This was really a revolutionary way of looking at reading instruction.

H: Exactly. And Ken went on with other principles: that language varies by the context of use; that language is learned *through* use; that language, by its very nature, is social; that learning is theoretically based; and that the hallmarks of learning are community and connectedness.

I think it's important to point out, though, that in addition to being a theory of language and a theory of learning, whole language is a theory of professional self-renewal. By using the child as our curricular informant, we have a self-correcting device built into our model of curriculum and curriculum development. It's really a call for teachers to reclaim their classrooms and participate in the development of a practical theory of language learning.

M: Of course. By definition, when you embrace whole language you embrace the notion of teaching as a true profession. The teacher becomes the expert, not the packaged program of the month.

H: Right. And you continue to grow.

What whole language teachers do, then, is take these principles and think about what they mean as they go about planning classroom instruction. I want teachers to understand these principles in practical terms as well as to understand their roots. The roots, like I mentioned before, are that the child is our curricular informant.

M: And as we learn more from the kids, whole language will change.

H: Yes, and that's what's wrong with seeing it as some sort of immutable orthodoxy. Some teachers think they can "do Graves" and they are doing whole language. To the extent that teachers buy a package and simply administer a new kit or instructional routine, whole language is lost.

M: It's more of a negotiation, right? When you lose that give-and-take, you lose the essence of whole language.

H: That's one of the problems in this field. The attitude that I encounter most often is that teachers want to be able to do it right or not do it at all. That's one problem. I think another one is what I just said: this notion of "Okay, I'm ready. Tell me what materials to use and I'll do it."

M: That's not a whole language problem, that's an institutional one we face. Everything we get comes in complete packages with questions and responses spelled out.

I was at one meeting and a teacher said, "Not to change the subject, but when are we going to adopt a spelling and a handwriting series?" And the coordinator said something like, "We'll be doing that in the '89–'90 school year." The teacher's response was, "Well, what are we supposed to do until then?" I thought, here's the logical consequence of a system that doesn't exactly encourage individual initiative.

H: The teachers that say, "I'm going to give whole language a try," and in the next breath ask, "What materials do I use?" need to understand that whole language is different.

Their problem is understandable. If you adopt a phonics program, you buy a set of materials and begin. If you buy a skills approach to reading, you adopt a new basal and begin. If you take a whole language approach, there is no set of materials. Whole language teachers see teaching and learning as a relationship. They assume that children are already readers and writers, that what we have to do is support and expand the reading and writing that already is in place. Other approaches assume that you have to teach kids to read and write. There's a world of difference there, and it's reflected in how you organize and conduct instruction in the classroom.

That reminds me of my favorite story along these lines—Gloria Kauff-man's response to Kathy Short. Kathy had been working with Gloria, a teacher, for three months. When Gloria was reporting on the study, she said, "I kept saying to myself, 'Why won't the woman just tell me what kind of materials to buy?'"

M: I think we need to talk more about this. If we want to address teacher concerns, I think we have to discuss packaged materials and how whole language teachers can use them.

This really struck a chord with me this past week when two teachers from Washington township visited my room. They were enthusiastic people and excited about whole language. I mentioned that I was only beginning to deal with teaching math in a whole language way. They were pretty high on *Math Their Way* and, I'll tell you, I'm more than willing to try this because I don't have a clear idea of where to start. This might be as good a place as any.

I don't think I'm alone. A lot of teachers new to whole language might need just such a springboard. They don't have to buy into these programs completely, but it gives them a way to start. There are a lot of materials available that are useful and a lot that are crap. It seems to me that the ability to separate the wheat from the chaff is a necessary step for an evolving whole language teacher. In the absence of like-minded colleagues or TAWL groups, teachers could start there and grow as they learn more about it.

H: Take yourself as an example. We're not talking about some ordered, linear process. You didn't wait until all your theories were neatly in place—you acted. When you act, you learn and your theories change. And when your theories of learning change, so, too, does your curriculum. This is an evolution you're dealing with—a *constant* evolution.

M: Sometimes it just seems to go so slowly. Given the fact that I operate in a limited time frame at school, I have to pick and choose my battles. I can't take on everything at once.

The wild card in all this is that I often have to deal with problems I didn't even know existed. Once, I was sitting in an authors' circle and the kids weren't making any productive comments: "It's good," "I like it." I was so frustrated, I shouted out, "How do you know when something is a good story?" And one of the kids said, "When *you* like it." I had set myself up as the judge, jury, and executioner of their stories.

So, I embarked on a crash course designed to get me to shut up and extend the audience for the kids' stories. We started doing small-scale puppet shows for the other classes, videotaping readings and plays and circulating them among the parents, publishing more books and putting comment sheets in them. I'm working on a grade-level magazine now that I hope works out well.

You get the point, though. I've got plenty of stories like this.

H: But that's the right tone. Stories make whole language personal and, it seems to me, that's the essence of whole language.

Try this. If I asked you, "What are the principles of learning that have guided you?" what would you say?

M: I guess my real concern in the classroom is to treat the children as I would want to be treated. Is that too biblical for you? It's true, though. That's my major guiding principle. If I was a kid in my class, would I like it? If I was learning this subject for the first time, what would I want to do?

That's putting a lot of faith in yourself and a lot of faith in your kids, but it works. I remember in the eighth grade, I was part of a group of kids that were pretty good readers, and the teachers wisely decided not to put us through a basal and said, "Do whatever you want. Do whatever you want, read whatever books you want, just give us a report on it." And the report could be in any form. We did plays, interviews, standard book reports — anything. I was thinking about that this morning and remembered that we read *All Quiet on the Western Front, Of Mice and Men, Uncle Tom's Cabin* — books we never would have touched under normal circumstances in that school. We thought we were hot stuff so we tried them. That was the year in my life when I probably read the widest variety of material. And it's because they just let us go.

H: So in some ways, what you're really saying is when people start to talk to you about whole language, there's a lot of resonance with your own experience.

M: With my experience and with my attitude toward the children.

H: Learning is finding those patterns that connect. Once teachers see how whole language clicks with what they know and believe about kids and learning, they take off.

We need to convince them to try. We need to let them know that we need to hear their voices, that we want to begin some new conversations. Your wife meeting your family is the message we want to leave them with.

M: Sure. Just jump in and start eating.

H: We've got a TAWL meeting Monday, right?

M: Yeah. We'll talk more then.

References

Baratta-Lorton, Mary. 1976. *Mathematics Their Way*. Reading, Mass.: Addison-Wesley.

McInerney, J. 1988. "Are We There Yet?" *Teachers Networking* 8(3): February.

Short, Kathy G. 1986. *Literacy as a Collaborative Experience*. Ph.D. diss., Indiana University, Bloomington.